THE
FORMATIVE
YEARS
OF SOCIAL SECURITY

THE
FORMATIVE
YEARS
OF SOCIAL SECURITY

Arthur J. Altmeyer

THE UNIVERSITY OF WISCONSIN PRESS

Madison, Milwaukee, and London, 1966

To my wife

Published by the University of Wisconsin Press
P.O. Box 1379, Madison, Wisconsin 53701

Printed in the United States of America
by American Book–Stratford Press, Inc.

Library of Congress Catalog Number 66–11801

Preface

This discussion of the Social Security Act and its administration will concentrate on the circumstances surrounding the preparation and passage of the Social Security Act in 1934–35 and the circumstances affecting its development throughout the years. No attempt will be made to describe in any comprehensive, schematic manner the provisions of the Social Security Act or its antecedents. Nor will there be an attempt to analyze the long-range economic, social, and political forces at work.

Rather, an effort will be made to shed some light on the considerations and personalities involved in the making of important policy decisions, concerning not only legislation but also administration. With this purpose in mind I shall discuss events of which I had personal knowledge, many of which are not matters of general public knowledge and are not usually given much attention.

When I speak of the Social Security Act of 1935, I have in mind chiefly those features which were entirely new in the field of federal social legislation and which came under the jurisdiction of the Social Security Board. Thus, less attention will be given to such features in the 1935 act as public health, maternal and child welfare, and vocational rehabilitation. However, it should be noted that the United States Public Health Service, which had been established in 1799, received considerable additional funds under the Social Security Act to carry on its work. So did the Children's Bureau, established in 1912, and so did the federal agency administering the Vocational Rehabilitation Act, passed in

v

1920. In each case the additional funds were for grants to the states. The United States Public Health Service had been making such grants to a limited extent for many years. The Children's Bureau had administered a Maternity and Infancy Act during the years 1922–29 which provided for federal-state cooperation in the promotion of welfare and hygiene during maternity and infancy. The Vocational Rehabilitation Act was also a federal-state cooperative program.

In order to understand why the Social Security Act took the form it did, it is, of course, necessary to know the general purpose President Roosevelt and his advisers had in mind. It is also necessary to know what considerations they deemed important in developing ways and means of achieving their purpose. But it is doubtful whether anyone today (including myself) can fully understand the relative importance of the various considerations which were involved in policy decisions that had to be made in 1934 under the conditions prevailing at that time. Nevertheless, an attempt will be made to present these considerations and the importance attached to them by those who were responsible for making the decisions and those who opposed these decisions.

Thus, it is hoped that this chronicle will clarify to some extent the reason why nine of the ten separate programs included in the Social Security Act are administered by the states; why chief reliance was placed on contributory social insurance; why we have a national system of old age, survivors', and disability insurance but a federal-state system of unemployment insurance; why Republican leaders opposed old age insurance; why permanent total disability insurance benefits were not provided until 1956; and why health insurance was not included in the 1935 Social Security Act.

I have considered it essential to discuss the administration of the Social Security Act as fully as the provisions of the act itself because, as John R. Commons, my teacher at the University of Wisconsin and the dean of labor economists for many years, used to say, "Administration is legislation in action." It is hoped that the importance of administration will be demonstrated in such matters as selecting and training qualified personnel; establishing proper organization and procedures; coping with the unique problems involved in the creation of the gigantic old age, survivors', and disability insurance system; strengthening our federal-state form of government; and, above all, exercising in an intelligent and responsible manner the power that lawyers call "administrative discretion."

Accordingly, this chronicle will illustrate how administrative decisions determined whether or not uniform old age pensions would become the dominant form of old age security; whether old age insurance records would be kept confidential and used only for administrative purposes; whether the United States Employment Service would be developed as the agency through which unemployment benefits were paid; whether public assistance payments would be made on an equitable and consistent basis throughout a state; and whether states would develop civil service systems.

Perhaps a brief biographical statement may help to explain my opinion concerning the inextricable relationship between a law and its administration, as well as other opinions I may later express. It will at least indicate, I think, that the origin in this country of what we now call social security will be found more largely in our labor legislation than in our poor-relief laws. This is in sharp contrast to Great Britain where the development of social security was influenced largely by dissatisfaction with the Poor Law. This difference in the relative influences of labor legislation and poor-relief legislation accounts for many of the basic differences to be found in the social security systems of these two countries.

My first interest in what is now called social security was aroused in 1911. At that time I was an office boy in my uncle's law office. One day the office received a pamphlet, issued by an insurance company, which described the new Wisconsin Workmen's Compensation Act, the first state law of this kind to go into effect in this country. When I entered the University of Wisconsin in the fall of that year, I naturally desired to learn more about workmen's compensation and other forms of labor legislation. I had already been told about the activities of John R. Commons. These included service as a member of the Wisconsin Industrial Commission which was charged with the administration of workmen's compensation. So I enrolled in Commons' classes. Later, in 1918, I became Professor Commons' research assistant. It may be of some interest to note that, while I was serving in that capacity, Professor Commons asked me to co-author a report entitled "The Health Insurance Movement in the United States." This report had been requested (and later published) by two of the state commissions which had been set up for the purpose of studying the desirability of enacting health insurance laws—the Illinois Health Insurance Commission and the Ohio Health and Old Age Insurance Commission.

In 1920 I became Chief Statistician of the Wisconsin Industrial Commission. In that capacity I began a monthly publication called the *Wisconsin Labor Market,* which included among other data an index of employment throughout the state. This Wisconsin index and a similar one published by the New York Department of Labor were the first two indices of employment published in the United States.

In 1922 I became Secretary of the Wisconsin Industrial Commission. In July 1927 I took a leave of absence from that position for a period of six months to serve the United States Employees' Compensation Commission as Deputy Commissioner for the Great Lakes Region in putting into effect the Longshoremen's and Harbor Workers' Compensation Act.

Both as Chief Statistician and as Secretary of the Wisconsin Industrial Commission, I was involved in the deliberations concerning an unemployment compensation bill which was under consideration by successive sessions of the state legislature from 1921 to 1932. On January 1932, the Wisconsin Unemployment Reserves and Compensation Act became the first such act to be passed in the United States. Both workmen's compensation (for accidents) and unemployment compensation, it should be noted, were regarded as labor legislation—what the Germans called "workers insurance."

In addition to the administration of the various labor laws, the Wisconsin Industrial Commission was given the responsibility in 1931 of supervising the administration of unemployment relief throughout the state. As Secretary of the commission, I was given the responsibility of establishing the necessary relations with the federal government so that Wisconsin could qualify for federal financial assistance when that became available in 1932. In February of that year Senators LaFollette and Costigan had been defeated in their efforts to secure passage of their bill to provide federal grants to the states for unemployment relief. However, in May of 1932 Congress did authorize the Reconstruction Finance Committee to make loans to the states.

On a number of occasions in the spring of 1933 I was requested by the Secretary of Labor, Frances Perkins, and officials in her department to go to Washington to assist in the development of effective working relationships with state labor departments. In November 1933 the Secretary of Labor asked me to accept the position of Director of the Labor Compliance Division of the National Industrial Recovery Administration. In that position I was responsible for enforcing the labor standards contained in the various industry codes.

Eighteen days after Franklin Roosevelt became President, he sent Congress a message, urging the passage of the Federal Emergency Relief Act, which authorized outright grants to the states to assist them in providing unemployment relief. In addition to securing some of this federal aid for Wisconsin, I was asked from time to time to assist officials of the Federal Emergency Relief Administration in the development of administrative procedures. I was also asked by them to assist in setting up the Civil Works Administration which provided work for over four million unemployed persons during the winter of 1933–34.

I had been granted a leave of absence from my post as Secretary of the Wisconsin Industrial Commission, but returned to that position in May of 1934. When I arrived back in Madison, I learned that the Secretary of Labor had been trying to reach me to offer me the position of Assistant Secretary. I accepted and was immediately assigned the task of assisting in the reorganization and expansion of the Department of Labor. However, within a month I was given the added responsibility of serving as Chairman of the technical board which was created by presidential order to assist the President's Cabinet Committee on Economic Security.

I was given the opportunity to participate in these various phases of the New Deal not simply because of my experience as a state official but more importantly because this experience had been acquired in a state noted for its progressive social legislation. Both the President and Miss Perkins were thoroughly familiar with this legislation and the philosophy underlying it. The President acquired this familiarity when he was a state senator and Governor of New York; Miss Perkins, as Commissioner of Labor for New York State.*

I am painfully aware of the tedious character of the year-by-year recital of legislative recommendations and legislative action. I can only hope that this detailed account will be of some value at least for reference purposes and that it will give some idea of how amendments to the Social Security Act occurred only after years of study, planning, and repeated recommendations.

Appendix I, "Significant Events of Social Security, 1935–65," may assist the reader who wishes to read selectively, while Appendix II, "Official Documents of Social Security, 1935–65," may be of some help to the reader who wishes more information on legislative history.

Arthur J. Altmeyer

Washington, D. C.
August 1965

---

* For a more complete account of these state activities and the similarity between the "Wisconsin Idea" and the New Deal, the reader is referred to the following publications by the writer: "The Industrial Commission of Wisconsin—A Case Study in Labor Law Administration," *University of Wisconsin Studies in the Social Sciences and History*, No. 17 (1932); "The Wisconsin Idea and Social Security," *Wisconsin Magazine of History*, XLII, No. 1 (1958).

Contents

Preface   v

List of Illustrations   xiii

1. The Enactment of the Law, 1934–35   3

2. Putting the Social Security Act into Operation, 1935–37   43

3. Improving the Social Security Act and Its Administration, 1937–39   74

4. A Year of Change, 1939   99

5. Social Security during the War Years, 1940–45   118

6. Social Security during the Postwar Years, 1945–48   152

7. The Crucial Years, 1948–52   169

8. The Uncertain Years, 1952–54   209

9. The Years Ahead   256

Appendix I. Significant Events of Social Security, 1935–65   277

Appendix II. Official Documents of Social Security, 1935–65   288

Appendix III. Memorandum for the President, 1937: Amendments to the Social Security Act   295

Appendix IV. Correspondence with Congressman Curtis of Nebraska, Chairman of Subcommittee on Social Security of the Committee on Ways and Means, U.S. House of Representatives, 1953: Investigation of Social Security   298

Index   302

List of Illustrations

Page 129

Draft of President Roosevelt's telegram to the governors of the states requesting the transfer of the state employment services

Between pages 162 and 163

Taking the oath of office as Assistant Secretary of Labor
The first meeting of the Social Security Board
Sir William Beveridge, author of the British "cradle to the grave" social security plan, and Arthur J. Altmeyer, Chairman of the Social Security Board, in New York
Arthur J. Altmeyer in front of the Social Security Administration's central office building in Baltimore

THE
FORMATIVE
YEARS
OF SOCIAL SECURITY

1.

The Enactment
of the Law, 1934–35

The term "social security" was not in common use either in this country or in other countries prior to 1933.* President Roosevelt did not use the term when he notified Congress on June 8, 1934, that "next winter we may well undertake the great task of furthering the security of the citizen and his family through social insurance. This is not an untried experiment. Lessons of experience are available from States, from industries, and from many nations of the civilized world. The various types of social insurance are inter-related; and I think it is difficult to attempt to solve them piecemeal. Hence I am looking for a sound means which I can recommend to provide at once security against several of the great disturbing factors in life—especially those which relate to unemployment and old age."

The President did not use the term "social security" when he created the Committee on Economic Security on June 29, 1934, to study the problems relating to economic security and to make recommendations for a program of legislation. Moreover, the bill drafted by the legal counsel for the Committee on Economic Security was entitled the "Economic Security Act." "Economic security" was a broader term than "social insurance," but it still was not comprehensive enough to cover all of the recommenda-

---

* However, interestingly enough, I discovered, while engaged in a project in Colombia, that "The Great Liberator," Simon Bolivar, in a memorable address at Angostura in 1819 used this very term, saying, "The system of government most perfect is that which produces the greatest amount of happiness possible, the greatest amount of social security, and the greatest amount of political stability."

tions of the President's committee. These recommendations included not only unemployment compensation, contributory old age insurance, noncontributory old age pensions, and public assistance for the support of dependent children, but also federal grants to the states to finance a greatly expanded nationwide public health program and federal grants to the states to finance maternal and child health and welfare programs.

But during the course of congressional consideration of the bill, several witnesses used the term "social security." Among them were William Green, President of the American Federation of Labor, and Abraham Epstein, Secretary of the American Association for Social Security. The Washington *Post* referred to the bill as the "social-security bill." Probably Mr. Epstein was the person most responsible for introducing the term. In the spring of 1933 he changed the name of his American Association for Old Age Security to the American Association for Social Security to indicate its broader scope. This association was in financial difficulties, and Epstein had exhausted all of his personal resources in keeping it alive. Therefore, an additional advantage of this particular change in its name was that the old letterheads could still be used by merely striking out "old age" and substituting "social." Neither Epstein nor anyone else at that time attempted to define what was meant by the term "social security." But obviously he was thinking primarily of social insurance, since he said in his book, *Insecurity, A Challenge to America*, published in 1933: "This book frankly advocates social insurance as a feasible method of social security."

Certainly President Roosevelt continued to regard social security primarily as a comprehensive system of contributory social insurance providing basic protection to Americans against all major personal economic hazards. In 1910 as a state senator he had supported the passage of a workmen's compensation law in New York. In 1930 as Governor of New York he stated, when he signed the old age pension law, that the problem of insecurity in old age could not be solved unless there was also a system of old age insurance. In 1931 at the Conference of State Governors he took a stand in favor of unemployment compensation.

In discussions with members of his Committee on Economic Security the President spoke of the possibility of every child's being issued an "insurance policy" on the day he was born to protect him against all the major economic misfortunes which might befall him during his lifetime. This is the reason that he displayed some irritation when Lord Beveridge was hailed in 1942 as the originator of the idea of "cradle to the grave" insurance when he made his famous report, "Social Insurance and Allied Services."

While social insurance was regarded as the chief instrumentality to be relied upon for protection against want, it was recognized that it would be necessary to supplement this protection in a certain proportion of cases by providing public assistance in accordance with individual needs. It was also recognized that public services of various kinds, such as rehabilitation, public health, and maternal and child welfare services, were also necessary.

So it can be said that those who had given particular thought to what came to be called "social security" in the 1930's used the term to describe a specific government program to protect and promote the economic and social well-being of workers and their families. They did not use the term to connote a fundamental reconstruction of economic and social institutions.

However, statesmen throughout the world seized upon this term to express the ideal objective of a government to assure the "Good Life" in all its phases for all its citizens. In this sense the term is even more sweeping, if that is possible, than the term "welfare state." Thus, we find the expression "social security" embedded in the Atlantic Charter, signed by President Roosevelt and Prime Minister Churchill in 1941. It may be of some interest to note that this inclusion was suggested by the first Chairman of the Social Security Board, John G. Winant, who later became United States Ambassador to Great Britain. The term was also included in the Declaration of the United Nations issued in 1942, and it can be found in the constitutions of many of the new nations which have come into existence since World War II.

Strangely enough, while throughout the rest of the world there is the tendency to use "social security" in an expansive sense, we in this country are inclined to use it more restrictively as the synonym for only one form of social insurance, namely, our federal old age, survivors', and disability insurance system. This restricted use undoubtedly is due to the spectacular growth manifested by this particular form of social insurance in terms of the number of persons insured, the number of persons receiving monthly benefits, the amount of benefits paid out, and the character of the hazards insured. Because of the many millions of persons insured and the billions of dollars paid out in benefits each year, it is unquestionably the largest insurance organization in the world.

I believe strongly that it is desirable to use the term "social security" to mean a specific governmental program designed to promote the economic and social well-being of individual workers and their families through providing protection against specific hazards which would otherwise cause widespread destitution and misery. There is at least a possibility that, used in this sense, the term will be comprehensive enough and still limited enough to be useful.

There is no question, of course, that sooner or later the same world-wide economic, social, and political forces responsible for the emergence of social security programs in 125 nations would have resulted in the development of a social security program in the United States. But, as U.S. Supreme Court Justice Holmes was fond of saying, the inevitable comes to pass only through the effort of individual human beings. Certain it was that the individuals charged by the President in 1934 with the responsibility of recommending a specific legislative program for the consideration of the Congress, which would convene within six months, could not wait for the inevitable to happen. So to me it seems obvious that the particular personalities involved and the particular circumstances which confronted them did affect the timing of the action that was taken and the form of that action.

If Franklin D. Roosevelt had not been President and if the nation had not been plunged into the Great Depression of the 1930's, action might not have been taken at that time or might have taken a different form. As it was, the President believed strongly that, besides taking the emergency measures necessary to relieve the human distress caused by the Great Depression, it was essential to develop a long-range program to protect the American people from the ill effects of unemployment and other personal economic hazards.

The President was fortunate in having at his right hand two persons who not only shared his convictions but also had the knowledge, experience, and skill necessary to develop such a program. These two were Frances Perkins, Secretary of Labor, and Harry Hopkins, Federal Emergency Relief Administrator. However, there were many other persons in and out of Congress who played an important part in the development of our social security program, as will be pointed out later.

In accordance with the instructions of the President, Secretary of Labor Perkins, and Mr. Hopkins, I prepared Executive Order No. 6757, signed by President Roosevelt on June 29, 1934. This order provided for the creation of a Committee on Economic Security, a technical board, an advisory council, and an executive director. The only change the President made in the original draft of the executive order was to substitute the Secretary of Agriculture for the Secretary of Commerce as a member of the committee. I believe this change was made because the President considered that the Secretary of Agriculture, Henry Wallace, and his associates were more interested in social legislation. Thus, the committee consisted of Frances Perkins, Secretary of Labor (Chairman), Henry Morgenthau, Jr., Secretary of the Treasury, Homer Cummings, Attorney General, Henry A. Wallace, Secretary of Agriculture, and Harry L. Hopkins, Federal Emergency Relief Administrator.

In accordance with the desires of Miss Perkins, I immediately proceeded to develop some suggestions on subjects to be studied and on the membership of the technical board. After the committee had considered a number of persons, I was authorized by Miss Perkins to offer the position of Executive Director to Dr. Edwin E. Witte, Chairman of the Department of Economics at the University of Wisconsin. This was done by telephone on July 24, and on July 26 Dr. Witte arrived in Washington, ready to begin.

Dr. Witte was uniquely qualified for the position of Executive Director. He was an outstanding expert in the field of labor legislation which, as already indicated, included social insurance. He had also served as Chief of the Wisconsin Legislative Reference Library for a number of years. Therefore, he had the ability to assemble and focus all the relevant information and the best thinking available within the very short period of less than six months before the committee was obliged to make its recommendations.

Dr. Witte kept a diary on the basis of which he prepared a 276-page confidential memorandum on the work of the Committee on Economic Security. This was prepared in 1937 but was not published until 1962.* Therefore, it is not necessary to describe in detail how the committee functioned. Rather I shall attempt to appraise the major policy decisions the committee was expected to make, the considerations which influenced the committee in making its decisions, and the personalities involved in making these decisions. But first it is necessary to mention in a general way the relationships which existed among the President, the committee, the technical board, the advisory council, and the Executive Director.

The committee itself, composed as it was of top officials in the Roosevelt Administration, was obliged to concentrate on the major policy questions presented to it and attempt to resolve these questions in accordance with what it considered to be the general thinking of the President. The technical board (of which, as already stated, I was chairman) was made up of federal officials who were experts in particular areas of significance to the committee. They conceived of their responsibility as twofold: on the one hand, assisting the Executive Director to develop a concrete program and, on the other hand, making certain that the committee members were apprised of all the considerations to be kept in mind in making policy decisions.

The advisory council consisted of 23 persons, five of whom were labor leaders, five employers, and the rest persons interested in social welfare. The function of the advisory council, as the President conceived it to be, was to convey to the committee the views of interested individuals and groups outside of the government, but the council was not expected to make a formal report.

It was specified in the executive order that the necessary studies and investigations would be under the immediate direction of the Executive Director, but "under the general direction of

---

* Edwin E. Witte, *The Development of the Social Security Act* (Madison: The University of Wisconsin Press, 1962).

the Technical Board." It was also specified that the Executive Director should appoint staff members "with the approval of the Technical Board." However, at the very outset the technical board adopted resolutions giving the Executive Director complete authority to employ members of his staff and to direct all of the work of the committee. In practice the Executive Director constantly consulted with me and other members of the technical board.

The advisory council functioned much more independently than had been originally contemplated. It also made a lengthy report which contained recommendations differing in some respects from the final recommendations of the Committee on Economic Security. These differences will be discussed later.

It has often been said that the Social Security Act was a child of the Great Depression, during which one-fourth of the workers of the nation was unemployed and one-fifth of the nation subsisted on direct relief or work relief. It is certainly true that the depression convinced the American people of the necessity for government action to relieve the human distress caused by unemployment, insecurity in old age, and widespread poverty. But while it is clear that public opinion demanded that the federal government take emergency action to relieve the existing human distress, it is not at all certain that the depression in and of itself caused the government to embark upon a long-range social program to prevent as well as relieve human destitution.

There was a strong feeling on the part of a large proportion of prominent persons, particularly those belonging to the political party not in office, that "recovery must precede reform." President Roosevelt flatly rejected this view, saying in his June 8, 1934, message to Congress: "It is childish to speak of recovery first and reconstruction afterward. In the very nature of the processes of recovery we must avoid the destructive influences of the past."

But the President, in rejecting the view that no long-range social program should be undertaken until recovery from the depression was complete, was also compelled to withstand strong pressures to accept panaceas of various kinds. One was the Townsend plan, so named after the retired doctor who began advocating it in 1932. However, no bill embodying the plan was actually introduced in Congress until after the President's message of June 8, 1934. This plan, as introduced, was called the "Townsend Old Age Revolving Pension Plan." The plan was very simple: It provided that every citizen of the United States, sixty years of age and over, should be entitled to receive $200 per month. The only requirement was that the recipient must spend this amount within thirty days. The cost (which, it was explained, would not be a real cost) would be met through a universal 2 per cent sales tax on all transactions. It was contended that the purchasing power thus injected into the economy would be multiplied many times as it passed from one individual to another, thereby automatically solving the problem of unemployment and all other economic problems.

Some writers have suggested that the popularity of the Townsend movement forced the President to develop some alternative plan. The President was, of course, concerned about the Townsend plan. But he was even more concerned about Senator Huey Long's "share the wealth" movement. The Senator was never precise about how he would go about sharing the wealth. And he made varying pronouncements about the resultant per capita amount of wealth that would be shared, although the different amounts he predicted were all large enough to appeal to the popular imagination, as was his slogan, "Every man a King!" In fact, a poll taken by the Democratic National Committee indicated that Long's strength was such that he might take enough votes from the Democrats to result in the election of a Republican President in 1936.

While the President was concerned about the political effect of the various panaceas being bruited about, he needed no prodding to develop a sound long-range program of social action. As already pointed out, his advocacy of social insurance and related forms of what we now call social security antedated his Presidency. However, the pressure of these movements, particularly the Townsend movement, was unquestionably helpful in securing congressional approval of the President's program.

Since these movements grew out of the depression, it can be argued that the President would have been unable to secure congressional approval for his long-range program had it not been for the situation created by the depression. However, these movements had no effect whatsoever on the kind of long-range program the President proposed.

As a matter of fact, the President emphasized in his June 8, 1934, message to the Congress that he favored financing any long-range program through a contributory social insurance system rather than by an increase in general taxation. At a meeting during the early days of the committee, he told Miss Perkins, Dr. Witte, and me that he was opposed to the Townsend plan or any other plan supported by general taxation. However, he recognized the necessity of using general revenues to finance assistance to people already old and without means.

The President's desire to place chief reliance on a system of contributory social insurance was due as much to his belief that it was a financially safe system as to his belief that it provided protection as a matter of earned right. He felt that requiring the benefits to be financed entirely by contributions furnished a built-in safeguard.

It is interesting to observe that these views of the President in the field of public finance were paralleled by his habits in his private finances. His friends and associates were intrigued and somewhat amused by his extreme frugality and the delight he got out of small savings, such as the number of shaves he was able to get from a single razor blade or the bargain he had made in the purchase of an old postage stamp or the length of time he had worn an old hat or sweater.

The President also emphasized in conferences which I attended, as he had in his June 8, 1934, message, that he wanted a program that was based upon a maximum of cooperation between the states and the federal government.

The President's desire to rely upon the states as much as possible was based upon his lifelong belief in our federal form, rather than a national form, of government. This conviction antedated his experience as a state senator and governor. It can be traced back to the influence of the great British Ambassador, James Lord Bryce, whom he knew personally and whose book, *The American Commonwealth,* had impressed him deeply. He was particularly interested in Bryce's thesis that a major advantage of our federal system was the opportunity it afforded for the individual states to serve as laboratories. Thus, when Miss Perkins came back from California to warn him that Upton Sinclair, who won the Democratic nomination, might be elected Governor of California on the strength of his EPIC program (End Poverty in California), the President refused to be disturbed, saying that the beauty of our state-federal system is that the people in a particular state can experiment. If the experiment fails, it will not have fatal consequences for the country as a whole; if it works, it will be copied.

President Roosevelt has often been charged with having had a desire to build up the central government at the expense of the state governments and also with having had little concern for the cost of the government programs he advocated. However, I am certain that this allegation was not true of his ideas concerning his social security program, which he often called the cornerstone of his Administration and the most enduring measure of the New Deal.

President Roosevelt has also often been described as a very complicated man. But as regards the sort of social insurance program he envisaged, he was very simple indeed. As already stated, he thought it should be possible to issue a comprehensive social insurance policy to every child on the day of birth. He thought the administration of such a program should be decentralized to the local community. Then a citizen could ascertain his rights and duties through a face to face conversation with a local official who would have authority to act. He would not have to depend upon correspondence with some faceless bureaucrat a long way off. To illustrate what he had in mind, he would describe how he thought Mose Smith, his farm manager, would deal with the manager of the local social insurance office just as he would deal with the cashier of the local bank. He felt that, if the federal government were involved, the local office should be in the post office because every one knew where it was located and was used to going there.

The President's solution to the problem of whether, as a long-range proposition, there should be a nationwide system of unemployment insurance or a nationwide system of work relief was equally simple. He said he did not see why there should not be both. He went so far as to say that, if a worker exhausted his unemployment insurance benefits and was still unemployed, he should automatically be given a green ticket which would entitle him to a work relief job. He did not explain why he thought the ticket should be green!

As has already been mentioned, the President, both in his message to Congress on June 29, 1934, and in later conversations, indicated that the Committee on Economic Security should attempt to develop a comprehensive social insurance system covering all major personal economic hazards, but especially the hazards of unemployment and old age. He also told the committee in August that he felt committed to both unemployment insurance and old age insurance.

Later, on November 14, in addressing a National Conference on Economic Security which the Committee on Economic Security had called, the President said, "I do not know whether this is the time for any Federal legislation on old age security. Organizations promoting fantastic schemes have aroused hopes that cannot possibly be fulfilled. Through their activities they increased the difficulties of getting sound legislation, but I hope that in time we may be able to provide security for the aged—a sound and a uniform system which will provide true security."

Some of the newspapers interpreted the President's statement regarding old age security to mean that he would not include old age security in the program he submitted to Congress. This aroused the Townsendites and others who felt very strongly that old age security was of paramount importance. Miss Perkins immediately issued a statement that there was no justification for this sort of interpretation. And two days later the President, in a communication to the National Conference of Mayors, said he would include both old age security and unemployment insurance in his recommendations to Congress.

One prominent columnist said that Dr. Witte had written the President's speech and that Miss Perkins blamed him for making a blunder. While it is true that Dr. Witte prepared a preliminary draft, a later draft which included the phrase quoted above was prepared by me after consultation with Miss Perkins.

The actual situation was that the President and his committee both felt that unemployment insurance should have top priority. In March 1934 the President had urged the enactment of the Wagner-Lewis Bill providing for a federal-state system of unemployment insurance before Congress adjourned. However, it later became apparent that it would be impossible for Congress to act on this measure and other important measures before adjournment.

Both the President and the committee thought it was necessary to avert the dangerous possibility that the widespread interest in old age security might obscure the need for unemployment insurance and other phases of a comprehensive social insurance program. They also thought it was important to indicate that it might be necessary to put the various phases of such a program into effect in stages. Thus, in this same address the President said regarding health insurance, "Whether we come to this form of insurance sooner or later, I am confident we can devise a system which will enhance and not hinder the remarkable progress which has been made in the practice of the profession of medicine and surgery in the United States."

The first meeting of the President's Committee on Economic Security was held on August 13, 1934. Dr. Witte, the Executive Director, had been at work since July 26 and had submitted to the technical board, on August 10, what he called a "Preliminary Outline of the Work of the Staff." This outline covered the subjects to be studied. It indicated that while these studies would encompass the whole field of protection for the individual against major economic hazards, they would need to be related to the existing emergency relief and unemployment situation. It emphasized that while a long-range program should be developed, the immediate problem was the preparation of specific legislative proposals for the consideration of the President and of the next Congress. The technical board and the committee approved of Dr. Witte's conception of the task.

It is difficult to appreciate, after the passage of over a quarter of a century, the uncertainties and difficulties confronting the committee in their resolution of these policy questions. If the committee had had the advantage of the experience acquired during this quarter of a century and had been able to pierce the veil of the future to ascertain the attitude of the United States Supreme Court, it undoubtedly would have made radically different recommendations in a number of respects.

But in 1934 the previous decisions of the United States Supreme Court had created considerable doubt as to how far the Constitution of the United States permitted the federal government to go in enacting social legislation. The Supreme Court had held two federal child labor laws unconstitutional. One of these laws had been based on the right of the federal government to regulate interstate commerce, and the other had been based on the taxing power of the federal government. The only favorable decision of the Supreme Court in the field of social legislation was one upholding the constitutionality of the Sheppard-Towner Act which provided for federal grants to the states to help finance maternity and child health programs (*Massachusetts* v. *Mellon; Frothingham* v. *Mellon, 262 U.S. 467*). However, this decision related to comparatively small federal grants financed out of general revenues and furnished no clue as to how the Supreme Court might feel about a nationwide social insurance system financed 100 per cent by specific federal payroll taxes.

How deep the concern of the committee was is indicated by an incident that occurred during the early days of the committee's deliberations. Miss Perkins had chatted with Justice Stone at his wife's tea one afternoon and had remarked about the difficulty of developing a nationwide social insurance system that would be constitutional. The next morning Miss Perkins came to her office highly elated to say that Justice Stone had commented that the taxing power of the federal government was sweeping indeed.

The committee, of course, felt bound to bear in mind the general ideas of the President in developing its recommendations. It also was compelled to give consideration to such major policy questions as constitutionality, administrative feasibility, and congressional reactions, as well as to the many technical problems involved.

The experts, both in the government and outside the government, who were called upon to advise the committee did not always agree about the technical aspects of the various alternative possibilities that were given consideration. Neither were they as concerned as the committee necessarily was regarding constitutionality, administrative feasibility, and congressional reactions.

Therefore, the committee did not arrive at its final recommendations without considerable travail. These recommendations envisaged the following program:

(1) The federal government would continue to assume responsibility for providing work for employable persons then unemployed.

(2) The federal government would make grants to the states to help them in providing public assistance to unemployable persons, consisting largely of needy old people and dependent children.

(3) There would be established a federal-state system of unemployment insurance, supplemented by a work program for those who remained unemployed after exhausting their insurance benefits.

(4) A straight federal system of old age insurance would be established for those who became aged in future years.

(5) The federal government would make grants to the states to help them finance public health and child welfare services.

(6) Eventually there would be established other forms of social insurance, particularly health insurance, providing protection both against wage loss due to sickness and against the cost of medical care.

The committee had in mind that social insurance should be the first line of defense against destitution and public assistance a second line to be relied upon to the extent the first line proved to be inadequate. In carrying out this idea the committee was obliged to devote most of its attention to policy questions involved in the development of an unemployment insurance system. However, the problems involved in the development of an old age insurance system also received considerable attention.

The committee's recommendation relative to federal grants to the states for the needy aged and dependent children was developed without the necessity for extended consideration. It implemented the views of the President as again expressed when he signed an executive order on May 6, 1935, terminating the Federal Emergency Relief Administration and creating the Works Progress Administration (which was not terminated until December 1942). He stated at that time that "work must be found for able-bodied but destitute workers" and that "the federal government must and shall quit this business of relief."

Similarly the committee's recommendations of grants to the states for public health and child welfare services did not require much discussion. Health insurance would undoubtedly have required much attention if the committee had not decided it would make no specific recommendations until Congress had acted on its other recommendations.

In its consideration of unemployment insurance the committee felt obligated to make every effort to carry out the views of the President as expressed in his June 8, 1934, message to the Congress, in which he said that he believed a sound system of security should be based on a "maximum of cooperation between States and the Federal government." Moreover, since the President had endorsed the Wagner-Lewis unemployment insurance bill, the committee felt that it should give particular attention to the type of federal system incorporated in that bill.

But before reaching a decision, the committee, of course, desired to have the advice of the technical board and the experts on the staff of the Executive Director. At its meeting on October 1 the committee received the "Preliminary Report of the Technical Board," discussing not only unemployment insurance but other subjects as well. About unemployment insurance the technical board said, "If constitutional, a nationally administered system of unemployment insurance is to be preferred to a State system." The only action the committee took on this report was to instruct the technical board and the staff to proceed with its studies along the lines suggested.

On November 9 the technical board made a report dealing exclusively with unemployment insurance. This report outlined the main characteristics of three major alternative plans: (1) an exclusively federal system; (2) a cooperative federal-state system on a federal subsidy plan; (3) a cooperative federal-state system on the Wagner-Lewis federal tax-offset plan.

The technical board presented the arguments in favor of each of these three plans and stated that its members were divided regarding which of these plans was preferable. The board's report requested the committee members to decide whether the committee favored an exclusively national system or a cooperative federal-state system, saying that an early decision on this issue was imperative. Furthermore, the report said it would be desirable, although less urgent, if the committee would indicate whether it had a decided preference between the two types of cooperative federal-state system (if such a system was preferred over an exclusively national system).

Behind the failure of the technical board to make a definite recommendation was the fact that its subcommittee on unemployment insurance, which previously had unanimously favored a straight federal system, had changed its opinion and now was unanimously in favor of a cooperative federal-state plan. However, a considerable number of the staff and some members of the technical board, who were not on this subcommittee, continued to favor a straight federal system.

The subsidy plan provided for the levying of a federal payroll tax of a fixed percentage. All except a small proportion of the proceeds of this tax would be paid back to the state in which it had been collected. This subsidy would cover 100 per cent of the cost of the benefits payable under a state law meeting specified minimum federal standards. The small proportion retained by the federal government would be used to establish a reinsurance fund, to provide benefits to migratory workers who had lost some of their rights, and to finance the United States Employment Service.

The plan contained in the Wagner-Lewis Bill also provided for the levying of a federal payroll tax of a fixed percentage, against which there would be allowed a credit to employers for the contributions they were required to pay under a state unemployment insurance law. The state law would be required to meet specified minimum benefit standards. The credit allowed would be a fixed proportion of the federal tax. The small proportion payable to the federal government would be used for the same purposes as under the subsidy plan. This plan came to be called the tax-offset plan.

The full committee was present on November 9 to consider the report of the technical board. After extended discussion the committee unanimously adopted a motion, made by Harry Hopkins, which urged that all thought of an exclusively federal system should be abandoned. There was no formal motion as to which type of cooperative federal-state system was preferred, but it also appeared to be the unanimous view of the committee that the Wagner-Lewis plan was preferable.

Miss Perkins immediately reported the committee's recommendation to the President. In his address to the National Conference on Economic Security on November 14, he affirmed this recommendation, saying that he would recommend "a cooperative federal-state undertaking."

This National Conference on Economic Security had been called both to give as many persons as possible an opportunity to express their views and to keep before the public the fact that the Administration was working on a legislative program to present to the next Congress. Immediately after the one day meeting of this conference, the advisory council held its first meeting.

The advisory council met for two days and spent all of its time discussing unemployment insurance. The council recognized that it was bound by the President's declaration favoring a cooperative federal-state system. Therefore, it proceeded to consider whether it should recommend basing such a system on the subsidy plan or on the Wagner-Lewis plan. Having reached no conclusion, the advisory council appointed a committee to report at its next meeting, which was held on December 6. At that meeting the council voted 9 to 7 in favor of the subsidy plan, but stated that all of the members recognized that both plans had distinct advantages.

Keeping in mind the views expressed by the advisory council, the committee continued to discuss the relative merits of the two types of federal-state plans but finally decided in favor of the Wagner-Lewis tax-offset plan. In reaching this decision, as well as the more basic decision to recommend a cooperative federal-state system instead of a straight federal system, the committee, of course, gave consideration to the views of the advisory council and the technical advice of the experts within and without the government. Nevertheless, the committee was obliged to make policy decisions which could not be left to interested individuals or groups or to technicians and, indeed, to weigh and choose factors whose merit only the future could determine.

The overarching policy decision of the committee to advise the President that his preference for a cooperative federal-state system would be feasible and effective, together with the subsidiary policy decision to recommend the tax-offset plan, involved first of all the question of constitutionality. It was absolutely essential that the system recommended should have the maximum likelihood of surviving the scrutiny of the United States Supreme Court. As already mentioned, Miss Perkins had reported that at a social occasion Supreme Court Justice Stone had remarked that much could be done through the taxing power of the federal government, but this comment gave no indication of exactly how the taxing power should be used.

The concern regarding constitutionality cannot be exaggerated. Actually, between January 1935 and May 1936 eight New Deal laws were declared unconstitutional. Following the presidential election of 1936, President Roosevelt made his dramatic proposal to increase the number of Supreme Court Justices. This led to the famous "court-packing" battle which the President lost. However, he apparently won the war, because in 1937 all of the Supreme Court decisions regarding the constitutionality of New Deal laws (including the Social Security Act) were favorable. One newspaper columnist, discussing this sudden reversal in the attitude of a majority of the nine Supreme Court Justices, commented that "A switch in time saves nine."

Reference has already been made to the favorable Supreme Court decision upholding federal grants to the states for maternity and child health programs. Offhand, this decision might suggest that the federal subsidy plan stood a better chance of being held constitutional than the tax-credit plan. However, there was one great difference: The federal grants for maternity and health programs were financed out of general revenues whereas the federal subsidies for unemployment insurance would be financed out of a specific payroll tax levied for that purpose. Moreover, the 100 per cent federal subsidies proposed would be unprecedented and would necessarily carry with them more federal control than did federal grants requiring the states to bear a substantial proportion of the costs involved.

As a matter of fact, in December 1935, only four months after the passage of the Social Security Act, the Supreme Court declared the Agricultural Adjustment Act unconstitutional. The subsidy plan for unemployment insurance involved constitutional questions practically identical with those presented by the Agricultural Adjustment Act. That act had two principal features: One was the levying of an excise tax on the processing of agricultural products, and the other was the appropriating of the proceeds from this tax to finance the payment of benefits to agricultural producers who complied with federal requirements relative to the use of their land. The Supreme Court held that the tax levied was not a tax within the meaning of the Constitution but a mere incident in the scheme of regulation which invaded the reserved rights of the states.

The committee believed the tax-offset plan was more likely to be upheld by the Supreme Court than was the subsidy plan since the tax-offset plan followed the method used under the Federal Estate Tax Act, which had been held to be constitutional years before (*Florida* v. *Mellon, 273 U.S. 12*). Under that act a tax-offset is allowed for taxes paid under state inheritance tax laws. As a matter of fact, it was known that Supreme Court Justice Brandeis had suggested the incorporation of this method in the Wagner-Lewis Bill. And, indeed, the Supreme Court cited that earlier court decision as a precedent when it later upheld the unemployment insurance feature of the Social Security Act.

Moreover, the committee believed that even if the Supreme Court eventually held the federal law unconstitutional, more states would be likely to continue to keep their employment insurance laws in effect under the tax-offset plan than under the subsidy plan. The committee reached this conclusion because under the tax-offset plan the states would be obliged to pass their own laws levying a payroll tax, which would continue to make their insurance plans self-sustaining. This was not true of the subsidy plan.

But, aside from the question of constitutionality, the committee favored the tax-offset plan in preference to a straight federal plan or the subsidy type of federal-state plan because it placed the maximum responsibility on the states. The committee considered this was necessary because there was considerable polarization of opinion among the advocates of unemployment insurance concerning such major substantive questions as what the scale of benefits should be and whether unemployment benefits should provide protection against short-term or long-term unemployment.

These advocates disagreed on whether the benefits should be relatively high in amount and of limited duration or relatively low in amount and of longer duration. They disagreed on whether protection should be provided for seasonal unemployment and partial unemployment. And they disagreed on whether there should be employee contributions and perhaps government contributions in addition to employer contributions. Finally, there was bitter disagreement over whether there should be "employer experience rating" and, if so, what kind. "Employer experience rating" was the designation applied to differential employer contribution rates related to the amount of unemployment sustained by the employees of the individual employer or a group of employers.

Under a straight federal system or even under a subsidy type of federal-state system, these substantive questions would have had to be answered for the entire country before there had been any actual experience. Moreover, the administrative problems involved in a federally administered nationwide system appeared staggering at that time.

The basic argument of those individuals and groups who favored a straight federal system was that the relief and prevention of unemployment was a responsibility of the federal government since unemployment is caused for the most part by conditions which are beyond the control of the states. They argued that the federal government could better discharge this responsibility under a straight federal system than under a cooperative federal-state system. The specific advantages they cited in favor of a straight federal system were the following:

(1) It would assure that adequate benefits would be paid throughout the country.

(2) It would assure that employees with equivalent wage losses would receive the same benefits regardless of where they lived.

(3) It would assure that all employers with the same unemployment experience would pay the same rate of contribution, thus preventing unfair interstate competition.

(4) It would assure the maximum spreading of the risk, thus providing the maximum protection at the minimum cost.

(5) It would assure better protection to workers moving from one state to another.

(6) It would assure simpler and more efficient administration because records could be centralized and standardized; also,

employers operating in more than one state would need to make payroll reports and contributions to only one government agency.

Those who favored a straight federal system for the above reasons also supported the subsidy type of federal-state system as their second choice. They did so because they felt that it could go further toward achieving the preceding advantages than could the tax-credit system.

It is interesting to note that the Business Advisory Council of the Department of Commerce was among those who took the foregoing position. It issued a statement saying, "We recommend that unemployment insurance take a national form and think the grants-in-aid type of legislation would more nearly meet that today, and in the future, than the form of the bill now before the Congress." The council listed as one of the advantages that "it would lend itself more readily to developing a national system should that become advisable." The council also urged that "provision should be made for employee contributions, just as the bill already provides for employee contributions for old age pensions.

There is no question that all of these arguments had intrinsic merit. However, they had to be balanced against the considerations already discussed. These countervailing factors had to be weighed by the committee in the light of the situation existing at that time, not in the light of the situation existing today, more than a quarter of a century later.

It is my opinion that the committee, having in mind these considerations, would have made the same recommendations even if the President had not indicated his preference for a cooperative federal-state system. However, my opinion may be affected by the fact that I joined with the Executive Director and the Chairman of the Committee on Economic Security in advocating that the committee make this recommendation. It is true, however, that Harry Hopkins, who, next to Miss Perkins, was the most active member of the committee, as well as Josephine Roche, who was Henry Morgenthau's alternate, and Henry Wallace all believed that unemployment was a national problem which created a presumption in favor of a straight federal system.

The position the committee took on employer experience rating was indicated in its final report which said, "The primary purpose of unemployment compensation is to socialize the losses resulting from unemployment, but it should also serve the purpose of decreasing rather than increasing unemployment. We favor leaving it optional with the States whether they will permit any 'contracting out' from State-pooled funds . . . ." The committee specifically recommended that, if a state did allow individual employer reserves or guaranteed employment accounts or lower rates of contributions on the basis of favorable experience, all employers should be required to pay at least 1 per cent into a pooled state fund.

It was alleged at the time that the "Wisconsin school" (meaning especially Dr. Witte and me) had influenced the committee to recommend the tax-offset plan because it would not interfere with the type of employer experience rating provided for under the Wisconsin Unemployment Compensation Act passed in 1932. Obviously, I cannot be objective in appraising this allegation. However, it is pertinent to point out that when the committee was discussing whether the states should be permitted to adopt a pooled fund system or an individual employer accounts system (as provided for under the Wisconsin law), it was I who suggested, as a compromise, that all employers be required to contribute at least 1 per cent of their payrolls to a pooled fund.

It is pertinent to note that the advisory council, which recommended the subsidy type of federal-state system, specifically stated in its report that states should be permitted to adopt any one of four types of laws, including "separate accounts for all employers (or groups of employers) provided contributions of not less than 1% of the payroll are made to a State fund." It is also pertinent to note that the Business Advisory Council of the Department of Commerce, which, as already stated, favored the subsidy type of federal-state system, gave as one of its reasons that the subsidy plan would provide "a clearer basis for experimentation [with employer experience rating] along interstate and even national lines."

As a matter of fact, all of the leading advocates of federal action on unemployment insurance, irrespective of their convictions about whether it should be a straight federal system, the subsidy plan, or the tax-offset plan, were in agreement in favoring some form of employer experience rating. The President had stated in his message to Congress of June 8, 1934, that unemployment insurance should be set up in such a way as to encourage stabilization of employment. He stressed this in his initial meeting with Miss Perkins, Dr. Witte, and me in August 1934. He mentioned it again in his November 14, 1934, address to the National Conference on Economic Security. He made the following significant addition to a draft of his message to Congress, transmitting the report of the committee, which I had prepared for him: "Moreover, in order to encourage the stabilization of private employment, Federal legislation should not foreclose the States from establishing means for inducing industries to afford an even greater stabilization of employment." This addition came as a complete surprise to all of us.

The committee recognized from the outset that there would need to be a two-pronged program to provide security for the aged, consisting of public assistance for persons already aged and in need and a social insurance system to provide benefits for workers who retired from the labor market in the years to come. The constitutional question of whether a straight federal system of old age security or a cooperative federal-state system was more likely to be upheld by the Supreme Court was of great concern to the committee. However, the committee decided it should recommend a straight federal system even though the risk of its being declared unconstitutional might be greater.

The reason was that the actuaries were unanimous in advising the committee against a state-by-state system. They pointed out that the great mobility of workers made it impossible to estimate the future age composition of the working population of each state or the length of time that individual workers would be working in a particular state before retiring. These estimates needed to be reasonably accurate in order to determine future costs.

The actuaries were of the opinion that this difficulty could be mitigated but not entirely overcome if each state was required to adopt a uniform system and to transfer records, wage credits, and contributions of individual workers who moved from one state to another. The committee was inclined to believe that the constitutionality of such an old age security system was open to as much doubt as a straight federal system. It was also appalled at the administrative difficulties that would be involved.

Therefore, the committee decided it was necessary to concentrate on the development of a straight federal system. However, the committee was not clear about how a contributory social insurance system could pay reasonably adequate benefits to workers already middle-aged, for whom not enough contributions would have been paid to cover the cost of these benefits.

The technical staff presented a plan to the committee which seemed to solve this dilemma. I well remember the November 27 meeting when the staff exhibited a wall chart which illustrated how the plan would work. It showed two lines: one declining year by year, which represented the declining number of old age assistance recipients; the other rising year by year, which represented the number of old age insurance beneficiaries. The two lines eventually crossed, demonstrating how the old age insurance system would gradually liquidate the old age assistance system.

The technicians explained that reasonably adequate benefits could be paid to workers reaching retirement age in the early years of the old age insurance operation by using some of the current receipts to pay the cost in excess of the contributions which had been paid on behalf of these workers. They said current receipts would be sufficient to cover the cost of current benefits for many years to come. Therefore, there would be no necessity for a government subsidy to pay for the excess cost of the benefits paid to these older workers until the time when receipts no longer exceeded benefits. When that time was reached, the cost of federal grants to the states for old age assistance would have decreased correspondingly. This would be so because the old age insurance system would be meeting the needs of old people who would otherwise have been obliged to seek old age assistance.

The committee was delighted with this plan because it made possible the payment of reasonably adequate benefits to older workers without requiring a government subsidy out of general revenues until many years later, when such a subsidy would be largely offset by the decreased cost to the federal government of old age assistance. Accordingly, the committee directed the staff to put the plan in final form.

As previously stated, the committee decided at the very beginning that it would not include any recommendations regarding health insurance in its report to the President, which had to be ready by the time Congress reconvened. The committee recognized that this was a very complex and controversial subject which might jeopardize speedy and favorable congressional action on its other recommendations.

But the committee did appoint a Medical Advisory Committee, composed of well-known physicians, including the President of the American Medical Association. The committee's staff also invited staff members of the American Medical Association to participate in the meetings of this advisory committee.

The attitude of the American Medical Association, as expressed in the *Journal of the American Medical Association,* which had previously been antagonistic to the committee, became very cooperative. Therefore, the committee was hopeful that its Medical Advisory Committee would be able to agree at least on the broad general principles that should be observed in any government health insurance system, regardless of whether some of the members might be opposed to the basic idea of government health insurance.

The President himself took a personal interest in these developments, not only because of his interest in the subject but possibly because one of the members of the Medical Advisory Committee was Dr. Harvey Cushing of Boston, a noted brain surgeon, who was the father-in-law of the President's son, James Roosevelt. He directed his personal physician, Dr. Ross McIntyre, to keep in close touch with the work of the Committee on Economic Security in this field. When it came time for the committee to complete its final report, it was agreed that the Medical Advisory Committee should have until March 1, 1935, to make its recommendations. However, the committee did decide to include in its report a statement that, in addition to the public health program which it recommended, it believed the next major step should be the application of the principles of insurance to risks arising out of ill-health.

The staff also persuaded the committee to say that, while it could not make any specific recommendations until the Medical Advisory Committee made its report, it believed it desirable to indicate broad principles and general observations which appeared to be fundamental to the design of a sound plan of health. The committee then proceeded to list these. As will appear later, this created something of a furor.

The various other recommendations made by the committee did not require any extended consideration. However, it should be noted that its recommendations of grants to the states for the needy aged and dependent children did not go as far as the recommendation of the advisory council. The council had urged federal grants-in-aid for all needy persons. But the committee believed, as stated in its report, that if all of its other recommendations were adopted, "the residual-relief problem will have diminished to a point where it will be possible to return primary responsibility for the care of people who cannot work to the State and local governments.

Miss Perkins and Mr. Hopkins met with the President on December 24 to discuss all of its contemplated recommendations. The President approved of all of the recommendations. So Dr. Witte proceeded to draft the committee's report which the executive order had stipulated was due on December 1.

This draft was completed and placed in the hands of all the members of the committee during the last week in December. Before signing the report, several members said they wanted their subordinates to examine both the language used and the policies recommended. This caused considerable delay, particularly on the part of the Secretary of the Treasury. He first stated he would not sign the report without a qualifying statement to the effect that he disagreed with the financing of the old age insurance program and favored employee contributions in unemployment insurance.

This attitude of the Secretary of the Treasury was due to several factors. He was extremely conscientious but cautious, and uncertain many times whether he was making the correct decision. In this instance he had been absorbed in other problems and had let the work of the committee fall largely on Josephine Roche, who was Assistant Secretary of the Treasury. He was beset by divided opinions over the report among his immediate staff members, some feeling the committee proposals were too conservative and some feeling they were unsound from a fiscal standpoint. This was exceedingly distressing to the Secretary because he was both socially minded and conservative by nature.

The Secretary finally decided to sign the report without insisting upon a qualifying statement, and the signed report was delivered to the President on January 15, 1935.

On the afternoon of January 16, after the President had already notified Congress that on the following day he would present a special message on economic security, he sent for Miss Perkins. He said there must be some mistake in a table which appeared in the report since he had not understood that a large deficit to be met out of general revenues would develop in the old age insurance system beginning in 1965. It is probable his attention had been called to this by the Secretary of the Treasury. When informed that the table was correct, the President said the report must be changed at least to the extent of indicating this plan was only one of several that Congress might consider. He also directed that the committee proceed to develop, as soon as possible, a completely self-sustaining old age insurance system.

The next day, January 17, the President forwarded the committee's report which incorporated the change suggested by him. It was accompanied by a message endorsing the recommendations made by the committee and urging immediate congressional action.

The President's committee felt that the two men in Congress who, in the previous session, had sponsored the unemployment insurance bill which the President had endorsed, should have the honor of introducing the Administration's economic security bill. Those men were Senator Robert F. Wagner of New York and Congressman David J. Lewis of Maryland. The committee had also hoped that the congressional leaders would set up a special joint committee of both the Senate and the House of Representatives to consider the Administration's bill. It turned out that these plans had not taken into account the strong procedural traditions of Congress. The House Committee on Ways and Means was particularly sensitive about its prerogatives.

The result was that in addition to the introduction of two identical bills by Senator Wagner and Congressman Lewis, the Chairman of the Committee on Ways and Means, Robert L. Doughton, insisted upon introducing a third identical bill. This was introduced after the first two bills, since Congressman Doughton had not been furnished a copy, but was nevertheless given a lower number.

The congressional leaders also flatly refused to set up a special committee and insisted that the bills should be referred to the standing committee in each house concerned with taxation. These were the House Committee on Ways and Means and the Senate Committee on Finance.

The Chairman of the Senate Finance Committee, Pat Harrison of Mississippi, did not insist upon introducing a bill in his own name. In the course of the hearings and executive sessions of his committee, he demonstrated great skill and loyalty to the Administration in securing approval of the main features of the Administration's program.

The Chairman of the House Committee on Ways and Means, Robert L. Doughton, although he had insisted upon introducing the bill as a matter of protocol, looked upon the bill as an Administration proposal for which he did not accept personal responsibility. This was largely due to the fact that his sense of caution and integrity inhibited him from endorsing novel proposals that he did not fully understand. However, he was completely loyal to the Administration and permitted two of the ranking Democrats of his committee to take the leadership in the committee consideration of the bill. These men were Fred M. Vinson of Kentucky, later Chief Justice of the United States Supreme Court, and Jere Cooper of Tennessee, who had been chairman of a subcommittee which held hearings on the Wagner-Lewis Bill during the previous session.

The referral of the Administration's bill to the Ways and Means Committee was bitterly opposed by William P. Connery of Massachusetts, Chairman of the Labor Committee, who wished to have the bill referred to his committee. He and Senator Clarence C. Dill of Washington had co-sponsored a bill which had passed the House in both 1933 and 1934, appropriating $10 million a year to finance grants to the states to cover one-third of the cost of old age pensions.

When he was rebuffed, he scheduled hearings on a sweeping bill, introduced by Congressman Ernest Lundeen of Minnesota, known as the "workers' unemployment and social insurance bill."

It was alleged that this bill had been prepared by Mary Van Kleeck, Director of Industrial Studies for the Russell Sage Foundation, who supported it as a representative of what was known as the Inter-Professional Association for Social Insurance. It was also supported by the Communist party in the United States. Although the Lundeen bill was actually reported favorably by the Labor Committee on March 15 while the Ways and Means Committee was still considering the Administration's proposal, it never reached the floor of the House.

The House Ways and Means Committee originally decided to begin its hearings on January 22. But when it heard that the Senate Finance Committee had scheduled its public hearings on the bill to begin on that day, the Ways and Means Committee insisted upon beginning January 21, although the Chairman of the Committee on Economic Security, Miss Perkins, was unable to appear on that day because of a long-standing commitment to speak at a Southern Labor Conference. Therefore, Dr. Witte began the presentation of the Committee on Economic Security, which lasted for two full days, after which Miss Perkins and other government witnesses appeared before the Ways and Means Committee.

The initial press reaction was favorable. But by the time the two congressional committees had concluded their public hearings in the middle of February, it had become distinctly unfavorable. There was considerable opposition to the omnibus character of the bill. Likewise, there was considerable protest leveled to the general effect that, while the objectives were commendable, there had not been thorough consideration. This reaction was probably caused to some extent by the disagreement over the relative merits of the subsidy type and the tax-offset type of federal-state unemployment insurance system.

This disagreement had been reported in the press as early as November when the advisory council was considering the subject. In the course of the public hearings, it was again given attention by the press since the Chairman of the advisory council and several other members of the council, as well as a number of other experts, testified in favor of the subsidy type. It is interesting to note that some of the experts who testified in favor of the subsidy type, such as Senator Paul Douglas, then a professor at the University of Chicago, and Abraham Epstein, Executive Secretary of the American Association for Social Security, a few months previously had supported the Wagner-Lewis Bill which incorporated the tax-offset device.

While the testimony in favor of the subsidy type may have had some effect on the press reaction, it had no apparent effect on either congressional committee. This was partly due to the belief of a number of influential members that it was not likely to be held constitutional. But, more importantly, the committee members realized that the chief reason the subsidy type was favored by its proponents was that they believed it would make possible more stringent federal controls over state unemployment insurance laws. As will appear later, the committees rejected a number of the minimum requirements for such laws, as recommended by the President's committee, and accordingly did not look with favor on the far more extensive requirements proposed by the advocates of the subsidy type.

What was of far greater interest to the committees was the attitude of various groups such as labor organizations, employers' associations, and Townsendites. The Townsendites were particularly vocal, being organized into hundreds of clubs and having a national publication, *The Townsend Weekly.*

Dr. Townsend appeared before the Ways and Means Committee to propose that his plan be substituted for the old age security titles of the economic security bill, although he did not oppose the bill as a whole. But his appearance and the flood of letters the committee received tended to create the idea that the real issue lay between the Townsend plan and the economic security bill.

Organized labor took little interest in the passage of the economic security bill until after it had passed the House and was reported out by the Senate Finance Committee. Indeed, when President William Green of the American Federation of Labor appeared before the congressional committees, some of the newspapers interpreted his testimony as an attack upon the bill. The reason was that he presented a long statement, probably prepared by his staff, making many suggestions for improving the bill. Later, however, when a struggle began in the Senate and continued between the Senate and House conferees over what was known as the Clark amendment, the American Federation of

Labor did everything it could to insure the final passage of the bill.

Employers' groups were divided in their attitude toward the proposed legislation. The employers who were members of the advisory council to the Committee on Economic Security, most of whom were also members of the Business Advisory Council of the Department of Commerce, favored the program. The United States Chamber of Commerce and the National Retail Dry Goods Association also supported the program. However, the National Association of Manufacturers, the National Metal Trades Association, the National Publishers Association, the Connecticut Manufacturers Association, the Illinois Manufacturers Association, and the Ohio Chamber of Commerce were opposed.

The American Association of Social Workers and social workers generally supported the proposed legislation. However, they urged that federal grants to the states include not only the needy aged and dependent children, but all needy persons.

As has already been mentioned, the inclusion in the report of the Committee on Economic Security of a discussion of health insurance, accompanied by a statement that the committee would make recommendations later, created something of a furor among the officers of the American Medical Association. A special meeting of its House of Delegates was called, the first since World War I. Resolutions were adopted condemning government health insurance and opposing the proposed maternal and child health services to be carried on by the Children's Bureau. However, an increased appropriation for public health work was endorsed.

The foregoing recital may provide some indication of the congressional situation and the public attitude as the Administration proceeded with the presentation of its proposals to the congressional committees. All of the government's witnesses had finished testifying before the Ways and Means Committee during the first week of its hearings except the Secretary of the Treasury, Henry Morgenthau, Jr. He appeared a week later to present the Administration's proposal for a completely self-sustaining old age insurance system which had been agreed upon by the Committee on Economic Security and approved by the President. Both the original plan and the new plan contained a schedule providing for a rising rate of contributions rather than a fixed rate. Also under both plans employees and employers each paid one-half of the combined rate. However, under the new plan the initial rate was set at 2 per cent instead of 1 per cent and rose to 6 per cent in 12 years instead of 5 per cent in 20 years.

The consequence was that an eventual reserve of $47 billion would be built up instead of $15 billion. The new plan was criticized by employers because it placed too heavy and sudden a burden on business and because it would create a dangerously high reserve. However, it was made a part of the bill recommended by the House Ways and Means Committee, and later by the Senate Finance Committee, and eventually became a part of the Social Security Act.

But the acceptance of the Morgenthau recommendation to make the old age insurance system self-supporting did not mean that either congressional committee favored the basic idea of a national old age insurance system. On the contrary, in both committees, there was strong opposition to the proposal. This opposition, plus the more general opposition already mentioned, prompted the leading members of the Ways and Means Committee to approach the President to ascertain whether he wanted the omnibus character of the bill kept intact and to tell him that the opposition to the old age insurance proposal was so great that it would not be possible to get a favorable vote on this feature of the bill. The President informed them that he wanted the whole bill passed and that old age insurance must stay in the bill. The final result was that a majority in the Ways and Means Committee could be secured for old age insurance only by inducing several wavering members to vote for its inclusion in exchange for the elimination of another feature of the bill providing for the sale by the Treasury of voluntary old age annuities. Apparently the reason this was considered a quid pro quo was that it removed at least one threat to private insurance companies.

There was an important change made in the eligibility conditions for an old age insurance benefit. This was the elimination of the provision that the individual "is not employed by another in a gainful occupation." The reason for the change was that the legislative draftsman considered this language too indefinite and no other language was found that was satisfactory.

There was also an important change made in the conditions

that a state must meet to qualify for the receipt of federal grants for old age assistance. This was the requirement that the state must furnish assistance at least great enough to provide, when added to the income of the aged recipient, "a reasonable subsistence compatible with decency and health." This requirement was objected to by southern members of the committee particularly. It was also objected to by a southern member of the Senate Finance Committee, as will appear later. The reason given was that it was too indefinite and gave too much authority to the federal agency administering the grants. Undoubtedly, the question of the relative standard of living of Negroes as compared with white people was a large factor involved in this objection.

There was no difference of opinion within either the House Ways and Means Committee or the Senate Finance Committee that the tax-offset type of federal-state system of unemployment insurance was preferable to the subsidy type. However, the leaders on the Ways and Means Committee did question the desirability of the employer experience rating provision which allowed employers to claim additional credit against the proposed federal unemployment tax in excess of the amount they had paid under a state unemployment insurance law, if the state law permitted them a reduction in their contribution rate because of their favorable unemployment experience. It was contended that this additional credit provision, by destroying the uniformity of the tax rate, not only would raise a serious constitutional question but would also expose employers to unfair interstate competition because of the varying rates that would be payable by their competitors under the various state laws. The result was that the Ways and Means Committee eliminated the employer experience rating provision.

There were two other important changes made by the Ways and Means Committee, both having to do with the administration of the new law. One was the elimination of a requirement that states would be required to establish a merit system for the selection of employees engaged in the administration of old age assistance, aid to dependent children, and maternal and child health programs. Instead there was inserted specific language saying that states must provide methods of administration necessary for efficient operation "other than those relating to selection, tenure of office, and compensation of personnel." The reason given by a leading member of the committee, Fred M. Vinson of Kentucky, who later became Chief Justice of the United States Supreme Court, was colorfully expressed as follows: "No damned social workers are going to come into my State to tell our people whom they shall hire."

The other change was to create a new and independent federal administrative agency to be known as the Social Security Board to administer old age insurance, unemployment insurance, old age assistance, and aid to dependent children. The Cabinet committee had recommended that a Social Insurance Board within the Department of Labor should administer old age insurance and unemployment insurance, but that the Federal Emergency Relief Administration should administer old age assistance and aid to dependent children. There was no disagreement between the Cabinet committee and the congressional committee that the Children's Bureau should administer the maternal and child health and welfare programs and the U.S. Public Health Service administer the public health program.

There was much to be said for the congressional committee's decision to make a single, permanent federal agency responsible for the administration of both the social insurance and public assistance programs included in the Social Security Act. The reason the Cabinet committee had separated the two was that it believed the social insurances were a phase of labor legislation which should be administered by the Department of Labor. The Cabinet committee felt that public assistance should be related to the work relief programs administered by the Federal Emergency Relief Administration, which, it expected, would eventually be succeeded by a permanent federal agency.

The congressional committee, in making the change, did so for a variety of reasons. It probably was impressed with the close relationship between social insurance and public assistance and also disliked placing the administration of a permanent program in the hands of an emergency agency. However, it must be recorded that influential members of both houses of Congress disliked the Department of Labor, because they considered it pro-labor, and also the Secretary of Labor. It is my opinion that the personal dislike of the Secretary of Labor was due largely to the fact that she was a woman and an articulate, intelligent woman at that, as well as to the fact that she was not sufficiently amenable to patronage needs.

The executive sessions of the Ways and Means Committee ended on April 5, at which time the committee took a vote on recommending the passage of the bill as amended. All of the Democratic members, except one, voted for the bill, and all of the Republican members voted against it. The Republican members filed a minority report in which they stated they were opposed to the old age insurance provisions of the bill. The reasons they gave, in addition to contending these provisions were unconstitutional, were as follows:

These titles impose a crushing burden upon industry and upon labor.

They establish a bureaucracy in the field of insurance in competition with private business.

They destroy old-age retirement systems set up by private industries, which in most instances provide more liberal benefits than are contemplated under title II.

In addition to these reasons, at least one of the influential minority members was inclined to favor the Townsend plan. It seemed incongruous at the time that a conservative should consider a universal pension plan paying a large, flat amount, irrespective of need, to be less of a threat to our existing institutions than a contributory social insurance system paying benefits related to wage loss.

The bill, as amended, was called the social security bill and was reported to the House on April 5. The debate in the House of Representatives lasted from April 11 to April 19. About fifty amendments were offered, none of which was adopted. The one which received the largest vote would have provided for federal grants to the states to cover the entire cost of $50 a month old age assistance grants without requiring any matching by the states. Amendments to substitute the Townsend plan or the Lundeen bill received about fifty votes each.

Some of the language used by leading Republican members in the debate was rather purple. Thus, in the debate on April 19, 1935, Congressman John Taber of New York said, "Never in the history of the world has any measure been brought here so insidiously designed as to prevent business recovery, to enslave workers and to prevent any possibility of the employers providing work for the people.

Congressman Daniel Reed, also of New York and a member of the Ways and Means Committee, predicted, "The lash of the dictator will be felt and 25 million free American citizens will for the first time submit themselves to a fingerprint test."

Congressman James W. Wadsworth, likewise of New York, alleged that, "This bill opens the door and invites the entrance into the political field of a power so vast, so powerful as to threaten the integrity of our institutions and to pull the pillars of the temple down upon the heads of our descendants."

The decisive motion to recommit the bill with instructions to eliminate the old age insurance provisions was made by Congressman Treadway, ranking Republican member of the Ways and Means Committee. This motion lost, although all the Republican members of the House who voted, except one, supported it. The final vote was 371 to 33 in favor of the bill. This large vote for the bill in the exact form recommended by the Ways and Means Committee was due in considerable part to the fact that this committee is undoubtedly the most powerful committee of the House. It not only has jurisdiction over all tax bills but is also the committee on committees which recommends to the House who shall serve as members of other committees.

While, as previously stated, the public hearings began simultaneously before the committees in the House and Senate, those before the Senate proceeded at a more leisurely pace. This was because of the custom in the Senate of holding committee hearings only in the morning, before the Senate convened.

There was a wide range in the general attitudes of the Senate committee members. At one extreme, concern was expressed that the proposed program substituted social security for the struggle for existence and took the private property of one individual to give it to another who, the government determined, needed it more. This point of view was expressed by blind Senator Gore of Oklahoma, who finally asked Miss Perkins this question (which does not appear in the printed hearings): "Now, Miss Perkins, wouldn't you agree that there is a teeny-weeny bit of socialism in your program?"

At the other extreme was the view of Senator Black (now Justice Black) that a considerable part of the cost of unemployment insurance and old age insurance should be met out of progressive taxes. He was of the opinion that sole reliance on payroll taxes resulted in persons with low incomes being obliged to pay, both as workers and as consumers, too heavy a share of the cost.

In the hearings before the Senate Finance Committee, as in the hearings before the Ways and Means Committee, it was necessary for Dr. Witte to testify ahead of Miss Perkins, because she had not yet completed her testimony before the Ways and Means Committee. Dr. Witte testified at length, both before and after Miss Perkins appeared. However, he did not have the opportunity that he had had in the House committee hearings of making a complete statement before questioning began.

Most of the questioning had to do with old age security, particularly old age assistance. Senator Byrd of Virginia focused his questioning on the requirement to be met by states, in order to receive federal grants for old age assistance, that a state plan must furnish assistance at least great enough to provide, when added to the income of the aged recipient, "a reasonable subsistence compatible with decency and health."

Dr. Witte pointed out that this provision was taken from the Massachusetts and New York laws and constituted a flexible standard related to varying circumstances throughout the country. However, Senator Byrd forced Dr. Witte to admit that in the final analysis this requirement meant that a federal official had the right to determine what constituted reasonable subsistence compatible with decency and health. The result was that the committee eliminated this clause from the bill.

The Senate Finance Committee completed its public hearings on February 20 but did not begin to hold executive sessions until the first week in May. At that time it proceeded to consider the social security bill as passed by the House, not the economic security bill as introduced by Senator Wagner. This was in accordance with its usual legislative procedure.

On May 6, a few days after the Senate Finance Committee began its executive sessions, the United States Supreme Court held the Railroad Retirement Act unconstitutional. This added to the difficulties encountered in obtaining a favorable vote on the old age insurance proposal. The Administration spokesmen undertook to differentiate between the act declared unconstitutional and the Administration's proposal, pointing out that the former had been based on the federal power to regulate interstate commerce whereas the latter was based on the taxing power. Nevertheless, the opponents in the committee used the decision as a final argument.

In addition, what was known as the Clark amendment caused great controversy. This amendment provided for exemption from the government old age insurance system of employers and employees participating in a private pension plan which was more liberal. On the face of it, this amendment appeared reasonable and desirable. However, the government experts considered the actuarial and administrative difficulties to be insurmountable.

The Chairman of the Senate Finance Committee deferred taking a vote until he considered it propitious to do so. When he did, the old age insurance section of the bill as passed by the House, but including a requirement of retirement from "regular employment" as a condition for the receipt of benefits, was approved by a substantial majority. But the Clark amendment failed of adoption by a tie vote.

As was true in the Ways and Means Committee, there was no sentiment for either a straight federal unemployment insurance system or the subsidy type of federal-state system. Moreover, the Railroad Retirement Act decision had raised constitutional doubts about how far the federal government could go in taking direct action or controlling the action taken by the states. Therefore, the committee adopted with little discussion an amendment offered by Senator LaFollette which allowed each state the freedom to have the type of unemployment insurance system it desired, including employer experience rating. In doing so, the committee did not include the condition recommended by the President's committee that a state law must require all employers to pay at least 1 per cent of their payroll into a pooled fund. As will be discussed later, this omission has had a profound effect upon the development of unemployment insurance in this country.

In addition to the foregoing changes, the committee added a title providing federal grants to the states for aid to the blind on the same basis as for old age assistance. It also added a permanent authorization for federal grants to the states for vocational rehabilitation. This replaced the previous practice of year to year authorizations.

Finally, the Senate Finance Committee voted to put the Social Security Board in the Department of Labor and to place the administration of aid to dependent children in the Children's Bureau. However, this was done not because the Senate committee members felt more kindly toward the Department of Labor than did the House committee members, but because of urging by the President. Moreover, the language of this change specified that the Social Security Board would have full authority to appoint personnel. Another indication of the attitude of committee members was the fact that the committee emasculated the requirement that the states must pay unemployment benefits specifically through public employment offices operated by the states in cooperation with the United States Employment Service. It added the qualifying phrase "to the extent that such offices exist and are designated by the State for the purpose." This was due to personal dislike for the Director of the United States Employment Service who not only resisted patronage requests but did so in what members of Congress considered an offensive manner.

The committee filed its report recommending passage of the bill as amended on May 20. However, the Senate did not take up the bill until June 14, largely because of a filibuster by Senator Huey Long. The debate lasted five days and most of it concerned old age insurance, particularly the Clark amendment. This amendment was finally passed by a vote of 51 to 35 on June 19. Later the same day the Senate passed the bill by a vote of 77 to 6. However, prior to this final vote, Senator Hastings, a Republican member of the Finance Committee, made a motion to eliminate the old age insurance provisions, saying that this legislation could "end the progress of a great country and bring its people to the level of the average European." This motion lost, although 12 of the 16 Republican members voting supported it. There were only 19 Republican members of the Senate at that time.

The conference committee of the two houses did not begin consideration until ten days later. The House conferees quickly accepted the Senate changes on unemployment insurance, except that the language relating to the use of public employment offices was modified to provide that payment of unemployment compensation must be paid through public employment offices or such other agencies as the Social Security Board approved. The House conferees also accepted the restoration of the provision that retirement from regular employment was required for the receipt of old age insurance benefits. They also accepted the addition of aid to the blind and the permanent authorization for vocational rehabilitation grants.

But the House conferees insisted that the Social Security Board should be independent and that the administration of aid to dependent children should be one of its responsibilities. The Senate conferees readily agreed to recede on these differences.

However, the situation was quite different as regards the Clark amendment to the old age insurance provisions. The President had indicated he would not approve the bill unless this amendment was eliminated. Nevertheless, the Senate instructed its conferees to insist upon its inclusion.

This stalemate continued until the first week in August, and there was some concern that Congress would adjourn without taking action. But the deadlock was finally resolved by an agreement to eliminate the Clark amendment, with the understanding that a special committee would be appointed to prepare a satisfactory amendment, embodying the principle of the Clark amendment, to be presented to the next session of Congress.*

Both the House and Senate promptly accepted the conferees' recommendations, and the bill was then sent to the President for his approval. He signed it August 14, 1935, and thus the Social Security Act became a part of the law of the land.

---

* It is interesting to note that, by the time the next session of Congress convened, interest in the Clark amendment had disappeared. The Senate Finance Committee appointed a subcommittee which drafted an amendment. Representatives of the Senate Finance Committee and the House Ways and Means Committee then met but took no action. This was because employers and insurance companies came to realize the difficulties and the probability that, even if these difficulties could be resolved, there would be stringent governmental controls imposed. These governmental controls would have been necessary to assure actuarial soundness, proper investment and control of funds, and protection of beneficiaries' rights.

2.

Putting the
Social Security Act
into Operation, 1935–37

Even before the President signed the bill, I had prepared a budget estimate of the probable cost of administration during the fiscal year ending June 30, 1936. This was necessary since it was anticipated that Congress would adjourn before the end of August. In order to save time, the Chairman of the House Appropriations Committee, James P. ("Buck") Buchanan, held a one-man hearing instead of calling his committee together. His parents had moved to Texas when he was less than a year old, and he was of the same breed as Sam Rayburn, the late Speaker of the House.

This first budget amounted to one million dollars. Today the budget for the administration of the federal old age, survivors', and disability insurance system alone amounts to one-third of a billion dollars. I must confess that this first budget was based entirely upon conjecture. But strangely enough, it turned out to be remarkably accurate!

To my dismay, the Chairman of the committee leaned back in his chair at the end of the presentation, put his feet on his desk, and said, "I don't understand a damned thing that you're saying and I don't believe you do, either." Then, after a pause he added, "But I'll give you the money anyway."

The President proceeded promptly to send to the Senate the names of the three nominees for members of the Social Security Board, including mine as one of the three. These were all confirmed by the Senate on August 23. But to the dismay of every one concerned, Senator Huey Long staged another filibuster on the closing day of the session while the last deficiency appropriation bill, which included the social security item, was still pending.

I well remember watching the hands of the Senate clock move toward midnight, when Congress would adjourn *sine die,* and hoping against hope that the Senator would end his filibuster which had no relation to social security. However, he was still talking when the presiding officer banged his gavel, signaling the end of the session.

The next morning the President called a conference to discuss what could be done to avoid calling a special session of Congress. Included in the conference were both leaders of Congress and members of the Administration. I was the only one of the newly appointed members of the Social Security Board who was present. The Comptroller General, John R. McCarl, furnished the solution. This was surprising, since he was a Republican, appointed for a 15-year term, and completely independent of the Administration, being solely responsible to the Congress. Furthermore, traditionally the Comptroller acts as the "watchdog of the Treasury," to make certain that federal funds are spent properly and only for the purposes authorized by Congress.

Mr. McCarl's solution was ingenious indeed and gratefully accepted by the President. Mr. McCarl pointed out that the work of the President's Committee on Economic Security had been financed as a research project by the Federal Emergency Relief Administration. He said that he, therefore, thought it entirely logical and proper to set up another research project to develop ways and means of putting the Social Security Act into operation!

So it came about that the much maligned Federal Emergency Relief Administration (which became the Works Progress Administration in 1935) again demonstrated its remarkable ability to cope with problems arising out of the Great Depression. Another resource was found in the National Industrial Recovery Administration. The National Recovery Act had been declared unconstitutional in May 1935. Therefore, it was liquidating as rapidly as possible and was only too glad to transfer office equipment and personnel to the Social Security Board. The personnel tranferred were continued on the payroll of the National Industrial Recovery Administration until funds were made available by Congress.

But one minor complication arose in the use of the emergency funds which had been made available. It was discovered that they could not be used for the payment of the salary of any person whose salary had been specified in any act of Congress. This meant that all the personnel, except the members of the Social Security Board, could be paid currently. Partly because of this fact and partly to retain my close contact with the Department of Labor as Assistant Secretary of Labor, I was not sworn in as a member of the Social Security Board until October 16, 1935, although I actually functioned as a member from the very beginning.

The first Chairman of the Social Security Board was John G. Winant, former Republican Governor of New Hampshire. His plan to cope with the problem of unemployment in his state and the record he had made in promoting progressive legislation had attracted nationwide attention. The third member was Vincent M. Miles, a lawyer from Arkansas, who had been Democratic National Committeeman from that state. The law required that not more than two members of the Board could be members of the same political party. Likewise, the President believed it desirable to have some one from a southern state who was known to southern members of Congress.

From the standpoint of speed and flexibility in the development of an administrative organization facing unprecedented problems, it was desirable to establish an independent agency such as the Social Security Board. It possessed great prestige since it was responsible only to the President. It was not obliged to obtain advance approval of any of its activities from a hierarchy of officials between it and the President. It was not bound by any precedents as are long-established governmental agencies.

Moreover, the fact that it was a board of three members, instead of a single administrator, was a great advantage. While, of course, the Board could not, if it would, escape responsibility for its actions, nevertheless its responsibility was a shared responsibility which gave both the Board members and those affected by its decisions greater confidence in those decisions.

But it must also be acknowledged that the board form of

organization had some disadvantages from the standpoint of establishing what administrators sometimes call a "chain of command." While the Board, at the very outset, agreed that it was necessary to delegate administrative authority to an Executive Director and that it should concentrate on policy matters, it did not actually do so in practice. This was due, in part, to the intrinsic difficulty of separating "policy" and "administration." It was also due to the human desire of individual Board members (including myself) to have a hand in making important decisions.

This inherent difficulty in the board form of organization was accentuated greatly by the inability of the Board members to agree upon the individual to serve as Executive Director. The result was that, in addition to the Executive Director, a "Coordinator" was appointed, both being separately responsible to the Board. It was agreed that the Coordinator would not have any administrative responsibility, but would confine himself to planning the organization and procedures, particularly those of budget and accounting. In practice it was, of course, impossible to distinguish between planning and administration. Therefore, this compromise arrangement was terminated by the resignation of the Coordinator when I succeeded the first Chairman of the Board in 1936.

The Board acquired an impersonal prestige which not only lent weight to its decisions but provided some protection from outside pressures. A little later these pressures concerned policy decisions of great importance. But in the beginning they involved the selection of personnel.

The pressures concerning policy decisions grew out of the very nature of the program itself. This program affected the daily lives of millions of Americans. Much of it involved cooperation between the federal and state governments, unprecedented in its complexity and scope. These pressures were most acute as regards the duty of the Board to withhold federal grants if it found, after an investigation and a public hearing, that a state law or its administration was not in conformity with the requirements of the Social Security Act. The withdrawal of federal grants meant that innocent beneficiaries would suffer because of the dereliction or maladministration of state officials. Therefore, effective cooperation between federal and state officials to avoid the necessity for such drastic action was the very essence of successful operation.

Regarding pressures about the selection of personnel, it must be remembered that the Great Depression was still a grim reality for millions of unemployed Americans. In their desperation they pursued every possibility that might lead to a job, including appeals to members of Congress. Thus beset, members of Congress naturally turned to this new and presumably gigantic federal agency as a source of thousands of jobs.

There was considerable protection from job-seekers and their sponsors in the fact that all personnel of the Board, except attorneys and experts, had to be recruited through the civil service system. This meant competitive examinations for all employees except the very small number of attorneys and experts whom the Civil Service Commission was willing to approve, provided they possessed exceptional qualifications specified by the commission. Likewise, there was some protection in the very fact that the Social Security Board would have no appropriation until the next session of Congress.

In an effort to lessen the deluge of job seekers, the Social Security Board publicized as much as possible the fact that during the first year and a half before the old age insurance provisions would go into effect, it would function with a very small staff, consisting for the most part of persons transferred from the staff of the Committee on Economic Security and from the National Industrial Recovery Administration.

The Board then proceeded to appoint an Executive Director and eight bureau chiefs who were given authority to select their respective staffs, subject to Board approval. These top officials were all persons of integrity with professional training and long experience in public administration and various specialized fields. They were given a free hand to select equally dedicated and qualified assistants who, in turn, were given the same freedom in the selection of subordinate officials, and so on down the line.

The Board's personnel policy immediately ran into trouble with important members of Congress both in the Senate and the House. Leading members of the House Ways and Means Committee were particularly affronted at not having been given the opportunity to have a hand in the appointment of key officials.

They called a meeting of all the Democratic members of the committee and notified me to appear. When I did so, they upbraided me for not consulting them in the selection of personnel since they were the ones who had been largely responsible for the legislation.

It developed that these congressmen were very familiar with key personnel actions that had already occurred. I did my best to convince the members of the congressional committee that the Social Security Board had meant no discourtesy in not having consulted with members of the committee. I told them the Board would give careful consideration to any recommendations they made, but reminded them as inoffensively as possible that personnel appointments had to be made in accordance with civil service regulations.

While some of the personal resentment of members of Congress was mollified as a result of this meeting and countless similar conferences with individual congressmen, the basic substantive conflict was really irreconcilable. The success of any organization, governmental or private, is largely dependent upon having officials who are completely committed to carrying out the purpose of the organization. If they owe their appointment to someone outside of the organization, there is always the danger of a conflict of loyalties affecting their actions.

Many other incidents in the course of the first year and a half of operations illustrate the political difficulties encountered in the appointment of personnel. One acute situation involved the recommendation of a wholly unqualified person to be Personnel Director. This was a position which required a person not only with high technical qualifications and long experience in government recruitment but also with dedication to serving the best interests of the Social Security Board, unbeholden to any outside individuals or group.

The congressman making the recommendation was the same member of the Ways and Means Committee, Fred M. Vinson, who had had inserted in the Social Security Act the provision that state agencies receiving federal grants-in-aid would not be required to include in their administrative procedures methods for the selection, tenure of office, and compensation of personnel. It was impossible to convince Mr. Vinson that his candidate was wholly unqualified. Nor was he interested in placing his candidate in a lesser position for which the candidate was qualified.

I vividly recall that after the final conference to discuss this matter, Mr. Vinson, the Chairman of the Ways and Means Committee, and I were walking down a corridor when an amazing incident occurred, which illustrated the intensity of the feeling surrounding patronage. In response to a point-blank question whether I would make the desired appointment, I replied rather self-righteously that I would have to act as my conscience dictated. Mr. Vinson lost his temper, pushed me against a wall, shook his fist at me, and shouted in emphatic expletives that he also had a conscience! Mr. Vinson was probably the ablest and certainly the most influential member of the Ways and Means Committee. As already mentioned, he later became Chief Justice of the United States Supreme Court.

In 1936 the Chairman of the Senate Appropriations Committee, Carter Glass of Virginia, insisted upon the appointment of a very nice woman who, the Social Security Board considered, could not qualify as an expert, since her only qualification was that she had been employed in a local welfare agency in a minor clerical capacity. It was finally agreed that the Board would obtain the opinion of the Civil Service Commission whose approval was necessary in any case. To the consternation of the Board, the commission stated that the lady could qualify as an expert. Nevertheless, the Board declined to make the appointment, believing that it would lead to increased insistence by other members of Congress to make similar appointments.

The result was that Senator Glass inserted a rider into the 1937 appropriation bill, providing funds for the Social Security Board, which required Senate confirmation of all attorneys and experts not appointed under civil service whose salaries amounted to $5,000 or more per annum. The President signed the appropriation bill but sent a letter to the President of the Senate, stating that he regretted the "unfortunate" provision and expressing the hope that legislation would be enacted at an early date to place these positions under civil service.

On July 1, 1937, the President sent to the Senate the nominations for the fifty-one positions which required Senate confirmation. All of these nominations were ultimately confirmed. However, the episode did affect the morale of key officials of the Board already employed and increased the difficulty of recruiting additional key personnel. Although the same provision was inserted by the Senate in the following year's appropriation bill, it was eliminated upon the insistence of the House conferees.

Still another acute situation developed in 1937 because of the insistence of Senator McKellar, the Chairman of the subcommittee of the Senate Appropriations Committee having jurisdiction over the Social Security Board's appropriation, that he be consulted on the appointment of all local old age insurance office managers in his state. He was particularly insistent that a prominent political protégé of his be made manager of the largest office. This person happened to be fully qualified for the position. Unhappily, however, the other senator from that state, George Berry, also insisted upon being consulted on these appointments, and he declared the prospective appointee absolutely unacceptable. This created an impossible situation, which was compounded by the fact that the Chairman of the Democratic National Committee, James Farley, wanted Senator Berry and the Governor of the state, who were political allies, to be satisfied. When I went to the President with my troubles, the President refused to be concerned and said jokingly, "Cheer up! The good Lord in his wisdom may solve your difficulty by calling the old boy to his reward." This did not happen, but another circumstance solved the dilemma. Senator Berry and his ally, the Governor, both failed to be re-elected in 1938!

A very ugly situation developed during these first two years out of a story that reached the ears of members of the Ways and Means Committee. This story was to the effect that a very large proportion of the personnel appointed by the Board was Jewish. I became aware of this rumor when I was told by a member of the Ways and Means Committee that the Board was appointing "too damned many New York Jews." The Chairman of the Ways and Means Committee also told me this in more kindly and diplomatic language, saying that he had a very high regard for "members of your race" but that he and his associates were disturbed at the large number the Board was hiring. He was quite surprised to learn that I was not, in fact, Jewish.

The President himself received a number of complaints on this score and asked me what the facts were. Upon being informed that, while no statistics had been kept, the percentage of Jewish employees was very small, certainly much less than 5 per cent of the total personnel, he remarked laughingly that that was a smaller percentage than at Harvard.

As I reflected on this story, I reached the conclusion that it probably arose from several entirely fortuitous circumstances. One was that the personnel director happened to be Jewish. The other was that one of the civil service registers used for the recruitment of personnel in a particular bureau happened to have, at the top of the list, a considerable number of young college graduates with Jewish names. In any event, this rumor eventually quieted down, although probably did not entirely disappear until November 1937 when the Personnel Director was transferred from what had become a more routine job to head up the State Technical Advisory Service, a new service to the state agencies receiving federal grants. This service furnished badly needed technical aid to the state agencies in setting up merit systems for their personnel.

Those who have not had occasion to serve as a bureau or agency head in the federal government are likely to be surprised to discover from this recital that the separation of the legislative and executive branches of government is not as absolute as the Constitution prescribes. A well-known political scientist, after making an extensive study of the parliamentary form of government in a number of European countries, concluded that they had actual although not nominal separation of powers while we had nominal but not actual separation. This is true not only in personnel appointments but in many other administrative matters, such as location of offices, contracts, and policy decisions.

Administrative officials who fail to recognize this situation and learn to live with it are apt to find that their appropriations and legislative programs suffer accordingly. The Social Security Board was no exception. However, it managed to restore reasonably amicable relations with members of Congress by following a policy of carefully explaining in every instance why it was not possible to appoint a person recommended by a congressman, instead of simply writing a perfunctory letter acknowledging receipt of the congressman's letter of recommendation. In many cases the person recommended was qualified for some position and in such cases could be appointed if he had the requisite civil service status.

It may be of interest to observe that my experience concerning political pressures in the appointment of federal personnel was that these pressures came entirely from members of Congress and not from the much publicized "patronage dispensers" such as Postmaster General James A. Farley or the Democratic National Committee. As a matter of fact, Mr. Farley and the officials of the Democratic National Committee were exceedingly helpful in lessening political pressures.

Even before I became a member of the Social Security Board, I had several personal experiences which demonstrated this. For example, when I talked with Mr. Farley regarding my proposed appointment as Assistant Secretary of Labor, he asked me about my political affiliations in Wisconsin. I informed Mr. Farley that I had none. I was then asked how I had voted. When I told him that I had usually voted the Progressive Republican ticket in state elections because the real contest always was between the Progressive and the Stalwart Republicans, he asked how I had voted in national elections. When I said I had always voted Democratic except when the senior Senator LaFollette had been a presidential candidate, Mr. Farley said if he had lived in Wisconsin, he would have done the same.

After I became Assistant Secretary of Labor, one of my first assignments was to clear with Mr. Farley the proposed appointment of Katharine Lenroot as Chief of the Children's Bureau. Miss Lenroot was the daughter of a Republican senator who could have had the vice-presidential nomination in 1920 if he had desired it. Mr. Farley said he would not think of interfering in a professional appointment of this character.

Various writers have commented on the success of the Social Security Board in developing a highly efficient organization in a surprisingly short period of time—an organization which has stood the test of time. I am naturally gratified that there has been so much praise and so little criticism of the administration of the Social Security Act. It is my opinion that this success has been due very largely to the initial appointment, on a nonpolitical basis, of a handful of dedicated and highly qualified top officials who were given a free hand to select equally dedicated and qualified staff members, and so on down the line. I cannot hope to give adequate credit to each of these splendid public servants. Therefore, I have reluctantly concluded that it is better not to mention any of them by name in connection with the important decisions and actions which spelled the difference between success and failure in this great administrative undertaking. Organization charts and written procedures are essential. But they are no substitute for the right kind of human beings whose responsibility it is to make certain that the administration of social legislation actually achieves its beneficent purpose.

It is true, however, that administrative relationships, particularly the relationship between staff and line officials, should be made as clear as possible. Thus, from the beginning, it was emphasized that the "staff" units, such as the General Counsel's office, the Bureau of Business Management (including the Personnel Division), and the Bureau of Accounts and Audits, should regard themselves as service units to assist the "line" units such as the Bureau of Federal Old Age Benefits, Bureau of Unemployment Compensation, and Bureau of Public Assistance in carrying out their operating responsibilities.

Another important reason for this success was the immediate establishment of an intensive training program for all administrative and professional personnel. This training program, which has been maintained throughout the years, includes not only specialized training classes for particular positions, but also basic training classes covering the historical background of the Social Security Act, as well as the economic and social considerations which created a need for this legislation. Pervading all of this training has been the effort to imbue each employee with his affirmative responsibility for carrying out the provisions of the Social Security Act.

Every effort was made to emphasize to employees involved in the federal-state programs that the role of the Social Security Board was that not of policeman but of partner in a great cooperative undertaking. Since nine of the ten different programs included in the Social Security Act were federal-state programs, the act represented a tremendous effort to take full advantage of the unique character of the American federal system of government. Moreover, these programs were unprecedented in their size and nature. The only previous federal-state program of any considerable scope was the highway construction program. That program involved the expenditure of some millions of dollars for financing an impersonal undertaking which had readily measurable results. But the social security programs involved the expenditure of billions of dollars for financing an undertaking which intimately affected the daily lives of millions of Americans and whose results could not be objectively measured. It was, therefore, of vital importance that federal officials recognize their affirmative responsibility to assist state officials in achieving their mutual objective.

In order to carry out its role of partner in this great federal-state undertaking, the Board made provision for a staff whose specific function was to provide technical assistance to the states, not only in the drafting of the necessary legislation but even more importantly in the development of the necessary administrative organization. These technical advisers included social workers, lawyers, constructive accountants, personnel experts, and other persons familiar with social legislation and programs in this country and abroad.

The result of this general policy has been that it has reduced to a minimum the necessity for the federal government to deny federal aid on the grounds of improper legislation or administration. In all of the years that the Social Security Act has been in effect, the federal government has been obliged to withdraw aid temporarily in only three instances because of improper or inefficient administration.

If this great experiment in federal-state cooperation had not been so successful, it would not have been possible for the Council of State Governments to report that, although American political science has predicted the decline and eventual demise of the state governments since colonial days, the opposite has happened, chiefly because of the system of grants-in-aid. The council concluded: "The administration of the grants-in-aid acts is, therefore, the most important aspect, from a fiscal point of view, of our federal government, one which inevitably affects the social, economic, and political welfare of the nation in a fundamental way."*

Employees who would come in direct contact with the public were impressed with the importance of making certain that people were given necessary assistance in understanding their rights and duties. This included assisting claimants in the preparation of their applications for benefits under the federal old age insurance system and ensuring that those who had valid claims received the benefits to which they were entitled.

At first the General Accounting Office took the position that under a federal statute of long standing, federal officials were prohibited from assisting citizens in the prosecution of claims against the government. However, it was pointed out to the General Accounting Office that the fundamental purpose of a contributory old age insurance system was to create a statutory right to specific benefits payable out of a special fund. Therefore, these claims were not of the same character as the usual claims against the government payable out of general revenues. The General Accounting Office finally decided that "it was not required to object."

Another factor that has contributed to the successful administration of the Social Security Act, as well as to the continued improvement in the provisions of the act itself, was the establishment of an adequate research unit at the very beginning. This unit had the largest technical staff of any federal agency carrying on economic and social research. The representatives of the President's Committee on Economic Security were successful in having Congress include in the act a section (702) which delegated to the Board the specific duty of "studying and making recommendations as to the most effective methods of providing economic security through social insurance, and as to legislation and matters of administrative policy concerning old-age pensions, unemployment compensation, and related subjects." The American Medical Association objected to the original language proposed which included specific reference to health insurance. However, elimination of that phrase still left the language broad enough to encompass health insurance.

---

* "The Growth of Cooperative Government," *State Government*, XVII, No. 1 (1944), 261.

The research program covered both "operational" research and basic research. The operational research included the collection and analysis of data secured as a by-product of administration. It also included research seeking solutions of administrative problems and ways and means of improving administration.

The basic research dealt with long-range economic and social factors affecting the need for social security and adequacy of existing provisions. It also included studies relevant to possible amendment of the Social Security Act. This basic research was justified not only by section 702 of the Social Security Act itself but also by the President's statement, at the time he signed the act, that the act was "a cornerstone in a structure which is being built but is by no means complete.

The value of a research program was demonstrated quite soon and in a rather dramatic fashion. The Justice Department, in arguing the case which decided the constitutionality of the old age insurance system (*Helvering* v. *Davis, 301 U.S. 619*), filed with its legal brief a study made by the Bureau of Research and Statistics of the Board, entitled "Economic Insecurity in Old Age." This, in effect, constituted an economic brief from which Justice Cardozo quoted in his opinion, handed down on May 24, 1937, holding that "Congress did not improvise a judgment when it found that the award of old age benefits would be conducive to the general welfare."

This decision of the United States Supreme Court was, of course, epoch-making and represented a complete reversal of the trend of previous decisions which had declared unconstitutional the Railroad Retirement Act, the National Industrial Recovery Act, and the Agricultural Adjustment Act. It came after the President had recommended that the court membership be increased in the hope of obtaining a majority on the court who would uphold New Deal legislation. The sharp reversal in the attitude of the court in the face of the President's proposal gave rise to a current quip that "A switch in time saved nine," which was the number of Supreme Court justices.

Since the language in section 702 was broad enough to include health insurance, the Board did direct its Bureau of Research and Statistics to carry on research regarding it. However, because of its preoccupation with the task of putting into operation the various programs included in the Social Security Act and because of the strong opposition of the American Medical Association to health insurance, the Social Security Board as a board did not give much attention to this subject. But as a member of the Interdepartmental Committee to Coordinate Health and Welfare Activities appointed by the President in August 1935, I did continue to give this subject my attention. If the President had indicated that he wanted to press for a health insurance program, there is no doubt that the Social Security Board would have given the subject more attention.*

---

* The President had told the Committee on Economic Security, in June 1935, to submit its report recommending a health program which included health insurance as well as other items, and he would then decide what to do with it.

Accordingly, the committee transmitted its report, "Risks to Economic Security Arising out of Illness," on June 15, 1935. This was while the social security bill was still pending. The letter of transmittal, signed by all members of the committee, said, "Although we realize that a difference of opinion exists as to the advisability of establishing compulsory health insurance, we are convinced, after reviewing experience in this country and abroad, that the compulsory feature is essential to the accomplishment of the end in view.

In a separate letter to the President accompanying the report, the Secretary of Labor, as Chairman of the committee, said, "In view of the controversial character of certain phases of the subject, I suggest that the report not be made public until the Social Security Bill, now pending before the Congress, has been enacted into law." After the committee had transmitted this report to the President, Dr. Witte, its Executive Director, received a letter from the committee's medical advisory board, recommending that any federal or state legislative action be deferred until the growing experience with voluntary health insurance in the United States and Canada could be analyzed.

In September 1935 the Secretary of Labor had a conference with the President about publishing the committee's report. He stated that he wanted no action in Congress the next year. Therefore, as Assistant Secretary of Labor (not yet having been sworn in as a member of the Social Security Board), I prepared a second letter of transmittal, dated November 6, 1935, which ended, "Our proposals on health insurance are especially cautious; they call for no drastic or hurried Federal action. In this field, we are, in effect merely proposing that the Federal government shall undertake to give small financial aid to those states which develop systems of health insurance designed with due regard to necessary safeguards. . . . However, the Committee does not believe that . . . legislation should be undertaken until there has been opportunity for extended discussion and further research by the Social Security Board."

I also prepared the draft of a letter for the President to send to the Chairman of the Social Security Board, transmitting the committee's report.

The most pressing task confronting the small administrative staff which the Social Security Board had been able to assemble during its first six months of operation was assisting the states to develop plans for the administration of public assistance and unemployment insurance. This was necessary in order to enable the states to qualify for federal grants as soon as Congress appropriated funds after it reconvened in January 1936.

This was a formidable responsibility to be placed upon the Bureau of Public Assistance and the Bureau of Unemployment Compensation, neither one of which had more than two dozen employees during the first six months of operation. The most rapid development occurred in public assistance since many of the states already had laws relating to aid for the needy aged, needy blind, and needy children. However, most of these were very inadequately financed and were optional so far as the counties were concerned.

The Social Security Act really represented a radical change in the character of these laws. Not only did it require that they be in effect throughout the state but it also required that assistance must be provided in the form of money payments and that individuals whose claims had been denied must be given a fair hearing. The Social Security Board, from the beginning, interpreted "money payments" to mean unrestricted cash payments and "fair hearing" to mean a hearing before an individual who had not been involved in the original decision. The Board emphasized that eligible claimants had a legal right to assistance based upon their need and were, therefore, entitled to "due process of law."

Another policy decision of the Board, which has had a continuing important effect on both public assistance and old age insurance, was the requirement that all records be confidential and used only for the administration of the program. In the case of old age assistance, this requirement was necessary since many

In this letter which the President approved and sent on January 14, 1936, he said, "You will note that the Committee suggests that there be further research in this field by the Social Security Board. I, therefore, request that you undertake such research as a part of your program during the balance of the present fiscal year and, if necessary, during the succeeding fiscal year."

state and local political office holders wanted to use them for political purposes.

By June 30, 1936, thirty-six states and the District of Columbia, in cooperation with the Bureau of Public Assistance, had developed public assistance plans which met federal requirements, and were receiving federal grants-in-aid to help finance one or more of the three types of public assistance included in the Social Security Act. It must be confessed that many of the plans were sketchy and the state and local matching funds inadequate to finance a reasonable minimum level of assistance. Moreover, the General Counsel of the Board stated that the Board could only approve or disapprove a plan, and that it could not approve a plan upon the condition that the state agency make certain improvements subsequently. Nevertheless, the Board did approve plans that were not completely satisfactory and did stipulate that the state agency (and in some cases the legislature) would be expected to make necessary changes as a condition of continued approval. The Board's approval under these circumstances allowed hundreds of thousands of needy old people, needy blind, and children dependent because of lack of parental support to receive somewhat more adequate assistance. It also meant that they received it in cash instead of in kind, thus encouraging the recipients to accept more responsibility in the management of their affairs.

Another effect of the public assistance provisions of the Social Security Act was that it introduced a higher degree of consistency and equity. It did this by requiring a state to have a statewide plan either administered directly by a state agency or at least supervised by a state agency if administered by the counties. Moreover, an applicant who believed his request for assistance had not been considered properly was entitled to an impartial hearing by the state agency.

But an insoluble problem of equity arose from the fact already mentioned that in many states the state and local matching funds were inadequate. The Board was powerless to require that a state legislature appropriate adequate funds, because of the language in the public assistance titles which Senator Byrd had insisted upon inserting. This language specified that the purpose of the federal aid was "to enable each State to furnish financial assistance as far as practicable under the conditions in such State." Moreover, it will be recalled that, upon the insistence of Senator Byrd, the requirement that the assistance furnished should be sufficient to provide "a reasonable subsistence compatible with decency and health" had been eliminated.

Therefore, when state and local matching funds were inadequate, the Board could only recommend to a state which of two undesirable alternative methods should be followed to allocate those inadequate funds to needy persons. One method was to spread these funds so that the same proportion of need should be met for every eligible individual. The other method was to meet the minimum need of eligible individuals in the order of their application for assistance. This second method would, of course, result in waiting lists of eligible needy individuals who would be receiving no assistance.

I supported the Bureau of Public Assistance in its view that the second method was the lesser of two evils and that it would be more effective in impressing upon the state legislatures the necessity of providing adequate funds because of the obvious existence of the waiting lists of eligible needy persons.

The second method may seem to be crueler than making a percentage reduction applicable to all eligible persons. However, the effect of a percentage reduction is actually more serious in the case of the most needy, who receive the maximum amount because they have little or no supplementary income, than it is in the case of the less needy, who receive only small amounts because they do have more supplementary income. In any event, most state public assistance agencies agreed with this line of reasoning, and it may be that some legislatures were thus induced to provide more adequate funds. But the fact remains that, in many states to this day, the state legislatures have still failed to appropriate adequate matching funds.

The most important policy problem that arose in connection with the approval of state public assistance laws concerned the question of whether the state law must stipulate that assistance would be furnished only on the basis of an individual's actual need. A few states proposed to pay uniform monthly allowances to all individuals over 65, regardless of need. Others proposed to pay fixed monthly allowances to all persons over 65 whose income did not exceed a fixed amount. This meant that an individual with no income would receive the same amount as an individual whose income just equaled the allowable maximum.

The General Counsel of the Social Security Board advised the Board that "it cannot be stated without question that a State plan must provide that recipients of assistance be in need." The reason was that, as already pointed out, Senator Byrd had been successful in having eliminated any definition of need—indeed, so successful that there was no mention of need in what the lawyers call the "operative" sections of the law. However, the Social Security Board believed that the history of the legislation and the language in the introductory paragraph of the public assistance titles of the Social Security Act clearly indicated that assistance must be based on individual need.

This probably was the most important of several instances in which the General Counsel, while expressing doubt, stated that the Board's decision would probably fall within the limits of its "administrative discretion." Thus was the policy-making function buttressed by legal doctrine. If the Social Security Board had approved state laws which specified the payment of a uniform amount to all persons over 65 regardless of need, it is quite likely that it would have fanned the flames of the Townsend movement, which was a factor in the 1936 elections and reached its peak of intensity during the 1938 congressional elections. The final result might very well have been to scrap the old age insurance system before it ever went into operation.

The development of state unemployment insurance laws was much less rapid than that of public assistance laws. This was due to several circumstances. The first was that only one state had any pre-existing unemployment insurance law, and in that state benefits did not begin to be paid until more than a year after the passage of the Social Security Act. Therefore, there was no experience in this country on which to build. Another circumstance was doubt as to the constitutionality of either federal or state legislation in this field.

Thus, by June 30, 1936, only ten states and the District of Columbia had unemployment insurance laws. But a year later, by which time the United States Supreme Court had upheld the constitutionality of unemployment legislation, all the states and territories had enacted unemployment insurance laws.

The administrative problems confronting the Bureau of Unemployment Compensation were somewhat similar to those of the Bureau of Public Assistance. However, there were only seven states that had passed unemployment compensation laws prior to the passage of the Social Security Act, and only one of these had been in existence long enough to permit the development of any administrative experience whatsoever. This meant that the Bureau of Unemployment Compensation was obliged to furnish far more technical assistance in the drafting of state legislation and in the establishment of state administrative machinery.

The Bureau of Unemployment Compensation was also obliged to scrutinize the state administrative budgets much more carefully than was true in the case of the Bureau of Public Assistance. This was because the Social Security Act provided that the federal government should pay 100 per cent of the cost of "the proper and efficient administration" of a state unemployment insurance law instead of 50 per cent as in the case of public assistance.

It was necessary to require the state agencies to submit "line item" budgets. As a result, differences of opinion were bound to develop between state and federal officials as to whether the amounts requested were actually necessary for proper and efficient administration. This involved consideration of the administrative organization and procedures themselves. Under such circumstances the utmost tact and understanding were required in order to maintain satisfactory working relations.

An important policy question confronting the Social Security Board was whether it would approve the payment of unemployment compensation through agencies other than public employment offices, as it was specifically authorized to do under the law. The Board decided at the very outset that it would approve only public employment offices affiliated with the United States Employment Service.

This was far from being an academic question. One state proposed to pay benefits through the poor-relief offices. Another state proposed to pay them through the state liquor offices "to avoid the extra expense of setting up separate offices." A number of states objected to being required to become affiliated with the United States Employment Service since this meant that they would have to pay 50 per cent of the cost of services not necessary for the administration of unemployment insurance. As late as 1939 a state legislature refused to make the necessary appropriation until after the state had been notified by the Board that the Board would not be justified in making a grant unless it was able to find that the state would pay benefits through public employment offices.

The Board took the position that, while the cost of operating public employment offices was a necessary expense involved in the administration of unemployment insurance, these offices would also serve employees and employers not covered by the state unemployment insurance law. It stated that it would consider the minimum matching required by the Wagner-Peyser Act (which established the United States Employment Service in 1933 on a cooperative federal-state basis) as representing the cost of service not related to unemployment insurance and would finance all of the cost above that.

The situation regarding the operation of public employment offices as an essential function in the administration of unemployment insurance was complicated by the fact that the United States Employment Service was administered by the U.S. Department of Labor. The Director of the United States Employment Service took the position that the "integrity" of the service must be maintained. By "integrity" the Director said he meant the assurance that all employers and employees would receive proper professional service in placing the best qualified workers in jobs that gave them the maximum opportunity to exercise their skills, and that positions should not be filled on the basis of whether or not the employee was entitled to unemployment benefits or whether or not it would cost the unemployment fund more or less in benefits.

The Board was in complete agreement with that policy. However, the Director of the United States Employment Service insisted that its implementation required a separate and direct line of administration extending from him, as federal director, to the state director to the manager of the local employment office. He also insisted that he should have the sole responsibility for approving separate state budgets covering the cost of operating the employment service.

The Board was of the opinion that two separate lines to the state agencies, one from the United States Employment Service in the Department of Labor and the other from the Board, would create a duality of authority and responsibility which would be fatal. The facts were that the largest share of the cost would be paid for out of the Board's appropriations to cover the cost of administering the unemployment insurance laws. Moreover, in all but two states the same agency administered both unemployment insurance and the employment service.

The Board believed it was essential that the United States Employment Service, which was a part of the Department of Labor, and its own Bureau of Unemployment Compensation should take joint action in planning for the participation of the state employment service in the administration of a state unemployment insurance law. It believed that without such joint action there was bound to be conflict and excessive administrative costs, as well as unsatisfactory service to clients in the local offices. At the state agency's headquarters, good administration required the integration of such activities as fiscal control, field supervision, personnel and matériel management, and research and statistics. In the local offices, good administration required that there be maximum flexibility in the use of personnel since the relative work-load of the employment service was likely to vary from time to time.

Therefore, despite the resistance of the Director of the United States Employment Service, the Board and the Secretary of Labor entered into the following agreement on March 30, 1937:

> In order to achieve integrated Federal action in rendering assistance to the States in the administration of State employment services, the Social Security Board, through the Bureau of Unemployment Compensation, and the Department of Labor, through the United States Employment Service, shall act as if they were a single agency, jointly and concurrently, with respect to all matters affecting a State employment service, including detailed plans of such State employment service financed under the Wagner-Peyser Act and the Social Security Act.

As a result of the policy of the Social Security Board of requiring the state unemployment insurance agencies to pay unemployment benefits through offices affiliated with the United States Employment Service, there was a rapid growth in the number of these offices during 1936 and 1937. This was, of course, absolutely essential since many of the states would begin paying benefits in January 1938.

A problem faced by both the Bureau of Unemployment Compensation and the Bureau of Public Assistance was that of inducing the state administrative agencies to establish a merit system for the selection of personnel, in the face of the language in the Social Security Act which excluded "the selection, tenure of office and compensation of personnel" from the definition of efficient administration. This was a very serious matter since in 1935 there were only nine states that had general civil service systems, and a number of these were quite ineffective in their actual operation. The Board decided to interpret this language to mean that it could not interfere in the appointment of a specific individual employee but could require a state to establish a merit system. The result was that, in spite of the legislative language just quoted, the Board was able to induce a considerable number of the state agencies to adopt merit systems. Thus, by June 30, 1937, of 47 jurisdictions having public assistance plans in operation, 23 selected at least their state staffs through some type of merit system. In the case of unemployment insurance, 19 of the administrative agencies had merit systems.

This result could never have been achieved if the Board had not recognized the necessity of furnishing professional assistance to the states through the State Technical Advisory Service which has already been mentioned. The Civil Service Assembly of the United States and Canada, at its meeting in 1949, passed a formal resolution lauding the contribution made during the previous ten years by this advisory service, not only to the field of personnel administration but to effective federal-state cooperative relations generally. Many political scientists have also expressed similar opinions, one commenting that, "It was little short of amazing that several States, where conditions approached a public scandal, should in a few months become the field for great technical advances."

The problems confronting the Board in the administration of the old age insurance system were quite different from those of the two federal-state programs that have been discussed. It was necessary for the Board to recruit personnel, set up an organization, and put into effect procedures for the administration of the largest insurance system ever undertaken in this country or any other country.

Fortunately, the Social Security Act deferred the date that this system would go into effect until January 1, 1937. This gave the Board a little over a year to get ready. The act also provided that monthly benefits would not begin to be payable until January 1, 1942. However, beginning January 1, 1937, lump sum refunds of contributions were payable to a worker who reached 65 years of age before having earned enough to qualify for monthly benefits and to the estates of deceased workers.

The administrative task of the Board was also eased by the fact that the Bureau of Internal Revenue was charged with the responsibility of collecting the payroll taxes levied on employers and employees. Therefore, the Bureau of Internal Revenue had the authority to decide what system of employer reporting should be used. However, the Social Security Board was naturally concerned about what system would be prescribed since it was charged with the responsibility of posting the wage information reported by employers to the millions of individual employee accounts upon which benefits were based. The Board was also concerned that the system used would be one that was likely to result in full and accurate reporting of wages paid. It was particularly concerned about obtaining proper reports from small employers who did not maintain systematic records.

The Board strongly urged that a stamp system be used, at least for smaller employers. The Board believed that a stamp system was feasible for larger employers as well, since they could use stamp meters. Under such a system every employee would have a stamp book which he would take with him if he changed employers and which would be sent in to the Social Security Board when filled. Employers would purchase the stamps at the post offices. This was the system which was in effect in Great Britain and had functioned successfully.

However, the Bureau of Internal Revenue refused to adopt this system, largely because it did not wish to share its tax collecting responsibility with the Post Office Department. But it indicated that it might be willing to turn the entire responsibility over to the Social Security Board, since it had considerable fear that this new tax collecting responsibility would adversely affect the collection of the taxes levied for general revenue purposes.*

Even though the Bureau of Internal Revenue collected the payroll taxes and the benefit provisions went into effect by stages, the immediate task confronting the Board was still unprecedented in complexity and size. Therefore, it was all the more unfortunate that the top officials selected by the Board to staff the Bureau of Federal Old-Age Benefits did not work effectively together and made little progress in the development of an administrative organization. Thus, by July 1, 1936, there were only 53 employees at work in that bureau. No definite plan had yet been developed for the first stage of operations which needed to be completed by January 1, 1937—namely, the assignment of social security numbers to the millions of workers who would be insured and the hundreds of thousands of employers who would be required to remit contributions after that date.

This situation had come about because of the inability of individual Board members to agree upon the selection of the person to be the permanent director of the Bureau of Federal Old-Age Benefits. The result was a compromise leading to the selection in January 1936 of Murray Latimer, the Chairman of the Railroad Retirement Board, to serve as temporary Director. This was not as strange an appointment as might appear since Mr. Latimer had been a leading member of the subcommittee of the technical board appointed by the President's Cabinet Committee on Economic Security. He served as Director of the Bureau of Federal Old-Age Benefits for a few months until the Coordinator already referred to was designated to succeed him. The new Director had not had sufficient large-scale administrative experience and relied too heavily upon an individual with an aggressive personality both in planning and in the selection of personnel. This individual, while possessing some ability, was highly political in his motivation, so that it was necessary to scrutinize

---

* It is interesting to note that today the Internal Revenue Service regards the collection of social security taxes as a great aid in the collection of general taxes, since social security taxes are likely to be paid more readily. It is also interesting to note that, while the payroll reporting system in general has worked remarkably well, there is still considerable failure of small employers to report wages paid to agricultural and domestic workers.

carefully all his recommendations for appointment of personnel. This untenable situation was partially resolved in 1937 by the appointment of a new Director, who relied almost entirely upon the Assistant Executive Director of the Board to administer the bureau. However, it was not until July 1, 1938, that the Assistant Executive Director was actually appointed Director of the bureau (the name of which had been changed to Bureau of Old Age Insurance in September 1937).

It was due to the unusual ability of this man that the administration of this tremendous social insurance system was finally established on such a successful basis.

But in July 1936, the situation was so desperate that, with the approval of the President, I asked the Postmaster General to assume the responsibility of assigning social security numbers to employees and employers. He agreed to do so, and in a few weeks plans were completed for carrying out this gigantic task through the 45,000 post offices, beginning November 16, 1936. I had urged that the assignment of account numbers should not begin until then in order to avoid becoming involved in the presidential campaign of that year. Another member of the board, Mr. Miles, had urged it to begin in October, and Chairman Winant had been undecided.

It was fortunate that the later date was selected because on September 27, 1936, like a bolt from the blue, the Republican candidate in a speech at Milwaukee denounced the old age insurance system. He said, "And to call it 'social security' is a fraud on the working-man. The saving it forces on our workers is a cruel hoax." The Republican member of the board, John G. Winant, a former Republican Governor of New Hampshire and later our wartime Ambassador to Great Britain, immediately resigned in protest, and the President appointed me Acting Chairman. In his letter of resignation Mr. Winant said, "Governor Landon has made the problem of social security a major issue in this campaign and I cannot support him. I do not feel that members of independent Commissions or Boards, such as the Social Security Board, should take an active part in politics and moreover, I was appointed and confirmed as the minority member. While I retain this position, I am not free to defend the Act.

A week before the election the Industrial Division of the Republican National Committee flooded employers with millions of pamphlets, posters, and pay envelope inserts attacking the old age insurance system. The pay envelope inserts were headed, "Notice—Deductions from Pay Start Jan. 1," and at the bottom were the following words in large black letters: "Social Security Board, Washington, D.C." This gave the appearance of an official notice. There was no mention of the benefits payable.

The Hearst press ran front-page stories the day before the election attacking the old age insurance system. They were illustrated by a picture of a man stripped to the waist, wearing a chain with a dog-tag. It was captioned "Snooping-Tagging" and carried this explanatory statement beneath: "Each worker would be required to have one for the privilege of suffering a pay cut under the Social Security Act, which is branded as a 'cruel hoax.'" Curiously enough this newspaper story apparently was based upon a proposal made by the Addressograph Corporation to furnish nameplates, which I had rejected, although its acceptance had been recommended by the planning officials of the Board. As a souvenir of this episode, I still carry with me the sample nameplate that was submitted.

Fortunately, the Social Security Board had prepared an explanatory leaflet for use in connection with the assignment of social security numbers. There were 50 million of these stored at various places throughout the country. Immediately upon learning of the distribution of the misleading and deceptive pay envelope inserts, it distributed the entire 50 million to workers at factory gates throughout the country, largely through the cooperation of labor unions. It also released explanatory movie films for use in theaters. One copy of this film was run continuously on Times Square the last day of the presidential campaign.

The Board had feared that the political attack might hamper the assignment of social security numbers. The Board also feared that many employers would refuse to cooperate because the constitutionality of the law had not yet been decided. However, this did not happen. A large proportion of the initial distribution of 26,000,000 application forms was returned during the ensuing three weeks, and by June 30, 1937, when the Social Security Board took over the task, 30,296,471 applications for social security numbers had been processed. Most of the credit for this success belongs to the postmasters, postal clerks, and mail carriers throughout the nation who distributed the forms, helped applicants fill them out, and answered questions about the new law.

Some of the success may also have been due to other factors. It was widely publicized that any information furnished by employees and employers would be confidential and used only for social security purposes. This was necessary because at the time there was considerable talk about the danger of a "police state," and workmen were concerned that employers might use information as to their previous work history for black-list purposes. This pledge of confidentiality has been kept throughout the years, the only exceptions having been a very few cases involving persons suspected of espionage or sabotage. The records remained confidential in spite of the fact that, during the period I was in office, nearly every Attorney General, at the urging of the Federal Bureau of Investigation, requested access to this information.

Likewise, every effort was made to use terminology that would inspire confidence rather than arouse suspicion. Thus, the process was called "assignment of social security account numbers" instead of "registration." The use of the word "registration" was avoided because it might connote regimentation. An analogy was drawn between the issuance of a social security account card and the issuance of a department store credit card, which was the only form of credit card in common use at that time.

While the problem of assigning social security numbers had been resolved, many other crucial problems were far from solution. These included the setting up of a centralized record-keeping establishment, the development of a headquarters staff, and the creation of a nationwide network of local offices. The Board turned to the large insurance companies for help in the creation of a centralized record system to handle the many millions of separate accounts that had to be established as the basis for calculating benefits. The Board found to its consternation that the record systems of these companies would be wholly inadequate for this unprecedented task. It, therefore, engaged the services of an outstanding expert in office lay-out and management who had been recommended by these companies.

After several months of study, this expert requested a full meeting of the Board. At the meeting, he solemnly informed the Board that the task was insuperable and recommended that the Board so inform the Congress! Much discussion ensued, and finally the expert said that the only possibility of success in the maintenance of individual records lay in amending the law to provide for a number of completely independent, self-sustaining regional organizations, small enough in size to be manageable. The expert stated that unless this were done, the Board would be smothered with a blizzard of millions of individual workers' pay slips sent in by employers every three months.

The Board rejected the proposal to fragmentize the old age insurance system in this fashion. But it was so disturbed that it decided to establish twelve self-contained record-keeping units (corresponding to twelve regions of the country) which would process the millions of individual workers' wage reports. However, it directed the expert to devise a single, centralized index system. This was absolutely essential to prevent confusion and duplication in the separate accounts which had to be maintained for individual workers.

The expert was obliged to solve unprecedented problems in the establishment of this mammoth central index which, by June 30, 1937, already covered more than an acre of floor space and contained 30,296,000 names, including hundreds of thousands of Smiths, Johnsons, Browns, Williamses, Joneses, Millers, Davises, etc. The index was based on the phonetic principle and so constructed as to make easily visible the millions of separate names. It enabled a clerk to locate a name in a matter of seconds and was so successful that it has been copied by many large insurance companies and other corporations. Full credit must be given to the expert who devised this index. At the meeting with the Board he had been seized with an attack of kidney stones which, he remarked, had been an affliction of Caesar, Napoleon, and other men of genius. In the light of his contribution, there may have been some significance to this remark!

The development of a headquarters staff moved along very well in spite of the previously mentioned difficulties concerning the Director of the bureau. By December 15, 1936, the headquarters staff numbered 2,307. Most of these had to be housed in an old warehouse on the waterfront in Baltimore. Employees were obliged to work at unfinished wooden tables whose rough lumber made slivers run into hands and arms. This deplorable housing situation continued for twenty-five years when an admirable new headquarters building was finally completed in 1960.

The field organization for the old age insurance system proceeded rather slowly. By December 31, 1936, only 74 offices had actually been opened. Studies had been made of factors affecting the number and location of offices, such as population, industrial concentration, and transportation facilities. Those who had been making these studies calculated that 2,000 offices would be needed. I was appalled at this recommendation. In order to gain some perspective, I calculated the number that would probably be needed in Wisconsin, my native state. After determining that 12 to 13 could fairly well serve the insured workers in that state, I multiplied the number by 40 and arrived at 500 as the number of offices that could serve the insured workers throughout the nation. The factor of 40 was based on the proportion of all insured workers who were working in Wisconsin.

Upon the basis of this crude, unscientific method, the Board approved of 500 offices. It is interesting to note that today, in spite of the increase in the coverage of the system, there are still only 619 local offices.

The foregoing progress in putting the various programs of the Social Security Act into effect, although uneven, was gratifying because it occurred in spite of considerable disagreement among Board members over personnel appointments. This disagreement, to which reference has already been made, became more serious when Governor Winant resigned as a member of the Board. As previously related, he resigned on September 30, 1936, as a protest against the Republican attack on the Social Security Act. After the presidential campaign was over, he again became a member of the Board, but resigned a second time on February 19, 1937, to become Deputy Director-General of the International Labour Office and the President appointed me to be Chairman. Mr. Winant's successor as a member of the Board was not appointed until August 6, 1937. So, for a period of almost six months, it was necessary for the two remaining Board members to reach agreement in order to avoid a stalemate in personnel appointments, administrative organization, interpretation of the law, and general policy decisions. This often caused delay and also resulted in compromises which were not always entirely desirable.

3.

Improving the
Social Security Act
and Its Administration,
1937–39

By the middle of 1937 it had become apparent that the Social Security Act would remain on the statute books. The United States Supreme Court in May 1937 had upheld the constitutionality of both the unemployment insurance and the old age insurance features. The cooperative federal-state programs were operating fairly well. It had been demonstrated that the initial problems involved in the administration of the gigantic federal old age insurance system could be solved. However, very serious administrative problems remained: The financial basis of the federal old age insurance continued to be attacked; and the need for improving the protection provided by both the public assistance and the social insurance provisions of the law came to be more clearly recognized as time went on. Therefore, it might be said that, while the ship had been successfully launched, problems of steering it and of making it more seaworthy remained to be solved.

In public assistance the number of states that passed legislation and submitted plans to take advantage of federal grants continued to increase, and by September 1938 all states, territories, and the District of Columbia had one or more of the public assistance programs in operation. But the administration of these plans in a number of states was quite unsatisfactory. As late as April 1939 only 19 states had both state and local personnel subject to civil service laws or departmental merit systems. Even in some states with civil service laws, the law had many loopholes which permitted the appointment of unqualified personnel on a personal or political basis. In states which allowed the counties to administer the program, there was especially slow progress in the adoption of civil service or merit systems because of the opposition of local elective officials.

The inefficiency or political motivation of personnel, of course, affected the cost of administration, but, far more seriously, resulted in inequity in providing assistance to needy persons on the basis of their actual need. The political motivation was particularly strong in old age assistance because of the strength of the Townsend movement.

In a number of states elective officials openly sought the support of recipients of old age assistance. This was particularly true of governors who sometimes wrote letters to recipients indicating concern for their welfare. These letters were usually written at Christmas time or when a governor took credit for an increase in the amount of assistance.

The administration was so bad in three states that the Board was obliged to withdraw grants. Two of the states, where the situation was due to plain inefficiency rather than political motivation, took immediate corrective action, so they actually lost no federal funds. But in Ohio, where a particularly scandalous situation existed, the state failed to take corrective action and did actually suffer the loss of federal funds. The Governor of Ohio had become increasingly active from 1936 to 1938 in soliciting the political support of old age assistance recipients. In 1936, during the primary election campaign, he directed a flat increase of $10 per month in each grant to be made without regard for individual circumstances. A "Certificate of Aid" was sent each one of 90,000 recipients with a typewritten notation in red, "Increased by order of Governor Davey." During the regular election campaign of that year, he sent several letters to each one of these old age assistance recipients, requesting that the recipient ask ten or fifteen friends to vote for Governor Davey. In December 1937, a 10 per cent increase was ordered by the Governor, and members of the staff of the state old age assistance agency were directed to deliver personally to each recipient a copy of the Governor's order.

In the Ohio primary election campaign of 1938 the Governor's activities reached a climax. On August 4 he ordered another $10 a month increase in each old age assistance grant. Not only the Governor but the Director of the Division of Aid for the Aged sent letters to recipients urging them to get three or four dozen friends to vote for the governor. Every applicant for old age assistance also received a letter from the Governor telling him that the Governor was taking a personal interest in his application and had assigned a special investigator "to work day and night, if necessary, in order to give your claim proper consideration at the earliest possible moment." In addition to this mail campaign, officials of the state Division of Aid for the Aged systematically visited the recipients to fill out, notarize, and seal absentee voter ballots. This occurred only a few days before the primary election. The Social Security Board announced that it would make an investigation of the situation. The result was that this became a main issue in the campaign, and the Governor was defeated for renomination on the Democratic ticket.

After the election the Governor refused to have any dealings with the Board. So the Board decided that it was useless to continue its efforts to persuade the Governor to cease violating the state civil service law and to permit the state agency to function on a nonpolitical efficient, and equitable basis. Therefore, as a last resort, the Board scheduled a hearing for August 29 to give state officials an opportunity to show cause why the Board should not withdraw federal grants on the grounds of improper administration.

The Governor ordered the state officials not to attend the hearing. Nevertheless, the hearing was held, a transcript of the hearing was furnished the Governor and other state officials, and they were advised they could make a reply if they so desired. No reply was received, and the Board made public its detailed findings regarding improper administration on September 29. The state Director of the Division of Aid for the Aged then informed the Board that he would proceed to correct conditions, whereupon he was immediately dismissed by the Governor.

The Social Security Act required the Social Security Board to cease making any further certification to the Secretary of the Treasury of grants to the state of Ohio until the Board could make a finding of proper and efficient administration. The Board was hopeful that corrective action would be taken by the state officials. In a press release issued at the time it made its findings regarding improper administration, the Board pointed out that, since the state had already sent out the old age assistance checks for September, there was ample time before the next checks would be sent out to make the necessary improvements in administration. However, the Governor continued his refusal to act until November 1. The result was that for the month of October the state of Ohio failed to receive a matching grant for old age assistance which would have amounted to approximately $1,300,000.

The Ohio episode illustrates the difficulties involved in the operation of a federal-state program whose success depends upon good state administration. The only sanction the federal government has available to secure good administration is the withdrawal of federal grants. However, this sanction is so drastic that it can be invoked only in extreme situations. Not only is public opinion in the affected state likely to be directed against the federal government, regardless of the necessity for such action, because of the loss of federal funds, but more importantly there is the danger that this loss may injure innocent recipients of assistance. Moreover, the application of this sanction is likely to become a political issue.

Fortunately, in this instance the state Control Board finally made state funds available to take the place of the federal funds withheld. Furthermore, the maladministration was so flagrant and well documented that public opinion supported the action taken by the Board. Finally, the action taken by the Board did not become a political issue between the two political parties. This was so because both the Governor's successful Democratic opponent in the primary election and the Republican candidate in the regular election supported the Board's actions.

The Governor, of course, blamed his defeat on the Social Security Board's actions, which he alleged were politically motivated. Therefore, it is interesting to note that the Democrats, who had opposed Governor Davey in the primary election and had supported the actions of the Board before the primary election, were also unsuccessful in their efforts after this election to persuade the Board to make the October grant (which they thought would be helpful to them in the November election).

When the Governor capitulated, public opinion in Ohio began to change, and many editorials appeared in newspapers throughout the state urging that the Board pay to the state the $1,300,000 which had been withheld for the month of October. In vain the Board pointed out that it was powerless to do so because this would require a finding that there had been proper and efficient administration during that month. The Board also pointed out that to do so would encourage a candidate for re-election as governor to use public assistance for political purposes during his campaign, knowing that after the campaign he need only agree to desist in order to obtain the funds which had been withheld. Furthermore, the Board emphasized that the federal government had lost far more than $1,300,000 because of maladministration during the long period it had been attempting to persuade the state officials to reform.

The uniform reaction to these arguments was that the Board should not punish the innocent people of Ohio for the sins of its elected officials. Moreover, the tolerance displayed earlier by the Board was turned against it by the argument that it had previously been making grants when the state administration was known to be unsatisfactory and in November had made a finding that the state was again in compliance with the federal law largely on assurances to improve administration rather than on the execution of the actual changes.

Actually, the final chapter in this lengthy Ohio story was not written until several years later when efforts were made to pass a bill to pay Ohio the $1,300,000 that had been withheld. At that time the sponsor of the bill, Republican Congressman Thomas Jenkins, alleged that politics had motivated the Social Security Board's action. I trust the foregoing account indicates that this was not so. However, it may well be that the Governor's successful opponent in the primary, who was, of course, a Democrat, was correct in his belief that, while the Board's action helped him in the primary, it contributed to his losing the regular election to his Republican opponent.

Suffice it to say at this point that in my judgment the decision of the Board in the Ohio situation was of profound importance. It demonstrated that states would be required to comply with the provisions of the Social Security Act or suffer the consequences. This did not automatically result in perfect administration but it probably did prevent similar situations from developing in other states. If comparable maladministration had occurred in other states, the entire program might have come into such ill-repute that it would have been discontinued by Congress.

The Ohio story also demonstrated that the Social Security Act should have been explicit in requiring state and local personnel to be appointed in accordance with recognized civil service standards and in guarding against the use of public assistance rolls for political or commercial purposes. It also demonstrated that the Social Security Act ought to provide additional sanctions less stringent than the complete withdrawal of federal grants to secure compliance with federal requirements.

The General Counsel of the Board believed that, after the Board had approved of a state public assistance plan as meeting the federal requirements (as it was required to do before it certified to the Secretary of the Treasury the amount of federal grant to be made), it had no power to take fiscal exceptions to any assistance payments made by the state unless they were in direct violation of a specific provision of the Social Security Act or the state plan. Nevertheless, the Board adopted the policy of taking exception to all individual assistance payments which its auditors considered were not supported by the evidence in the case record. In some states these individual exceptions ran into the thousands.

The Board recognized that this was a negative approach to the problem of securing good administration. Therefore, from the very beginning the Board provided constructive accounting services to state agencies to help them set up the necessary accounts and accounting controls to guard against careless or dishonest fiscal practices.

But, of course, action to assure proper accounting did not meet the real problem, which was to assure that the rights and needs of each public assistance applicant or recipient were properly determined by trained social workers so that there would be no need to take individual exceptions on the grounds of ineligibility. Therefore, the Board also proceeded to organize a field staff which would provide professional assistance to the states in establishing the necessary administrative organization, including trained social workers and supervisors. It was the hope of the Board that eventually, instead of accountants examining millions of individual payments, there would be the need only for a joint "administrative audit" whereby professional state and federal personnel would determine the general adequacy of administrative procedures, studying only a representative sampling of individual cases in making this determination. However, this objective was not actually achieved until 1939.

Even with reasonably efficient administration, it became clear that the substantive provisions of the federal and state laws did not assure adequacy and equity in public assistance payments. First and foremost was the absence from the public assistance titles of the Social Security Act of any definition of need, as has already been mentioned. The Social Security Board's insistence that public assistance payments must be related to individual need resulted in every state's specifying either in its law or by administrative regulation that eligibility was dependent upon the establishment of need. However, the states varied widely in their criteria for determining the extent of need in individual cases. The amount of income and resources which was exempted in the consideration of need varied. Likewise, the extent to which relatives would be held liable for support varied.

In addition to these variations in the treatment of resources, there was great variation in determining the amount necessary to cover the cost of a minimum standard of living. Many states omitted entirely allowances for such items as medical care and clothing. The determination of what constituted a minimum food budget and a minimum rental allowance varied widely.

Not only were there wide variations among the states in the determination of need but there was wide variation within a state when the law made local governmental units responsible for administration. The Social Security Board was obliged to warn the states that in the absence of an objective standard for determining the extent of need in all local units of governments, the variation in the grants made to individuals in equal need might be so great as to result in a series of local plans instead of a single statewide plan as required by the Social Security Act.

The Social Security Board urged the states to establish objective budgetary standards for the guidance of all case-workers in determining need. Considerable progress was made in this respect in states where public assistance was administered by the state itself. But in states where public assistance was administered by local units of government the progress was much slower. In fact, many years were to elapse before the last state having a locally administered program finally issued regulations requiring local public assistance officials to follow state-established standards in determining need.

The basic argument advanced by state public assistance agencies against statewide uniform standards for determining resources and budgetary needs was that conditions varied throughout the state. This argument was supplemented by the contention that the provision in the Social Security Act that a state plan "shall be in effect in all political subdivisions" did not require uniform standards to be applied throughout the state. The Board rejected this argument and contention, pointing out that uniform standards did not mean uniform payments, if the cost of living varied throughout the state, but only that persons with the same resources and needs should be treated the same. Actually, it was demonstrated in the course of time that the wide variations in payments within a state bore little relationship to variations in the cost of living. In fact, it was discovered that with the exception of rent, the variation in the cost of living was surprisingly small throughout a state, even between rural and urban areas.

In some states the variation in the average assistance payment in a particular category was such that the average in the highest-paying local governmental unit was more than double that in the lowest-paying unit. The amount of variation has been reduced considerably in the course of time, as the states have been induced to prescribe standards to be observed by the local units of government. However, the variation among states in the average assistance payment in a particular category was far greater—the highest average being more than five times the lowest average. There has been some reduction in this variation as the years have gone by. But even today the highest state average in old age assistance is three times the lowest, and in aid to dependent children the highest is more than four times the lowest.

The basic reason for this continuing wide variation among the states in average assistance payments is due to the wide variation in average per capita income of the inhabitants of the various states. The wide variation in average per capita income affects the fiscal ability of a state to pay its share of the cost of public assistance; it affects the number of persons in need of public assistance; and it also affects the level of what is considered to be a minimum subsistence budget (because a state with a low per capita income has a generally lower standard of living than a state with a high per capita income).

The failure of state legislatures to make adequate appropriations for public assistance resulted in long waiting lists in many states. While this created highly visible evidence that the legislative appropriations were inadequate, it also created a question of conformity with the provision in the Social Security Act requiring an opportunity for a "fair hearing" for any person to whom assistance has been denied. Since the Social Security Act also defined the purpose of the public assistance titles as enabling each state "as far as practicable under the conditions in such state to furnish financial assistance," the Social Security Board did not press the issue of conformity to the point of withdrawing federal grants.

Concerning unemployment insurance, it should first be noted that the Railroad Unemployment Act was approved June 25, 1938, and went into operation July 1, 1939. It provided for the transfer of wage credits acquired by railroad workers and transfer of the contributions collected on wages earned by railroad workers.

While all the states had enacted unemployment laws by July 1937, Wisconsin was the only state which actually began the payment of benefits before January 1, 1938. On January 1, 1938, 21 other jurisdictions began benefit payments, and by July 1939, all states had begun.

Local facilities for receiving benefit claims and applications for work had been developed during this period. The number of local public employment offices affiliated with the United States Employment Service had increased from 215 in June 1935 to

1,263 in June 1938. The personnel in these offices had increased from 1,527 in June 1935 to 16,955 in June 1938. Most of this increase occurred after July 1, 1937, when funds were made available under the Social Security Act. These were permanent offices with permanent personnel, as contrasted with what was known as the National Reemployment Service. The latter was a temporary organization with temporary personnel operated directly by the federal government to serve primarily as the placement agency for the various emergency public works programs. Therefore, it was regarded by many as a part of the relief program rather than as a public employment office service for private employers and workers generally.

The Director of the United States Employment Service was also the Director of the National Reemployment Service. As the public works programs were reduced and the offices of the United States Employment Service were increased, the National Reemployment Service facilities were decreased, and it was finally liquidated in 1939.

Unfortunately, in September 1937 unemployment, which was still large, began to increase, so that by January 1938 it was estimated that ten million workers were unemployed. When the doors opened for the filing of claims, the public employment offices were deluged with claimants. Emergency offices were established in armories and other large public buildings. Employment service personnel joined unemployment insurance personnel in receiving the claims which totaled 3,554,669 during the first three months of 1938.

In spite of the temporary adverse effect on the operations of the employment service, the lasting effect was beneficial. Thus, the Secretary of Labor could report on June 30, 1938, "As a result of a close link between these two functions of Government, the Employment Service receives among its applicants, all unemployed workers in insured occupations and industries, thus building up the active files of local employment offices both in quality and quantity. Moreover, because of the interest of employers in the conservation of the unemployment-reserve funds, there exists an increased motivation for the use of employment offices by employers.

The agreement of March 30, 1937, whereby the Department of

Labor and the Social Security Board undertook to "act as if they were a single agency, jointly and concurrently, with respect to all matters affecting a State employment service," helped to achieve this result. However, this agreement did not automatically eliminate differences of opinion by any means. In fact, the Director of the United States Employment Service, because he continued to hold strong views about the best way to protect the integrity of the service, created so many difficulties that the President, in January 1939, suggested to the Secretary of Labor that he be asked to resign. The Director, being both an able and a determined man, requested an opportunity to hear from the President's own lips the reason for asking him to resign. His request was granted, and the President, while expressing appreciation for his devoted and valuable service, told him the reason was simply that he did not have "a happy ship." Even if he had not resigned, the problem would have been solved when the United States Employment Service was transferred to the Social Security Board a few months later.

There was more progress made by the state unemployment insurance agencies than by the state public assistance agencies in establishing merit systems for personnel. By January 1939, 39 state unemployment insurance agencies and 19 state public assistance agencies were operating under a general state civil service law or in accordance with a statewide merit system established by the agency itself. The slower progress made by the state public assistance agencies was perhaps due to the fact that many of them had been in existence before the Social Security Act was passed and were unwilling to change their personnel practices. Moreover, in states where local units of government administered public assistance, the state agency was also confronted with their opposition to the establishment of a merit system.

As contrasted with public assistance, there was practically no political influence brought to bear in the payment of unemployment insurance benefits. This was, of course, due to the fact that both the amount of the benefit and the eligibility for its receipt were specified in the law itself and were dependent upon the wage record of the applicant. Therefore, there is far less discretion involved in the payment of benefits.

Moreover, in contrast to public assistance, there was no problem arising out of variation in the per capita income of the individual states. There was, of course, wide variation in per capita income and in the general wage level. However, since both contributions and benefits were geared to payroll, the benefits were self-financing and not dependent on legislative appropriations out of general revenues. Likewise, it was possible for each state to pay the same benefit for the same wage loss and thus maintain consistency and equity, regardless of variations in the general wage level.

However, it was soon discovered that the unemployment insurance title of the Social Security Act suffered from a fundamental defect somewhat analogous to the defect in the public assistance titles of not incorporating any definition of "need." That is to say, there were no minimum benefit standards to be observed by the states.

The benefits provided under the original state laws were deliberately established on an extremely conservative basis so that there would be no danger that the 3 per cent payroll tax would be insufficient. Even when there had been only one year's experience, a number of states began to feel that they were building up excessive reserves. But instead of improving the benefits, they sought to have the federal unemployment tax law amended so that they could reduce the state general contribution rate. Only Wisconsin's law had been in effect long enough to permit reduction in individual employers' contribution rates in accordance with their individual compensation experience.

The failure of the federal law to contain minimum benefit standards was especially serious because the law included a provision allowing employers credit against their federal unemployment tax for contributions they had been forgiven from making under a state law because of their individual "compensation experience," i.e., the relation between benefits paid out to contributions paid in. Thus, the federal law actually created a powerful incentive for individual states to keep benefit rates low. Indeed, the federal law, instead of achieving its fundamental purpose of protecting employers in a state with an adequate unemployment insurance law from the danger of unfair interstate competition by employers in other states with inadequate laws, actually increased that danger.

The recommendation of the President's Cabinet Committee on Economic Security that all state unemployment insurance laws impose a minimum contribution rate of 1 per cent, if Congress had accepted it, would have done much to protect the states from the danger of unfair interstate competition. This is so because the average contribution rate for all states has never exceeded 1⅛ per cent of total payrolls in the last twenty years.

The administrative organization of the Bureau of Old Age Insurance developed smoothly during this period after the faltering start previously described. The name of the bureau was changed from the Bureau of Old-Age Benefits as soon as the United States Supreme Court had upheld the constitutionality of a federal system of contributory old age insurance. The bureau had established 175 local offices by July 1, 1937, when it relieved the Post Office Department from the task of assigning employee account numbers. The number of offices increased steadily and was 327 by July 1, 1939. Its total number of employees was 6,992 by that date. Of these, 3,294 were located outside of central headquarters and 3,698 at headquarters. Of those at headquarters 3,151 were engaged in accounting operations. Their task was to maintain the mammoth central index system and to maintain the millions of individual employee accounts.

Besides the assignment of employee account numbers, the bureau had the task of paying small lump sums which were due after January 1, 1937, to insured workers who became 65 years of age without meeting the minimum eligibility requirements or to their estates if they had died before drawing monthly retirement benefits amounting to as much as the lump sum. The number of these lump sum payments was 80,000 during the calendar year 1937.

But the real test of the ability of the bureau to administer this tremendous social insurance system came in September 1937 when the bureau began to receive from the Bureau of Internal Revenue the 1,700,000 employer reports for the first half of 1937 covering 36,000,000 employee wage items. Each one of these employee wage items had to be placed on punch cards and then posted mechanically to the individual employee's account.

The bureau was able to keep up with the processing of wage items as they were transferred from the Bureau of Internal

Revenue. However, employee account numbers were not shown for about 12 per cent of the wage items contained in employers' reports for the first half of 1937. This percentage, it should be said, rapidly declined in subsequent reports.

Because of the omission of account numbers and inaccuracies in employers' reports, a large number of wage items, dubbed "John Does," could not be posted immediately during the years 1937, 1938, and 1939. However, by June 30, 1940, 99.2 per cent of the 312 million wage items reported in those years had already been posted to 50 million individual employee accounts. The remaining .8 per cent were placed in a "suspense" file, and continued efforts were made to identify them and post them to the correct employee accounts.

For the first year and a half after employers were required to make reports, the bureau maintained twelve self-contained record-keeping units corresponding to twelve geographical areas of the country. However, as accounting problems were solved through actual experience, it was possible to consolidate all twelve of these "production lines." This process was facilitated by changing from a reporting system which required an employer to send in an individual slip for each worker, to a payroll reporting system, which remains in effect to this day.

At the time this accounting operation was set up it was dubbed "the largest bookkeeping job in the world." The cost of maintaining a worker's account was twenty cents a year at the outset and is now considerably less.

Today it is hard to realize the magnitude of the accounting problems that existed in 1937. The first electronic computer in the world was not constructed at Harvard until ten years later. Electronic data-processing equipment using magnetic tape for maintaining the tremendous volume of records was not developed until twenty years later. And it was not possible to convert the National Employee Index to microfilm until 1959, when a microfilm printer was developed which transferred information directly from magnetic tape to microfilm. By that time the index contained 163 million names.

There was, of course, a continuing necessity to coordinate the Board's interpretation of the coverage of the old age insurance system with the interpretation of coverage made by the Bureau of

Internal Revenue. This was because, for constitutional reasons, the benefit provisions in the law had been made independent of the tax provisions, although identical language was used in defining the employment covered. Failure to coordinate might result either in collection of contributions on wages for which no benefit credits would be given or in the payment of benefits based on wages for which no contributions were collected. The latter possibility was the more likely because the Bureau of Internal Revenue was concerned about being reversed by a court if the bureau held that the employer was liable, whereas the Social Security Board was concerned about the worker losing benefit rights if the Board did not hold that the wages were subject to the law. But because of good will and the desire to avoid creating an anomalous situation, the two agencies were able to harmonize their interpretations, and this successful cooperation has continued to exist throughout the years.

While the administration of the old age insurance system was moving along successfully, there was continuing criticism of the large reserve which would be accumulated during the early years when receipts from contributions would exceed benefit disbursements. It was estimated that this reserve would amount to $47 billion in 1980, when current disbursements would equal current receipts from contributions and from interest earned on this reserve. The law required that this reserve be invested in federal government obligations, so the opponents contended this was a mere fiction because the government would be paying interest to itself. It was this criticism that the Republican candidate for President in 1936 meant when he called social security "a fraud on the working-man" and said, "The saving it forces on our workers is a cruel hoax.

Senator Vandenberg of Michigan introduced a concurrent resolution as soon as Congress convened in January 1937, when the memory of the 1936 presidential campaign was still fresh. This resolution called for the abandonment of what it called "the full reserve system," to be accomplished either by raising benefits or reducing payroll taxes, and for extension of coverage to other groups. A hearing on the resolution was held by the Senate Finance Committee on February 22, 1937, at which I, as Chairman of the Social Security Board, testified. I pointed out that the reserve would consist of government obligations which presumably would otherwise be in the hands of private investors. Therefore, if there were no reserve, the government would have to pay out in 1980 twice as much, i.e., a subsidy to the old age insurance system equivalent to the interest that would have been earned on a reserve and also a similar sum in interest to the private investors holding the government obligations which would otherwise have been in the reserve account. I also stated that so long as the old age insurance system covered only 50 per cent of gainfully occupied persons, I considered it unwise and unfair to require the excluded group to pay, through general revenues, any part of the cost of benefits to the covered group. I also pointed out that if there were no reserve to earn interest and no government subsidy in lieu of interest, the schedule of contribution rates would have to be raised, so that the eventual combined employer-employee contribution rate in 1980 would have to be 10 per cent instead of 6 per cent.

I did remark to Senator Vandenberg, off the record, that if the Senator really was worried about the future government debt's being larger than the present debt, he could insert a provision requiring the Treasury to invest the excess in sound private securities. The Senator threw up his hands in mock horror, saying, "That would be socialism."

Unfortunately, the persuasiveness if not the validity of my presentation was blunted by the fact that it envisaged a government debt amounting to $47 billion in 1980 whereas the government debt in 1937 was only $27 billion. At any rate, at the end of the hearing Senator Vandenberg inquired whether I would have any objection to "a concurrent inquiry by a congressional commission into this fundamental question." I replied that I thought probably as good progress could be made if Congress would suggest persons to serve on advisory committees to the Social Security Board. It was finally agreed that the Board, in consultation with the Chairman of the Finance Committee, would create an advisory group to study the problem and report to both the Board and the Senate Finance Committee.

Subsequently in May 1937, the Board joined with a Special Committee on Social Security of the Senate Finance Committee in the appointment of an Advisory Council on Social Security which consisted of representatives of labor organizations and employers' organizations, as well as actuaries and economists. The terms of reference were made broad enough to cover not only such questions as the advisability of increasing the payroll taxes less rapidly and the size, character, and disposition of reserves, but also such questions as the advisability of commencing the payment of retirement benefits sooner, increasing the size of monthly retirement benefits, and extending coverage to include groups then excluded. It was agreed that the Board would make all the necessary studies and furnish all necessary technical assistance.

When the Democratic members of the House Ways and Means Committee heard of this, they were very much disturbed, partly because they felt the committee's prerogative in initiating social security legislation had been infringed, and partly because they felt that I had yielded to a partisan Republican maneuver. I was called before a meeting of the Democratic members of the Ways and Means Committee to justify my action. I explained that I could not very well oppose the suggestion that the Board appoint a representative advisory group to advise it on this subject as similar advisory groups had on other subjects. However, Mr. Vinson, the same congressman who had demanded that the Board appoint his candidate for personnel director, indicated his extreme displeasure by replying forcefully, if somewhat inelegantly, "What you are saying is that you finally let your milk down."

Because of this situation the Board did not take any immediate steps to call a meeting of the advisory group. Instead I talked with the Chairman of the Senate Finance Committee several times, and it was finally agreed that a meeting should be called, but that I should discuss the matter with the President before doing so.

Accordingly, I prepared a memorandum to the President, dated September 11, 1937, dealing not only with the question of what to do regarding this advisory group but with the basic question of what the Administration should do regarding amendments to the Social Security Act. This memorandum suggested that current political attacks should be utilized to advance a socially desirable program. It recommended a series of amendments to the old age insurance system speeding up and liberalizing the benefits and converting it into an old age, permanent invalidity, and survivors' insurance system. It also recommended that the unemployment insurance system should be extended to include unemployment due to temporary disabilities which were not covered under workmen's compensation laws.

I then met with the President who agreed that the advisory group should begin to function and that a small, unpublicized group of government officials should also be formed to explore the problems involved in the development of an expanded social security program. Because the changes in the old age insurance system recommended in the memorandum furnished the basis for the deliberation of the advisory group, the memorandum is presented in full as Appendix III.

In spite of the rather inauspicious circumstances surrounding the appointment of this advisory group, it functioned very successfully. In order to stimulate the advisory council to develop its recommendations before the 1939 Congress would convene, and to assure these recommendations would include liberalizing the benefit provisions in addition to the financing provisions, I requested the President to send me a letter indicating his interest. This letter, dated April 28, 1938, read in part as follows:

I am particularly anxious that the Board give attention to the development of a sound plan for liberalizing the old-age insurance system. In the development of such a plan I should like to have the Board give consideration to the feasibility of extending its coverage, commencing the payment of old-age insurance annuities at an earlier date than January 1, 1942, paying larger benefits than now provided in the act for those retiring during the earlier years of the system, providing benefits for aged wives and widows, and providing benefits for young children of insured persons dying before reaching retirement age. It is my hope that the Board will be prepared to submit its recommendations before Congress reconvenes in January.

The advisory council submitted two interim reports on coverage and financing. On December 10, 1938, it submitted its final report. The report was in accord with the memorandum submitted to the President on September 11, 1937, and the letter of the President just quoted. It recommended that monthly retirement benefits begin January 1, 1940, and that they should be

liberalized in amount during the early years. It also recommended payment of monthly benefits to aged wives and to
survivors, including aged widows, children, and young widows
with children in their care. But it recommended that the eventual
annual cost of these benefits not exceed the cost of the benefits
stated in the existing law, this result to be achieved in part by
reducing the monthly retirement benefits payable in later years to
single workers and by reducing the large lump sum death benefits
to a nominal amount. It stated that all members of the advisory
council regarded the provision of benefits for permanent and total
disability as socially desirable but differed as to when they should
begin.

As regards coverage, the advisory council recommended that
the chief groups of employees of private employers then not
covered, namely farm and domestic employees and employees of
nonprofit organizations, be covered. But it did not recommend
coverage of self-employed persons until a solution of the administrative problems could be found.

With regard to financing, it recommended that, with the
broadening of the coverage of this social insurance system, the
eventual cost should be borne by approximately equal contributions from employers, employees, and the government out of
general revenues.

Concerning the reserve fund question which had led to the
creation of the advisory council, the council issued a statement on
April 29, 1938, to which it referred in its final report. This
statement, which was unanimously approved, concluded by saying, "The members of the Council, regardless of differing views on
other aspects of the financing of old-age insurance, are of the
opinion that the present provisions regarding the investment of
the moneys in the old-age reserve account do not involve any
misuse of these moneys or endanger the safety of these funds."
The final report did, however, state that "with the changes in the
benefit structure here recommended and with the introduction of
a definite program of governmental contributions to the system,
the Council believes that the size of the old-age insurance fund
will be kept within much lower limits than are involved in the
present Act."

At the same time that this advisory group was giving its

attention to old age insurance, a Special Committee to Investigate Unemployment and Relief was functioning. This special committee was created in August 1937 pursuant to Senate Resolution 36, offered by Senator James F. Byrnes of South Carolina, who became its chairman. It was recognized that the emergency work relief program known as the Works Progress Administration was not a permanent solution of the unemployment problem, and it was hoped that, with the continuing recovery from the Great Depression, a permanent solution could now be found. However, in September 1937 the curve of unemployment started to turn upward. So the committee decided the time had not yet arrived when it would be feasible to replace existing emergency programs with permanent ones. But the committee did submit a preliminary report in April 1938 which made several recommendations for improving the Social Security Act. Concerning old age insurance, it recommended that monthly retirement benefits be commenced earlier. As regards unemployment insurance, the committee pointed out that, while it was too early to say what effect it would have on relief and work relief expenditures, it was "apparent that some far-reaching modifications in the present system will have to be made before this type of benefit can serve the purposes for which it was designed." It recommended that the United States Employment Service be transferred from the Department of Labor to the Social Security Board. It also recommended that every state be required to put into effect a merit system for personnel as a condition for receiving a federal grant under the public assistance and unemployment insurance titles. It is interesting to note that the committee rejected a suggestion made by Harry L. Hopkins, Administrator of the Works Progress Administration, that the aid to dependent children program be broadened to include children of unemployed parents as well as children dependent because of the death, disability, or absence from the home of a parent. It was not until a quarter of a century later that Congress adopted this suggestion for a temporary period only.

The Interdepartmental Committee to Coordinate Health and Welfare Activities, of which I was a member, was also active during this period. This committee had been created by the President in August 1935. While the social security bill was still pending in Congress, Dr. Harvey Cushing, Chairman of the Medical Advisory Committee appointed by the Committee on Economic Security, had written a letter to the President suggesting the desirability of coordinating the various health activities of the federal government. The President referred Dr. Cushing's letter to the Secretary of Labor with a note asking her to explore the possibility of setting up "an interdepartmental committee of coordination of the existing health and welfare activities." As Assistant Secretary of Labor, I was asked for my ideas. I suggested the establishment of a steering committee composed of members of the "Little Cabinet" (i.e., assistant secretaries) to concentrate on specific situations. Accordingly, a memorandum was sent to the President, recommending such a committee "instead of setting up an interdepartmental committee with blanket authority, or which would in any way smack of a super-bureau." The President accepted this recommendation and issued a statement, which I had prepared, that included the sentence, "I am confident that this procedure will facilitate the consummation of a series of appropriate agreements between the various departments of the government.

The President appointed the following persons as members of this interdepartmental committee: Josephine Roche (Chairman), who was Assistant Secretary of the Treasury and had the U.S. Public Health Service under her jurisdiction; Oscar Chapman, Assistant Secretary of the Interior; M. L. Wilson, Assistant Secretary of Agriculture; and myself, as Assistant Secretary of Labor.

For the first year and a half this committee gave its attention to promoting coordination of existing health activities. But early in 1937 it turned its attention to a comprehensive survey of health needs of the nation and the development of a national health program to meet these needs. This came about largely because of the interest of Miss Roche and myself. It was done, of course, with the approval of the President.

The President's interdepartmental committee appointed a Technical Committee on Medical Care to make the survey and draft recommendations. The advantage of this procedure was that none of the government agencies represented on the interdepartmental committee would be committed in advance to support the recommendations.

The report of the technical committee was submitted in February 1938. The report presented the health needs of the nation and a series of recommendations to meet those needs. These recommendations were as follows:

(1) An expansion of public health and maternal and child health services under existing titles of the Social Security Act.

(2) Federal grants-in-aid to the states for the construction of hospitals and for defraying operating costs during the first three years.

(3) Federal grants-in-aid to the states toward the costs of a medical care program for medically needy persons.

(4) Federal grants-in-aid to the states toward the costs of a general medical care program.

(5) Federal action to develop a program of compensation for wage loss due to temporary and permanent disability.

Harry L. Hopkins, the Administrator of the Works Progress Administration, although not a member of the interdepartmental committee, was much interested in the development of this program. In fact, it was he who first suggested a nationwide hospital construction program as a necessary preliminary to a nationwide health insurance system.

Miss Roche and I met with the President to discuss what should be done with the technical committee report. The President decided that the section of the report dealing with the health needs of the nation should be made public immediately and that later a National Health Conference should be called which would include representatives of the medical profession and other interested groups. Those attending this conference would be asked to discuss the full report of the technical committee.

The conference was called on July 18, 19, and 20, and the President, who was out of the country on a cruise, sent a long message indicating his great interest. In that message he took occasion to say that he was glad that the conference included so many representatives of the general public because the problems were in a real sense public problems. He concluded by saying, "I hope that at the National Health Conference a chart for continuing concerted action will begin to take form."

The conference was such a great success in arousing public support that Miss Roche sent a cable to the President on July 23 reading as follows: "Cannot resist sending you word amazing public support at National Health Conference for National

Health Program and which is mounting daily as evidenced by press comment, telegrams and letters. Our technicians are working with all speed to develop specific proposals which we expect to have ready for you on your return. Meanwhile we are following your instructions to make no public commitments as to future program.

Representatives of the American Medical Association asked to meet with members of the President's interdepartmental committee on the Sunday following the conference. At that meeting they offered to support recommendations 1, 2, 3, and 5 of the technical committee's report if recommendation 4, proposing federal grants-in-aid to the states toward the costs of a general program of medical care, were abandoned. The members of the interdepartmental committee declined to agree with this proposal. Even so, the House of Delegates of the American Medical Association, meeting in special session in September 1938, adopted its committee report approving of all the recommendations except recommendation 4.

Miss Roche and I met with the President, after he had returned from his cruise, to discuss the next step. The President was so enthusiastic about the public response to the proposed National Health Program that his first inclination was to make it an issue in the congressional campaign which was then under way. However, he then said he thought it would be better to make it an issue in the 1940 presidential campaign. It did not occur to me at that time that this might be an indication the President was thinking of running for a third term.

While these various groups were considering matters of concern to the Social Security Board, the Board itself was giving consideration to the changes in the Social Security Act which it would recommend to the President and the Congress when it convened in January 1939. On December 30, 1938, it submitted its recommendations to the President, covering old age insurance, unemployment insurance, public assistance, and health.

The recommendations regarding old age insurance were in general agreement with those of the advisory council, although more specific in recommending a method whereby larger retirement benefits could be paid in the early years without increasing the long-range cost of the system. The Board was also more explicit in stating that, while it believed that contributions should eventually be made out of federal taxes other than payroll taxes, such contributions should not be substituted for any part of the payroll taxes provided in the existing law. The Board also recommended that such contributions should not begin until annual benefit disbursements began to exceed annual payroll tax collections plus interest earnings. As regards coverage, the Board recommended extension of coverage to large-scale agriculture, to domestic service, and to nonprofit organizations. The Board also stated it thought the coverage should include not only federal employees but also state and local government employees if constitutional difficulties could be overcome. The Board's recommendation concerning benefits for permanent total disability was equivocal, merely stating that, if such benefits were provided, they should be linked to old age insurance instead of unemployment insurance.

In the area of unemployment insurance, the Board recommended extension of coverage to coincide with the coverage recommended for old age insurance, except that it excluded agricultural employment because of the administrative difficulties and federal employment because the need was not urgent. The Board recommended also that employers of one or more should be included, and that a maximum of $3,000 should be placed on wages subject to the payroll tax, the same as in the case of old age insurance.

The Board felt that there was a great advantage in having the same maximum for both taxes since it would facilitate combining the two federal tax returns into one. But in retrospect it is clear the Board made a grievous error in not recommending instead that the maximum of $3,000 under the old age insurance system be removed so that there would be no maximum under either system. The imposition of a maximum not only has made the employee payroll tax regressive but has had a serious effect throughout the years in preventing a rise in the level of benefits commensurate with the rise in the general wage level.

The Board also recommended that the administration of unemployment insurance and of the United States Employment Service be unified in a single federal bureau. It did not specify where this bureau should be located.

To improve the public assistance provisions, the Board recommended that the federal grant-in-aid for aid to dependent children be raised from 33⅓ per cent of the state payments to 50 per cent to make the proportion of federal aid the same as that for old age assistance and blind assistance. The Board also recommended that the federal grant-in-aid for administrative expenses for old age assistance and blind assistance be changed from an additional 5 per cent applied to the assistance payments to 50 per cent of actual administrative expenses, as in the case of aid to dependent children.

The Board took advantage of the bad experiences of several states in the political use of public assistance records and political appointment of personnel to recommend that public assistance plans be required to include provision for protecting the confidential character of records and that a state be required to establish merit systems for personnel in both public assistance and unemployment insurance.

The most important recommendation for amending the public assistance titles was that the uniform percentage of federal matching be changed to a percentage which would vary inversely with the economic capacity of a state to meet its share of the cost. The Board pointed out that, "The present system of uniform percentage grants results at best in an unnecessarily large amount of money flowing in and out of the Federal Treasury, and at worst in increasing the inequalities which now exist in the relative economic capacities of the States."

In the field of health the Board endorsed the national health program recommended by the interdepartmental committee. The Board stated that it was not making a positive recommendation regarding protection against wage loss due to permanent and total disability because of the difficult administrative problems and the cost considerations involved. It said, however, that it did not consider the administrative problems insuperable and that the cost could be kept within reasonable limits if a fairly strict definition of disability were adopted. It added that this protection should be linked to old age insurance. Finally, the Board suggested that, if a program of protection against wage loss due to temporary disability were inaugurated, it should be placed on a state basis, following the precedent of unemployment compensation.

4.

A Year of Change, 1939

The President, on January 16, 1939, shortly after the new Congress had organized, transmitted the Board's recommendations with a message which not only constituted a general endorsement but which also explicitly endorsed all of the major recommendations. The House Ways and Means Committee scheduled hearings to begin on February 1 to consider the many bills which had been introduced to amend the Social Security Act. Since the Townsend movement still had considerable strength, it was decided at a preliminary conference between the Democratic members of the committee and myself that it would be best for me to present the Board's recommendations at the opening session but defer committee questioning until the Townsendites and all other witnesses had been heard. Both the committee members and I would then be in a better position to discuss the Board's recommendations in the light of the criticisms and suggestions made by the various witnesses.

The strength of the Townsend movement was demonstrated by the fact that more than fifty congressmen and two senators testified in support of it. While the ranking minority member of the committee indicated a desire to find some common ground between the Townsend plan and the recommendations of the Board, there was no active support of the plan by either minority or majority members of the committee.

The general interest in social security and the thoroughness with which the Ways and Means Committee considered all the suggestions it received was demonstrated by the fact that 2,612 pages of testimony were taken. My testimony and the questions asked me by the committee alone occupied 13 sessions of the committee, 12 of which were consecutive.

The questioning of the committee was friendly throughout, although several minority members took occasion to repeat the criticisms regarding the size and character of the old age insurance reserve fund. Congressman Vinson, who had been critical of the personnel policy of the Board and of the Board's acceptance of the proposal to create an advisory committee, was no longer a member of the committee. If he had been, the attitude might have been different although my later contacts with him had been friendly.

However, the physical characteristics of the hearing room made the extended appearance before the committee something of an ordeal. The room itself measured approximately 100 feet by 150 feet with a high ceiling. The dais upon which the 25 members of the committee sat measured approximately 75 feet and was slightly curved. The witness sat about 25 feet from the Chairman and about 40 feet from the members at the far ends of the dais. There was no microphone, and the acoustics of the room were such as to make even a shout almost inaudible. Moreover, Robert L. Doughton, the Chairman, was very deaf and disdained the use of a hearing aid.

I can never forget how the elderly Chairman would say, "Speak up, young man, speak up," although I was shouting at the top of my voice at the time. However, at the conclusion of the extended hearings, the Chairman was kind enough to say, "And especially would I thank Dr. Altmeyer for his very able, patient, and full presentation of the recommendations of the Board. I do not believe I have ever known any witness to more completely cover the case in which he was interested or more fully or intelligently discuss the subject under consideration. It is a very heavy responsibility which has fallen upon him, and I am sure each and every member of the Committee appreciates the valuable service which he has rendered to the Committee during the course of these hearings."

Most of the testimony and questioning was devoted to the consideration of the old age insurance system. I related the benefit changes recommended to their effect on the long-range cost of the insurance system and consequently the size of the reserve fund which would be built up, hoping in this way to win the support of both the advocates of increased benefits and the advocates of a smaller reserve fund. I repeatedly used the analogy of a teeter-totter. The following quotations from my testimony are typical:

In other words, your present annual benefit cost goes up steeply, so that you have got one end of the teeter-totter way down and the other end of the teeter-totter way up, taking one end as 1940 and the other end as 1980. Our recommendation, in effect, raises the lower end of the teeter-totter and lowers the upper end. The increased benefits in the early years will be slightly more costly than the saving in the decreased benefits in the later years, so that your level premium cost will be a fraction more, but not much more.

. . . .

I should say, Mr. Congressman, that in considering this problem [i.e., reserve fund] it is necessary to consider the two phases; first, of benefits, and secondly, how you are going to finance them. They are interrelated. As I tried to point out, the teeter-totter of the new pattern of benefits is less steep than the present pattern in the Social Security Act. Now, to that extent it is what you might call a safer system, because you are not promising so much for the future as you are under the present system. Consequently you are giving more aid in the early years than you have promised under the present system. To the extent that you bring home the cost of the system in the early years and have leveled down the cost of the system for the long time future years, you have a safer system, because the people then appreciate what the system is costing and is likely to cost.

The increase in the total benefits payable in the early years and the reduction in the steepness of the annual increase in the cost of the benefits paid in future years were brought about chiefly in two ways: The retirement benefit payable to a single worker (called the primary benefit) was related to the previous average monthly wage of the worker and not to the cumulative wages he had earned before he retired; survivors' benefits, also related to the previous average monthly wage, were payable to widows and orphans (or dependent parents, if there was no surviving wife or child) instead of a lump sum to the estate of a deceased worker, amounting to 3½ per cent of his cumulative wages.

Since a monthly benefit was also payable to the wife of a married worker who retired (if she was at least 65 years of age), the new pattern of benefits could be characterized as family protection rather than individual protection. Therefore, the new pattern of benefits had the basic social advantage of relating the benefits to the probable need as indicated by the existence of dependents. From a financial standpoint it could be said that it provided maximum protection at minimum cost.

This increased social adequacy was not achieved at the expense of individual equity since the change in the benefit formula also provided an increase in the monthly benefit of 1 per cent for every year that a worker had been in covered employment. The effect of this annual increment was that it assured that every worker, whether married or single and regardless of how much he had paid in contributions, would receive at least as much protection as he could have purchased from a private insurance company with the same contributions. However, it is true that this annual increment represented a smaller increase in the benefit amount than would have occurred under the original cumulative wage formula.

The face value of the survivors' benefits payable under the new plan was estimated to be equal to the face value of all the private life insurance written in the United States. This is still true today. But after all these years there still prevails a considerable lack of awareness of the existence and importance of these survivors' benefits. I recall vividly that the widow of Joseph Smart, President Truman's Press Secretary who had died of a heart attack, was quite unaware of the sizable benefits to which she and her young children were entitled, based on her husband's previous employment in a covered occupation.

Besides accepting the Board's recommendations on benefits (and indeed adding surviving parents' benefits), the Ways and Means Committee approved various administrative changes which the Board recommended, such as specifying that a claimant dissatisfied with the Board's decision should be entitled to a hearing and court review. The failure of the 1935 act to provide for a hearing under this social insurance system was an oversight. There was such a provision included in the unemployment insurance and in the public assistance titles. I felt very strongly that this was essential to protect the statutory right to benefits. The committee also approved of the Board's recommendation that the confidential character of the Board's records should be protected.

The committee declined to extend the coverage of the old age insurance system. In fact it broadened the exclusion of agricultural employment by applying the exclusion to the processing of agricultural products. I well remember the reply of the Chairman when I saw him in his office to urge the inclusion of farm workers: "Doctor, when the first farmer with manure on his shoes comes to me and asks to be covered, I will be willing to consider it."

The committee also decided to eliminate the increase in the contribution rate which was scheduled to take place January 1, 1940, from 1 per cent each payable by employers and employees to 1½ per cent each. But it retained the later scheduled increases to 2 per cent, 2½ per cent, and 3 per cent on January 1 of the years 1943, 1946, and 1949, respectively. This was one of four alternatives suggested by Secretary of the Treasury Morgenthau. The Secretary had testified that four years' experience had shown that the benefits of the act would be so widely diffused that supplemental funds from general revenues might be substituted for a considerable proportion of the expected interest earnings from a large reserve. He also had recommended only a contingency reserve fund, amounting to not more than three times the highest prospective annual benefits in the ensuing five years. This, of course, represented a complete reversal of his attitude in 1935.

The committee took no action on providing benefits for permanent disability. This was not surprising because, when pressed, I had informed the committee that the Board recommended that Congress not make such benefits effective at the same time as the proposed changes in old age and survivors' benefits, but that it was reasonably certain it could administer permanent disability benefits if they became effective one or two years later.

Neither did the committee take any action on the Board's suggestion that, if action were taken to provide protection against wage loss due to temporary disability, it be along the same lines as unemployment insurance. Actually the committee gave little attention to unemployment insurance since the Board had made only two major recommendations: one, that the coverage should be extended to coincide with that of old age insurance; the other, that the administration of unemployment insurance and of the

United States Employment Service be unified in a single federal bureau. Since the general attitude of the committee was against extension of coverage under either old age insurance or unemployment insurance, that subject was disposed of without any discussion. The committee did give some attention to the question of the unification of unemployment insurance and the United States Employment Service but took no action because a reorganization plan involving this had been presented by the President and was awaiting action by the entire Congress.

However, a member of the committee from Massachusetts, John McCormack, now Speaker of the House, raised the question of reducing the unemployment tax because he contended that Massachusetts and a number of other states were collecting more than they needed to pay benefits. A reduction in total contributions would eventually occur in the 30 states having employer experience rating in their laws at that time. But Wisconsin was the only state whose law had been in existence long enough to bring the employer experience rating into effect.

I recommended against any reduction in the unemployment tax because there had not been sufficient experience with the payment of benefits to establish that the cost of adequate benefits would be less than 2.7 per cent, which was the general rate payable under state laws. However, the Congressman from Massachusetts, when the committee met in executive session, pressed for an amendment that would permit a state to make a reduction in the 2.7 per cent rate. I suggested that, if such a provision were enacted, it ought to require a minimum reserve and minimum benefit standards as a condition for reducing the general tax rate, and also as a condition for permitting an employer experience rating system to reduce the total contributions below 2.7 per cent. This suggestion was accepted by the committee and came to be called the McCormack amendment. However, the minimum benefit standards included in the bill reported by the committee were considerably lower than those I had recommended.

Concerning public assistance, the committee accepted the Board's recommendation that the federal grant-in-aid for dependent children be raised from 33⅓ per cent to 50 per cent, to make the percentage the same as that for old age assistance and blind assistance. But the committee rejected what the Board considered its most important recommendation: that the uniform percentage of federal matching be changed to a percentage which would vary in accordance with the economic capacity of a state to meet its share of the cost. I have always felt that the use of the label "variable grant," instead of a more attractive label such as "equalization grant," was a serious handicap in achieving understanding and favorable action.

The committee failed to approve the Board's recommendation that the state public assistance plans be required to include a merit system for personnel, although all except 3 of the 25 members of the committee came from states that had a merit system. However, the committee did approve the Board's recommendation that these plans include provision for protecting the confidential character of records. Curiously enough, the committee also approved the Board's recommendation to increase the participation in administrative expenses as far as blind assistance was concerned, but neglected to do so for old age assistance.

The Board had not made a formal recommendation that the public assistance titles be amended to make it clear that a state plan must give consideration to any other income and resources in determining need. This was because it did not want to give the Townsendites the impression that there was any ambiguity in the existing law. But I did suggest, when the committee was in executive session, that this be done, and the committee agreed.

The committee proceeded to prepare its report to the House of Representatives, but the Democratic members decided that it would be best to dispose of the Townsend bill which had been re-introduced and labeled "general welfare act," the same title as was given to another bill introduced by another organization called the General Welfare Federation of America. This latter group's proposal was similar to the Townsend proposal except that the amount of the flat pension would be limited to a minimum of $30 and a maximum of $60 a month, depending upon revenues from a 2 per cent tax on the gross volume of payments for goods and services. The minority members of the committee were offered the opportunity of supporting the Townsend bill, but did not do so, so the bill was reported to the House without recommendation.

There were four hours of debate, divided equally, with the

ranking minority member of the committee assigning time to supporters of the Townsend bill and the Chairman of the committee assigning time to the opponents. The final vote on approval of the bill was taken on June 1, 1939, and was 97 yeas and 302 nays; so the bill was rejected.

The following day the committee made its report on amendments of the Social Security Act to the House and submitted a bill incorporating its recommendations. The minority members did not oppose the bill, stating that, while it was not completely satisfactory, it at least made certain improvements in the present law which justified supporting it.

The minority took credit for the abandonment of "the staggering and illusory" $47 billion reserve fund for old age insurance and the consequent three-year postponement of the scheduled increase in the payroll tax. It also criticized the abandonment of the large "money-back" lump sum payments to the estates of deceased workers although this abandonment made possible the payment of survivors' benefits without increasing the cost of the system. While the minority called the abandonment "confiscation," it said, "We do not wish to be understood as opposing the liberalization of the present old age insurance provisions."

After several days of debate in the House on the bill presented by the committee, a motion made by a minority member of the committee to recommit the bill was rejected, and a motion made by the Chairman of the committee to approve the bill was adopted by a vote of 364 yeas and 2 nays on June 10, 1939. The bill then went to the Senate where the Finance Committee scheduled hearings to begin June 12, 1939.

The Chairman of the Senate Finance Committee invited Senator Byrnes, the Chairman of the Special Committee to Investigate Unemployment and Relief, to sit with the committee. Senator Byrnes' committee had submitted what it called a "final report" on January 14, 1939, but had held hearings in February at which I had testified, endorsing its recommendations which were in accordance with the Board's recommendations. In one respect the committee's recommendations went further by including minimum benefit standards to be observed by the states in their unemployment insurance laws.

I was the first witness called by the Senate Finance Committee.

I repeated the Board's recommendations which had been presented to the House Ways and Means Committee, including the recommendation that the federal grant to the states for public assistance be related to the economic capacity of each state to bear its share of the cost. To my amazement, the Washington, D.C., *Evening Star,* in its noon edition, had a front-page headline reading, "Altmeyer Recommends Variable Grant."

The venerable Chairman of the Ways and Means Committee telephoned me that afternoon upbraiding me for making this recommendation after his committee had rejected it. He called me ungrateful "after all that the committee had done" for me and told me never to appear before his committee again. This incident occurred hardly a month after he had eulogized me. In vain I tried to explain that I felt obligated to present the same recommendations to the Senate as I had to the House. Fortunately, by the time the Senate had passed the bill with certain amendments and had returned it to the House, I had been able to make my peace with the irate Chairman.

On the second day of the Senate committee hearings, I was appalled by being subjected to detailed questioning by Senator Robert M. LaFollette of my own home state. All of his questions were designed to show the effect of what he called "arbitraries" in the proposed minimum eligibility requirements for benefits under the old age and survivors' insurance system. Thus, he brought out that it was conceivable that a worker could fail to have earned the minimum required amount of wages by only one cent and be ineligible for benefits; that the minimum eligibility requirements increased with the passage of time; and that the benefits paid in relation to contributions became less liberal as time went on.

I tried to explain that under any contributory social insurance system it was necessary to have specified minimum eligibility requirements; that these requirements should be less stringent for workers already old than for younger workers who would have more opportunity to meet higher requirements; and that it was also necessary to pay higher benefits in relation to contributions in the early years than in the later years, if they were to be significant in terms of wage loss.

After having asked about 50 questions from a list, Senator LaFollette handed me his entire list of 105 questions and asked that both the written questions and answers be inserted in the record. These questions were so detailed and technical that it was clear the Senator had been furnished them by an expert in social insurance.

I was naturally concerned about the possible unfavorable public reaction, so I invited to my house a half-dozen persons whom I had reason to believe might have been involved in the preparation of the questions. They included a brother-in-law of a brother of the Senator, who was a top economist in the Treasury Department and who later became a White House adviser; another economist in the Treasury Department who later became a high official of the International Monetary Fund; the Chairman of the Railroad Retirement Fund; and two lawyers who worked as a team on legislation that the President was interested in. The purpose of the meeting was to ascertain whether it would be possible to reach an agreement on some alternative plan.

It soon became clear that the group was opposed to any contributory social insurance plan and favored a uniform pension financed out of general funds of the Treasury, as did the Townsendites. The two economists from the Treasury were apparently the main advocates of this radical change in the existing system. They were both ardent Keynesians and were desirous of using social security as a device to stabilize the business cycle. Therefore, they believed it was imperative to abandon the payroll tax method of financing and substitute a method of financing which would have a strong contracyclical effect.

The Director of the United States Employment Service had estimated that there were 10 million unemployed at that time, which was 17 per cent of the labor force, so their concern that government fiscal operations should stimulate the economy was understandable. The collections under the old age insurance system were, of course, far larger than benefit payments. As already explained, these consisted only of small lump sums amounting in all to about $8 million, whereas contributions amounted to $390 million. The net excess of contributions over benefit payments under the state unemployment insurance systems was about $390 million. Moreover, it could be argued that, even if benefit payments and contributions were equal, the payroll tax itself was regressive.

I did point to the fact that the federal government was paying out more than $3 billion in grants for public assistance and in wages under the various work programs. I also pointed out that the federal budget deficit was $3 billion so that government fiscal operations as a whole were contracyclical.

Of course, my fundamental argument was that a contributory social insurance system with both the benefits and the contributions related to wages was a safer and more equitable system than a system which paid a uniform benefit not related to either need or wage loss and which was dependent upon annual congressional appropriations out of general revenues. I also pointed out that the wide differentials in wages and in standards of living would make it impossible to select any particular benefit amount which would be generally satisfactory, so that whatever amount was selected would inevitably become a political football.

Thus, there was a basic policy question at issue which was whether any temporary economic advantage inherent in a system financed out of general revenues outweighed the inherent long-range social, psychological, and political advantages of a contributory social insurance system under which both benefits and contributions were related to wages. This sort of question in its very nature could not be resolved by experts since it involved incommensurable value judgments which in a democracy must ultimately be resolved by the elected representatives of the people.

The final dialogue with one of the economists from the Treasury was rather heated and went something as follows:

"Just what do you mean by a flat pension?"

"A pension geared to the business cycle."

"Well, what do you mean by that?"

"What we mean is that, when we're in a slump, we step up the flat pension, and when we have inflation threatening us, we cut back.

"What kind of a social program would that be; where would you get any security for the individual out of a program like that?"

"We don't give a damn about how it's done as long as you shovel out the money when it's needed to iron out the business cycle.

"Don't you think there is any value in relating benefits and contributions to wages?"

"That's just a lot of ⸺ [an obscene expression that cannot be recorded].

A number of years later the two economists were accused before congressional committees of having been associated with a Communist group. I have no reason to believe that this was so. However, I do know from personal experience that they did have a great urge to manipulate and influence prominent officials in making decisions of considerable public importance.

This group also sent a memorandum to the President, captioned "Political Repercussions of Pending Social Security Act Amendments," which the President sent on to me. I felt that the matter had become serious because of the possible effect of the LaFollette type of criticism on public opinion and the possible use the Townsendites might make of such criticism to strengthen their cause. I was also concerned about this dissension within the Administration. Therefore, I asked for an appointment with the President.

To my great relief the President said he did not think the situation was dangerous. Characteristically, he reached that conclusion quickly by applying the so-called arbitraries to a situation with which he was thoroughly familiar. He said, "Why, take Mose Smith, for example [Mose Smith being his farm manager]. If Mose barely missed qualifying for these benefits, there would be any number of people in Duchess County who would give him enough work to do so that he could qualify." Thus, by personalizing a complicated problem, he was able to dispose of it simply and effectively.

Interestingly enough, Senator LaFollette never again referred to this question of "arbitraries" but merely inserted my written answers in the record. The only other matters discussed at any length during the remainder of the public hearings were the McCormack amendment to the unemployment insurance title of the Social Security Act and variable grants for public assistance.

I was pressed by Senator LaFollette to say whether I favored the McCormack amendment. I stated that, in view of the short period of experience, the Board would be reluctant to endorse any proposal for the reduction of contribution rates, but that, if

Congress believed it desirable to reduce contribution rates, the McCormack proposal was less dangerous than an outright flat reduction, since it required as a condition for reduction that a state maintain a minimum reserve and observe minimum benefit standards.

On June 29 the Senate Finance Committee concluded its public hearings and went into executive session. The McCormack amendment was eliminated, after brief discussion, because of the uniform opposition of representatives of state unemployment insurance agencies to the requirement that contribution rates average at least 2.7 per cent unless federal minimum benefit standards were observed. The variable grant proposal was discussed at considerable length. Finally, Senator Connally proposed an amendment which would provide two-thirds federal matching for the first $15 of the average monthly old age assistance payment in a state and one-half federal matching of the balance (up to a total state average payment of $40). This proposal did not represent the recommendation of the Board that the federal matching ratio should vary with the economic capacity of each state. It had the effect of increasing the proportion of the cost of old age assistance borne by the federal government in all states but to a greater extent in the low-income states, since these, for the most part, had low average old age assistance payments. Although the Chairman of the committee favored the proposal, it was nevertheless rejected by the committee.

The Senate Finance Committee reported the bill on July 7, including in it the Board's recommendation that state public assistance and unemployment insurance agencies have a merit system for personnel. The Senate debated it on July 11 and 12. The only change that was made in the bill as reported by the committee was the adoption of the Connally amendment and a further amendment by Senator Johnson of Colorado requiring the states to contribute at least $10 a month for each recipient. The vote for passage of the bill as amended was 57 to 8.

The bill then went to conference. The conferees from the Senate and House remained deadlocked for several weeks, chiefly because of the Connally amendment. In an attempt to break the deadlock, I drafted an amendment which would continue the 50–50 matching basis, but provide that the minimum monthly federal grant would be $7.50 per recipient. This compromise amendment was satisfactory to the Senate conferees. It would cost the federal government only $10 million a year additional which would be received by 14 states, mostly low-income states, as compared with $120 million under the Connally amendment.

The conferees remained deadlocked, and there was grave danger that Congress would adjourn without taking action. So again I was obliged to seek the President's assistance. I explained the compromise amendment to the President and suggested that the President send a letter to the chairmen of the House Ways and Means Committee and Senate Finance Committee indicating that he favored the compromise.

To my consternation the President said he was absolutely opposed to it. When I pointed out that the cost was a small price to pay to get through this important piece of legislation, he said, "Not one nickel more, not one solitary nickel. Once you get off the 50–50 matching basis, the sky's the limit, and before you know it, we'll be paying the whole bill."

What made it all the worse was that, when I explained that it had somewhat the same effect as variable grants related to the economic capacity of the states, he said, "What you are talking about are lopsided grants and I'm opposed to them."

This placed me in an extremely embarrassing position. I had been told by the Chairman of the House Ways and Means Committee never to come back again because I had continued to advocate variable grants before the Senate Finance Committee and now I had to tell the Senate Finance Committee that the President opposed variable grants. When I did so, Senator Connally wanted to know what was going on at the other end of town. Another senator said, "Do you usually make important recommendations that you haven't cleared with the President?"

As a matter of fact, the President had said in his message dated January 16, transmitting the Board's recommendations, "The report suggests a twofold approach which I believe to be sound. One way is to begin the payment of monthly old-age insurance benefits sooner, and to liberalize the benefits to be paid in the early years. The other way is to make proportionately larger Federal grants-in-aid to those States with limited fiscal capacities, so that they may provide more adequate assistance to those in need. This result can and should be accomplished in such a way as to involve little, if any, additional cost to the Federal government. Such a method embodies a principle that may well be applied to other Federal grants-in-aid."

It is true that I had prepared the President's message. Unfortunately, he apparently had not noted this important recommendation. However, I had also sent the President a memorandum on June 2, telling him that the Democratic members of the Ways and Means Committee wanted to know whether he had any objection to increasing the federal matching along the lines later proposed by Senator Connally. In that memorandum I pointed out that he had approved the principle of variable grants, but that the members of the committee did not think that varying grants in accordance with the per capita income of the states would be completely understood or satisfactory to the richer states. The President at that time indicated his opposition to the Connally type of matching, but I did not understand he was opposed to the fundamental principle of variable grants related to the economic capacity of the various states.

The Senate conferees realized that they could not prevail in the face of the President's opposition. So they receded on the Connally amendment (as well as the Johnson amendment which was never seriously considered). Senator Connally was very bitter that Senator LaFollette had changed his vote in conference, saying on the floor of the Senate that, "The price to kill the Connally amendment in the Conference Committee was the $695,000,000 taken out of the old-age insurance fund for people who get to be 65 this year." He was referring to a further liberalization in the eligibility requirements for persons already 65 years of age which the Senate Finance Committee had added to the bill as it came from the House.

The House conferees receded on the McCormack amendment. The bill was then passed by both houses without further debate and was signed into law by the President on August 10, 1939.

I prepared a statement which the President issued at the time he approved the bill. The statement pointed out that the original Social Security Act had been passed exactly four years ago on the fourteenth day of August and that these amendments illustrated the manner in which a great program of social legislation should be improved in the light of additional experience and understanding. I included in the statement specific mention of the fact that the social insurance benefits were related to wage loss, as contrasted with any system of flat pensions, and that public assistance would continue to be furnished on the basis of individual need.

Because I was still concerned about the activities of individuals within the Administration in advocating a uniform pension, I also included an announcement that the President was asking the original Cabinet Committee on Economic Security (with the addition of myself) to continue its life and to make active study of various proposals which may be made for amendments to the Social Security Act.

My thought was that this Cabinet committee would furnish a broad and effective base not only for considering proposals but also for assuring that subordinate officials in the respective departments under the Cabinet secretaries would act in a responsible manner. Actually, an occasion arose almost immediately for calling the Cabinet committee together.

I learned that the National Resources Planning Board (of which the President's uncle, Frederic A. Delano, was Chairman) was contemplating a study of public social services, broadly defined, and particularly relief and work relief. This board included, as one of its members, Charles E. Merriam of the University of Chicago, who was also active in the Public Administration Clearing House, which in turn worked closely with the American Public Welfare Association and the Council of State Governments.

I suggested to Mr. Frank Bane, Executive Director of the Council of State Governments (who had previously served as Executive Director of the Social Security Board), and Mr. Fred Hoehler, the Executive Director of the American Public Welfare Association, that the Social Security Board could make the study more expeditiously and more satisfactorily than an ad hoc research staff. I also pointed out that an embarrassing situation would arise over the important judgmental decisions that would have to be made, because the President's Cabinet committee would be formulating recommendations as to what the government's policy should be in this field.

The Cabinet committee did meet in November 1939 to discuss the situation but decided not to oppose the National Resources Planning Board in making the study. It was intended that the study would be completed within a matter of months. Actually, it was not completed until December 1941. Therefore, it will be discussed in connection with other events that occurred during the war years.

All that needs to be said at this point is that the group interested in making this study had no relationship to the group involved in the LaFollette questioning episode. It might also be observed that the Cabinet committee never did undertake an active program. This was due to the fact that neither the Secretary of Labor nor I, who were the members most interested, found it necessary for the Cabinet committee to do so.

However, the Interdepartmental Committee to Coordinate Health and Welfare Activities did continue after the National Health Conference held in July 1938. After the elections of that year were over, Miss Roche, the Chairman of the committee, and I again talked with the President. He directed Miss Roche to transmit the report and recommendations of the committee to him and said he would send it to Congress with a message indicating the need for a national health program and commending the general approach proposed by the committee. However, he indicated he did not want to go further at that time. Accordingly, the final paragraph of the message was drafted to read as follows:

I recommend the report of the interdepartmental committee for careful study by the Congress. The essence of the program recommended by the Committee is Federal-State cooperation. Federal legislation necessarily precedes, for it indicates the assistance which may be made available to the States in a cooperative program for the Nation's health.

This message was sent to Congress on January 23, 1939. I arranged with Senator Robert F. Wagner of New York to introduce a bill incorporating the interdepartmental committee's recommendations. On January 30 he announced in a long radio address that he would introduce such a bill and took care to include the following paragraphs:

Again and again I have been asked: "Do you propose a plan of compulsory health insurance?" To my mind the projection of this question to the forefront of discussion emphasizes controversial issues, to the exclusion of matters on which there is universal agreement. Broadly speaking, millions of consumers of medical services want compulsory health insurance; on the other hand, the medical profession is divided as to the wisdom of compulsory features. But there is substantial agreement among all groups and all classes on every *other* aspect of the program including provisions for public health, maternity and child care, disability insurance, and medical care for the needy.

The question of compulsory health insurance arises only in connection with State plans of general medical care. The answer is simple and clear: The bill will not impose a Federal strait-jacket upon the development of State plans. Subject to necessary basic standards, each State will be at liberty to set up a plan of its own choosing and geared to the needs of its own people. The plan may be supported by contributions from beneficiaries or by general taxation, or both. It may be limited to some phase of medical care or be more inclusive. It may cover only the relief population or include other groups higher in the economic scale.

On February 28, Senator Wagner introduced the bill itself, S. 1620, which was referred to the Committee on Education and Labor. Hearings were held by a subcommittee of which Senator James Murray of Montana was Chairman and Senator Robert Taft of Ohio one of the members. It is interesting to note that both of these senators from that time on took an active interest in health matters.

Representatives of agriculture, labor, civic, welfare, and other public groups testified in favor of the bill. However, representatives of the American Medical Association opposed the bill in toto despite the fact that a meeting of its House of Delegates, held only a few months before, had approved four out of the five programs recommended by the interdepartmental committee. Representatives of various dental and hospital associations took positions which ranged from complete opposition to endorsement of some of its provisions. Government officials, including myself, testified in favor of the bill.

The subcommittee made a preliminary report on August 4, 1939, stating, "This subcommittee, having studied this bill, held numerous public hearings and accumulated a large volume of testimony and supplementary information, reports that it is in agreement with the general purposes and objectives of this bill. However, the subcommittee wishes to give this legislation additional study and to consult further with representatives of lay organizations and of the professions concerned. The subcommittee intends to report out an amended bill at the next session of Congress."

This seemed to indicate that the prospect for comprehensive health legislation was very good. However, when Miss Roche and I talked with the President in late autumn, he said he wanted to have only a hospital construction bill, which indicated that he had changed his mind about making a national health program an issue in the 1940 presidential campaign.

Besides the foregoing legislative developments, important administrative changes took place during 1939. Reorganization Plan No. 1, prepared by the President and approved by Congress, created the Federal Security Agency (now the Department of Health, Education, and Welfare) and placed the Social Security Board within that agency. This brought the Board into closer working relationships with other components of the agency which administered programs under the Social Security Act and other social programs, notably the United States Public Health Service, Office of Education, National Youth Administration, and Civilian Conservation Corps.

This reorganization plan also transferred the United States Employment Service, which had been consolidated with the Bureau of Unemployment Compensation, to form a new bureau under the Social Security Board, called the Bureau of Employment Security.

The reorganization plan became effective July 1, 1939, and the appointment of the first Federal Security Administrator, Paul V. McNutt, former Governor of Indiana and later High Commissioner of the Philippine Islands, was confirmed by the Senate on July 12, 1939. The only internal administrative changes that were made in the organization of the Social Security Board were to transfer the office of the General Counsel and the personnel functions of the Bureau of Business Management from the Board to the office of the Administrator where they served all units of the agency. The prestige of the Board and the willingness of the Administrator to permit the Board to function as freely as it had previously disguised the long-range importance of the change in status of the Board. This will be discussed later.*

---

* Before the President sent the reorganization plan to Congress, he had called me to his office to tell me that it would not result in any change in my status or my relations with him.

5.

Social Security
During the War Years,
1940–45

During the war years the President and the Social Security Board continued to point out the need for improving the Social Security Act. This may have helped to acquaint the public and the Congress with the necessity for eventual action. But it was evident that the prosecution of the war was the primary concern of the President, the Congress, and the public.

A person concerned only with the legislative history of the Social Security Act would probably consider these war years as unimportant; and it is true that there was no important permanent social security legislation enacted during this period. However, there was social security legislation proposed but not passed, some of which, I believe, would have been of great value and some of which, I believe, would have been highly detrimental to the future development of a contributory social insurance system providing benefits related to loss of income.

There were some temporary wartime programs of great importance which took advantage of the existing programs and administrative organization developed under the Social Security Act. The most vital was the national manpower program, which could not have functioned without the United States Employment Service. There was also developed a program of servicemen's readjustment allowances which could not possibly have been so successful if it had not used the existing federal-state system of unemployment insurance.

During the year immediately following enactment of the 1939

amendments, the Social Security Board, of course, devoted most of its time and attention to putting these amendments into effect. The number of field offices of the Bureau of Old Age Insurance (whose name was changed to Bureau of Old Age and Survivors Insurance) was increased from 327 on July 1, 1939, to 469 by June 30, 1940. The number of employees of the bureau was increased from 6,992 to 8,918 during the same period.

Monthly old age and survivors' benefits were payable beginning January 1, 1940. By June 30 of that year, 111,000 claims for monthly benefits had been processed. Today this seems like a trifling accomplishment, since 2½ times that number are now processed every month. However, in 1940 it was necessary to interpret and establish precedents for the interpretation of the various provisions of the law. It was also necessary to establish administrative procedures for the initial determination, for the review of this determination, and for the preparation and certification of the monthly benefit roll to the Treasury Department for payment. It must also be remembered that electronic processing devices had not yet been devised.

Besides undertaking this new task, the bureau continued to process a large number of claims for small lump sums payable when an insured worker died, leaving no eligible survivors. It also continued with its task of posting the millions of wage items reported by employers to the correct individual employees' accounts.

The Bureau of Public Assistance was able to make considerable progress in inducing and assisting the state public assistance agencies to improve their administrative organizations and procedures. Much of this improvement was due to the fact that the 1939 amendments had made it clear that employees must be selected under a merit system, that public assistance rolls could not be used for political purposes, and that the amount of assistance provided should be on the basis of individual need, taking into consideration any income and resources possessed by the individual.

The Bureau of Public Assistance was also able to expand its field staff sufficiently so that it was possible to substitute a sampling administrative review of state and local operations in place of the detailed field audits made by accountants. This administrative review was carried on cooperatively with each state agency for the purpose of ascertaining what, if any, administrative improvements should be made to assure that the eligibility of applicants and the extent of their need were properly determined. The advantage of this affirmative approach was that it was likely to prevent improper payments from occurring. The disadvantage of the previous detailed post-audit was that it was essentially negative, resulting in hundreds of thousands of "exceptions" being taken to payments already made. This caused endless argument, much irritation, and considerable financial loss to state agencies.

The Bureau of Employment Security was able to function more satisfactorily in its relations with state agencies than when the Bureau of Unemployment Compensation and the United States Employment Service were located in separate federal agencies. However, federal-state relations were becoming less cordial, since the Board had begun to criticize what it considered the inadequacy of state unemployment insurance benefits. Moreover, in its 1939–40 annual report the Board suggested that, "As a means of ensuring reasonably adequate provisions throughout the country, States might be required to establish minimum benefit standards. . . ." It pointed out in that report that "in general, States where benefit expenditures have been low in relation to contributions are those in which benefits are relatively inadequate." It also called attention to the fact that more than 2,500,000 insured workers exhausted their benefit rights while they were still unemployed.

The effect of World War II was being felt by the United States Employment Service, which was experiencing increasing difficulty in filling employers' requests for skilled workers. It received an additional appropriation from Congress on June 27, 1940, of $2 million for special assistance to the state employment services in "selection of workers and their placement in occupations essential to national defense." This appropriation contained a proviso which made it available to the Social Security Board to carry on this activity if any state employment service was found unable to do so. As will be discussed later, this proviso turned out to be of considerable significance.

A *Dictionary of Occupational Titles* which contained detailed job descriptions covering more than 17,000 job titles was issued in 1940. It was used to determine what particular skills of peacetime workers could be used for wartime production. It was also used to break down intricate jobs into simpler operations which could be performed by unskilled or semiskilled workers.

Besides its strictly operating functions that have just been described, the Board and I personally were also involved in policy matters in both the administrative and legislative spheres. Within the administrative sphere several unfortunate major disagreements arose between the Board and the Federal Security Administrator only a few months after the Administrator had taken office.

One of these disagreements concerned a bill introduced by Congressman Thomas Jenkins of Ohio which would have required the Social Security Board to make a grant to the State of Ohio covering one-half of the cost of old age assistance during the month of October 1938. It will be recalled that the Board had made a finding of gross maladministration existing during that month. Shortly after Robert A. Taft was elected to the Senate in 1939, he called upon me to argue in favor of this bill. Mr. Taft did not dispute the facts of maladministration but argued that, after the maladministration had been corrected, the law required the Board to reimburse the state for one-half of the cost of the regular assistance payments which the state had made during the month of October. However, when I offered to cooperate in a friendly court action to determine the validity of his legal argument, Mr. Taft dropped the matter.

But the Jenkins bill, which was entitled "An Act for the Relief of the State of Ohio," passed both houses of Congress and was sent to the President for his approval. I had appeared before the House Committee on the Judiciary to oppose the bill, but the Federal Security Administrator, who took office subsequently, informed supporters of the bill that he would not oppose it.

This placed me in a dilemma because, while I was a presidential appointee, the Social Security Board was subject to the supervision of the Federal Security Administrator. However, I felt obligated to recommend a presidential veto and submitted a draft of a message to accompany the veto. The President accepted my recommendation and signed the message which I had drafted. This message read in part as follows:

> I am withholding my approval of the bill under consideration because of my belief that an expeditious, effective, and non-political administration of the provisions of the Social Security Act is indispensable to the conduct of operations thereunder, and that approval of the measure would be inconsistent with this objective and create a precedent that would seriously endanger the success of the entire Social Security program.
>
> If this bill were to become law it would at least make it possible for a State agency to violate civil-service laws, to give blanket increases to some and deny aid to other needy applicants, to discriminate in the handling of complaints, and to maintain a faulty accounting system, all in the belief that if the Social Security Board were to withhold Federal funds because of this, the State agency could later go to the Congress of the United States and receive a special appropriation in proportion to the amounts the State had put out.
>
> The State authorities would have this bill as a precedent. It is needless for me to say that if I were to sign this bill, the precedent of it could be extended to other forms of Federal aid—aid for highways, aid for widows, and aid for dependent or crippled children. It would mean that States no longer would be compelled to maintain the standards set up by the Congress, but could violate these standards with impunity and still get their money.

Another of these major disagreements between the Board and the Federal Security Administrator involved the Administrator's support for a federal uniform universal old age pension, financed by a graduated personal income tax, to replace both the federal-state old age assistance system and the federal contributory old age insurance system. The Social Security Board learned of this through receipt of an advance mimeographed copy of a speech to be delivered before the National Industrial Conference Board the evening of March 28, 1940. This copy was received by the Board the day before the speech was to be delivered. The next morning I sent a memorandum to Stephen Early, the President's Press Secretary, calling his attention to the fact that only a few months previously the President had rejected a less drastic similar proposal made by two members of the group who had met at my home when the 1939 amendments were pending. The President at that time had called the proposal a "Baby Townsend plan which would be sure to grow up."

Mr. Early telephoned me to say that the President did not want the Administrator to deliver the speech as written and specifically did not want him to advocate a flat old age pension regardless of need. The Administrator had already taken the train for New York, so it was necessary to prepare a substitute speech which was handed him by a member of the Social Security Board, who had flown to New York, just a few minutes before he was to speak.

This incident indicated that the group within the administration which favored a noncontributory uniform old age pension was still active and felt that the Federal Security Administrator could be induced to support their proposal. A probable reason for this belief was that the Federal Security Administrator was a leading candidate for President at that time (President Roosevelt not yet having indicated he would run for a third term) and would want to attract the support of Townsend plan sympathizers.

Another indication that this group was still active in its opposition to a contributory old age insurance system was the appearance of newspaper stories, beginning the latter part of 1939, which greatly exaggerated the extent and importance of unposted wage items. These stories spoke of millions of such items which would seriously affect the eligibility of workers for future benefits. Of course, as has already been pointed out, these unposted items constituted only a fraction of one per cent of the total wage items reported. The actual effect on individual benefit rights would be negligible even if later efforts to secure correct employers' reports were unsuccessful. As a matter of fact, any claimant whose benefit rights might be affected would be assisted in establishing his wage record by obtaining supplementary information from his past employers.

Some of these newspaper stories were to the effect that the Social Security Board was under attack by persons within the Administration not only because of these unposted wage items but also because of the Board's opposition to uniform old age pension payments. These stories said that I was the chief target and that efforts were being made to dislodge me by abolishing the Board and substituting a single director under the immediate control of the Federal Security Administrator. The following excerpt from a rather colorful story sent out by two nationally syndicated columnists (Drew Pearson and Robert S. Allen) is illustrative:

> The SS Board has been under fire from two powerful groups for some time. They are:
> (1) New Deal insiders and congressional leaders, who are sore at Chairman Arthur Altmeyer for his diehard opposition to liberalizing old-age pension payments. Although vast sums in social security taxes are piling up in the Treasury, Altmeyer has grimly fought against amendments to increase monthly checks to oldsters. This, of course, has added fuel to the agitation of Townsendites and other "funny money" schemers.
> (2) Administration executives who are up in arms over the high-handed bureaucracy which dominates the Social Security Board, and concerned over the discovery of millions of unidentifiable "John Doe" records in the SSB files.
> With pension payments due to start January 1, these unidentified records are loaded with political dynamite, especially for McNutt, who is a red-hot presidential white hope.

This disagreement within the Administration was all the more serious because the Senate Finance Committee, a few weeks after the President had directed the Federal Security Administrator to alter his speech, appointed a Special Subcommittee to Investigate the Old Age Pension System. Senators Vandenberg and LaFollette and five other senators comprised this subcommittee. Senator Vandenberg said the action in creating the subcommittee was taken "primarily at the instance of the Chairman of the full Committee." But Senator LaFollette said that the Townsend organization and others interested in an "adequate" old age pension system would give Senator Sheridan Downey of California, a leading Townsendite, full credit. Senator LaFollette added, "I have been convinced for some time that a broad national system of old age pensions must be provided." It may have been of some significance in explaining Senator LaFollette's attitude that he was running for re-election that year and that there were Townsend Clubs in various parts of Wisconsin.

Of course, the Social Security Board from the very beginning had given consideration to whether any common ground could be found for a uniform old age pension and a pension related to wage loss. Because of the activities of the group within the

Administration and because of the continuing public interest, I decided to give concentrated attention to the problem. The result was what was dubbed a "double-decker system"—that is, a basic uniform pension with graduated insurance benefits superimposed thereon. I sent a memorandum to the President's Secretary, General Watson, on May 7, 1940, telling him that such a plan had been developed, so that the President would be aware of it if he were approached by persons interested in substituting a uniform pension system for the existing system.

The general idea underlying the so-called double-decker approach was simple. Under the old age insurance system, as amended in 1939, the monthly retirement benefit was calculated as a percentage of the previous average monthly wage. This percentage was 40 per cent of the first $50 of the average wage and 10 per cent of the portion of the wage above $50 (up to a maximum monthly wage of $250). Under the double-decker proposal, all aged persons, whether insured or not, would receive $20 a month (i.e., the equivalent of 40 per cent of $50), and insured persons would receive in addition 10 per cent of their previous average monthly wage.

There was, of course, the problem of how such a plan should be financed. The possibility of substituting a "value added" tax (roughly, a tax on gross income minus cost of material, etc.) for the employers' payroll tax and of substituting a personal "old age income tax" for the employees' tax on wages was suggested.

I discussed the double-decker approach with various top government officials, particularly officials in the Treasury Department and the Bureau of the Budget. A presidential economic adviser who continued to favor a uniform universal old age pension was also furnished information regarding the double-decker approach.

The Social Security Board felt that the disadvantages outweighed the advantages of the double-decker approach. It was true, of course, that in the early years of the old age and survivors' insurance system the value of the retirement benefits payable would be far in excess of the value of the retired workers' contributions. Therefore, it might be argued that it was unfair to pay such "unearned" benefits to only those persons who had been lucky enough to have worked in insured employment for the required minimum period, and deny benefits to the unlucky persons who had not. The argument that these "unearned" benefits were paid for out of the total amount of employers' payroll taxes and represented credit for past service was not entirely persuasive.

However, the Social Security Board was concerned that political pressures might inevitably result in a continued increase throughout the years in the basic uniform amount payable under a double-decker system, thus weakening and eventually destroying the rationale of a contributory social insurance system under which benefits, contributions, and wage loss were interrelated.

The President never specifically recommended legislation which would substitute the double-decker plan for the old age assistance system and the old age insurance system. But he did include in his famous speech to the Teamsters Union on September 11, 1940, the following paragraph:

Yes, it is my hope that soon the United States will have a national system under which no needy man or woman within our borders will lack a minimum old-age pension which will provide adequate food, adequate clothing, and adequate lodging to the end of the road without having to go to the poorhouse to get it. I look forward to a system coupled with that, a system which, in addition to this bare minimum, will enable those who have faithfully toiled in any occupation to build up additional security for their old age which will allow them to live in comfort and in happiness.

In the field of health the President did send a message to Congress on January 30, 1940, as he had previously said he would do, recommending only a modest program for the construction by the federal government of small hospitals in needy areas of the country, especially in rural areas. This message, which I assisted in drafting, was based on a report made by the Interdepartmental Committee to Coordinate Health and Welfare Activities, which contemplated that the Works Progress Administration would do the work, as advocated by Harry Hopkins several years before. However, it differed in one important respect from the recommendations of the interdepartmental committee in that it did not recommend any federal aid for the maintenance of the hospitals constructed. The interdepartmental committee, in an unpublished report to the President dated January 10th, had informed him that, even though he had stated there should be no federal aid for maintenance, without such aid the most needy communities would not be able to avail themselves of the hospital construction program. This attitude on the part of the President grew out of his desire to transfer ultimately the complete responsibility for these hospitals from the federal government to the localities.

Senators Robert F. Wagner of New York and Walter F. George of Georgia introduced a bill, S. 3230, to implement the President's message. The bill was referred to the Committee on Education and Labor which made two important changes. One change was that only in the first year of a six-year program would the federal government bear the entire cost of construction; during the remaining five years the cost would be shared with the locality. The second change was that a federal grant for maintenance was provided, beginning at $300 per year per bed and declining to $30 per year per bed by the fifth year.

The bill, as amended by the committee, had bi-partisan support. Senator Robert A. Taft spoke for the minority party when the bill was debated and passed by the Senate on May 30, 1940. Unfortunately, other matters being considered by the House prevented enactment of the bill into law before the adjournment of Congress.

The only other event of some interest which occurred during 1940 was a report on migratory labor, submitted to the President by the Interdepartmental Committee to Coordinate Health and Welfare Activities. This report recommended federal grants to the states for public assistance to needy persons not included in the existing categories of public assistance for which the Social Security Act already provided federal aid. The proposed grants would be related to the economic ability of the states and would have safeguards to prevent discrimination against migratory labor. This was the last report ever made by the interdepartmental committee and did not result in any legislation's being proposed.

In 1941 the President did not send any special messages to Congress concerning social security. However, in his Budget Message of January 3, 1941, he did say, "I deem it vital that the Congress give consideration to the inclusion in the old-age and survivors insurance system and the unemployment compensation system of workers not now covered." He repeated this recommendation in his January 6, 1941, Message on the State of the Union and added, "We should widen the opportunities for adequate medical care.

The only other important public statement made by the President during 1941 relative to social security was contained in the Atlantic Charter, which he signed jointly with Prime Minister Winston Churchill on August 14, 1941, reading as follows: "They desire to bring about the fullest collaboration between all nations in the economic field, with the object of securing for all improved labor standards, economic advancement and social security." I was told by John G. Winant, the first Chairman of the Social Security Board, who was Ambassador to Great Britain and aboard ship when the Atlantic Charter was signed, that the reference to social security was included at his suggestion.

While there was no substantive legislation passed in 1941, there was some important activity going on. Early in the year Senator Sheridan Downey, Chairman of the Senate Committee to Investigate the Old Age Pension System, and other Townsendites began pressing the President to support a federal old age pension of $30 a month for every person over 60 years of age. The President suggested to Senator Downey that he discuss with me a "new plan" which the President told Senator Downey I had been working on.

I avoided presenting a detailed plan to Senator Downey because this might have given the impression that the President and the Social Security Board were endorsing it, which was not the case. However, I explained the double-decker approach and offered to furnish any data and technical assistance the Senate committee desired.

The Senate committee made a report on August 28, 1941, which in effect proposed a double-decker system, specifically as follows: (1) that the existing federal-state system of old age assistance be abolished and that the federal government pay a uniform pension to all persons over 60 years of age; (2) that the existing old age insurance system be liberalized and cover all employed persons working for others. The financing provisions were brief and somewhat indefinite, proposing the use of payroll

United States Employment Service
12/18/41

<u>Telegram</u> - *to the Governors of the State* *The Governor of Hawaii The Governor of Alaska*

Now that this country is actually at war it is more than ever necessary *see other copy*
that we utilize to the fullest possible extent all of the manpower and woman-
power of this country to increase our production of war materials. This can
only be accomplished by ~~one~~ central *izing work into one* recruiting agency, ~~the United States~~
~~Employment Service.~~ At present, as you know, the United States Employment
Service consists of fifty separate State and territorial employment services
whose operations are loosely coordinated by the Federal Government. In order
that there may be complete responsiveness to the demands of national defense
and speedy, uniform, effective action to meet rapidly changing needs, it is
essential that all of these separate employment services become a *uniformly and of necessity* nationally
operated employment service. I have, therefore, given instructions to the
proper Federal officials that the necessary steps be taken to accomplish this
purpose at once. I ask that you likewise instruct the proper officials of
your State to transfer to the United States Employment Service all of the
present personnel, records, and facilities required for this operation.
Inasmuch as the Federal Government is already paying practically one hundred
percent of the cost of operation and the State personnel has been recruited
on a merit basis, there will be no difficulty in transferring State employees
into the Federal service. These employment offices will continue to serve the
unemployment compensation agency so that there will be no need to set up
duplicate offices. I shall appreciate your advising me at once of your full
cooperation so that the conversion of the present employment service into
a truly national service may be accomplished without delay.

FDR

*Draft of President Roosevelt's telegram to the governors
of the states, requesting the transfer of the state employment
services to the federal government under the direction of the
United States Employment Service (December 18, 1941)*

taxes to the extent not needed to finance the insurance benefits, matched by an equal sum from general revenues.

Senator Theodore Green of Rhode Island submitted a minority report, prepared largely by George Bigge, a member of the Social Security Board, who had previously been a professor at Brown University. The minority report confined itself to recommending the extension and improvement of the contributory social insurance system.

In the early part of October I made inquiry as to what the President wanted done about a social security message which had been under discussion for some time. He instructed me to confer with the Secretary of the Treasury and the Director of the Budget concerning the Social Security Board's recommendations for an expanded social security program and the preparation of a presidential message. He said that he would like to read a draft over the weekend, and this was sent him on October 11. However, other matters occupied his attention, and he did not take any action until January of 1942.

An administrative development of great importance that occurred during 1941 was the action taken by the President immediately after Pearl Harbor, transferring all of the state affiliated offices of the United States Employment Service from the states to the federal government. This was accomplished simply by the President's sending a telegram to all governors on December 19, 1941, requesting their "full cooperation so that the conversion of the present employment service into a truly national service may be accomplished without delay." The original draft of the telegram with the President's handwritten corrections is reproduced on page 129.

I was bitterly denounced by state officials for having surreptitiously secured the inclusion of a proviso in an appropriation bill which enabled the President to act so swiftly. There is no question that I had recommended to the President on June 11, 1941, that the following proviso be included in the 1941–42 appropriation of $62,500,000 to the Social Security Board to cover the cost of grants to the states for unemployment compensation administration: "Provided further, that such portion of this appropriation, as may be necessary shall be available to the Social Security Board for all necessary expenses incurred by the Board, including personal services in the District of Columbia and elsewhere, in connection with the operation of employment office facilities and services essential to expediting the national-defense program.

However, the key members of both the House and Senate appropriations committees were fully informed as to the purpose of this proviso. Thus the President, at my request, wrote Senator James F. Byrnes, who was a member of the Senate Appropriations Committee, asking him to sponsor the inclusion of this proviso in the appropriation bill which had already passed the House. In his request, the President explained the purpose of the proviso, saying, "I think it is essential that the Federal Government should have the power to operate directly the public employment offices in any locality, state or for the country as a whole, as the labor requirements of the national defense program may indicate to be necessary." The effect of the proviso was also explained in a letter written by me to the Chairman of the Senate Appropriations Committee and in a letter written by the Federal Security Administrator to the Chairman of the subcommittee of the House Appropriations Committee, who had charge of the bill.

It is probable that the appropriation of $2 million already mentioned, which was included in a previous appropriation act to enable the Social Security Board itself to engage in the selection of workers and their placement if any state was found unable to do so, served as a helpful precedent. However, this previous proviso making available such a small amount did not arouse the opposition of state officials. If they had been consulted regarding this subsequent, more sweeping proviso, they undoubtedly would have lobbied vigorously against it and would probably have been able to defeat it since they would have had more time. As it was, they supported an amendent offered by Senator Danaher of Connecticut which they (mistakenly) thought would have the effect of nullifying this proviso. The Danaher amendment was eliminated by the House and Senate conferees due to the confusion as to its actual effect.

I have no regrets over my decision not to consult with the state officials. It was of vital importance to the national defense program that the federal government have the authority and funds to operate the United States Employment Service directly, if any states were unable or unwilling to do so, in complete accordance with national defense plans and operations. Only in this way could the labor force of the nation be utilized to the maximum advantage. State officials inevitably were inclined to think of defense labor needs in terms of local and state interests, rather than in terms of the national interest. They were inclined to permit their employers in nonessential or less essential industries to hoard the supply of skilled workers who were greatly needed in defense industries throughout the country. And, of course, as state officials, they would feel entitled to oppose any federal directives with which they disagreed.

The charge that state officials made, alleging that the Social Security Board obtained this proviso as a part of its desire to "federalize" the entire existing federal-state unemployment insurance system, is not supported by the record. Actually, the two Associate Directors-General of the Office of Production Management, William S. Knudsen and Sidney Hillman, and the top officials of the War Department responsible for defense production advocated federal operation of the United States Employment Service before the Social Security Board did. Thus, on August 28, 1941, the Board stated in a memorandum covering its recommendations concerning defense labor policies and defense labor supply, "While it would be possible to transfer all State employment service employees to the Federal payroll without examination since they have all been appointed in accordance with State merit systems, federalization would still be a drastic step and should be taken at the same time, and only if, action is also taken to control new hirings in scarce defense occupations. If the situation is not deemed serious enough to control such new hirings, it is not serious enough to warrant federalization."

My position on the general policy question of substituting a straight federal unemployment insurance system for the existing federal-state system was expressed in a statement I made to the Executive Committee of the Interstate Conference of Employment Security Agencies on November 7, 1941. This statement was made extemporaneously but, as I learned later, was taken down in shorthand. It was in part as follows:

In this field of unemployment particularly, we think, and I hope you think the same, we must prepare quickly, thoroughly, and intelligently to meet what we believe is going to be the supreme crisis of democracy when this post-defense period comes upon us. If our democracy can't meet the problem of unemployment when this defense effort, which has distorted so terrifically all of our economic machinery, is over, we are headed for economic collapse and chaos.

What should we do? Should we take the Social Security Act as we saw it in 1935, as permanent and perfect, or should we have a constant self-appraisal to build a strong first line of defense against the terrific unemployment that will come upon us? We all know the confusion and difficulty that there was in trying to work out ways and means of meeting the emergency situation in the early relief days. We have to set up a first line of defense so next time we will have a few months to achieve a few more fundamental things that can be accomplished under unemployment insurance. I think we all agree that unemployment insurance can only be a first line of defense but if we can build it so it is a strong first line then we have made a contribution. If we don't do that we will be swept aside like autumn leaves before a gale. We are just simply instruments, and pretty poor instruments all of us, of a social purpose. If we don't do our part we deserve to be swept aside and we will be. I'm saying this from the heart because I think we are missing a great opportunity to think together and to work together. So far as Washington developments are concerned there have been no conclusions reached with the President. . . .

The Social Security Board doesn't know what the conclusions will be. I don't think anybody knows. If it is what you call federalization you can be sure it will be after weighing the pros and cons we are convinced that is the best solution in this particular field of the problem of the defense against unemployment. You can be sure we will recommend fundamental changes in the present system of unemployment insurance regardless of whether you join with us, such as federalization, or minimum federal standards with reinsurance. We see it to be our duty to lay our thinking before the President and before Congress. Perhaps it won't make much difference what our thinking is. But we believe it is our duty at any rate to make available our best thinking and the alternatives as we see them and let the President and Congress, representing the people of this country, decide what they want to do. So far as we all can work together in developing alternatives I think we are performing a service we should perform and for which we are being paid. To the extent we don't we are subject to criticism and worse; we are no less than traitors to this country. We are in the field that is going to be the most critical in the post-defense period. I don't know what more I can say.

As previously stated, the Social Security Board had sent the President a draft of a message on social security on October 11,

1941. However, in the above statement I still could only speak in general terms since the President had not yet indicated what he intended to do. But I did make it clear that the question of "federalization" was under consideration and that the Social Security Board would make its recommendations regardless of whether the state officials concurred.

Actually, the draft of the presidential message recommended a single comprehensive social insurance system which would include unemployment insurance. Other proposals contained in the draft included the following: the extension of old age and survivors' insurance not only to all employees but to self-employed persons as well; protection against wage loss due to either temporary or permanent total disability; per diem cash hospitalization benefits; and federal aid to the states on a variable matching basis for public assistance to all needy persons.

The reason for including unemployment insurance in a single social insurance system was based not only on the inherent general advantages of consistency and avoidance of overlaps or gaps in the various benefits as well as maximum administrative efficiency. It was also due to the fact that the Social Security Board had become disillusioned regarding the operation of the federal-state system. This disillusionment was expressed in its 1940–41 annual report, submitted to the Federal Security Administrator on October 31, 1941, as follows:

The Board believes also that action is needed during the war to strengthen the unemployment compensation system so that it can effectively carry the post-war burden of unemployment. . . . A Federal system would obviate the marked disparities in the proportion of workers protected under State laws and the degree of protection afforded. . . . Although the States have made progress in broadening the protection afforded unemployed eligible workers since the inception of the program, the division of revenue among 51 separate funds limits the protection that can be provided under the existing Federal-State program. In 1940, more than half of the beneficiaries were still without jobs when they exhausted their benefit rights. . . . A Federal program, moreover, would equalize the cost of unemployment compensation among employers. The diversity of experience-rating provisions under State laws has resulted in the fact that competing employers in various States contribute at different rates even when their unemployment experience is identical. . . . This situation works out to the financial disadvantage of employers in States which are endeavoring to deal adequately with workers' risks of unemployment and undermines the basic purpose of the unemployment compensation program.

The President decided not to send a special message on social security but to include his recommendations in his Budget Message, which was sent to Congress on January 5, 1942. It included the recommendations made by the Social Security Board, except the one regarding public assistance. Following are the paragraphs on social security:

I oppose the use of pay-roll taxes as a measure of war finance unless the worker is given his full money's worth in increased social security. From the inception of the social security program in 1935 it has been planned to increase the number of persons covered and to provide protection against hazards not initially included. By expanding the program now, we advance the organic development of our social security system and at the same time contribute to the anti-inflationary program.

I recommend an increase in the coverage of old-age and survivors' insurance, addition of permanent and temporary disability payments and hospitalization payments beyond the present benefit programs, and liberalization and expansion of unemployment compensation in a uniform national system. I suggest that collection of additional contributions be started as soon as possible, to be followed one year later by the operation of the new benefit plans.

Additional employer and employee contributions will cover increased disbursements over a long period of time. Increased contributions would result in reserves of several billion dollars for post-war contingencies. The present accumulation of these contributions would absorb excess purchasing power. Investment of the additional reserves in bonds of the United States Government would assist in financing the war.

The existing administrative machinery for collecting pay-roll taxes can function immediately. For this reason congressional consideration might be given to immediate enactment of this proposal, while other necessary measures are being perfected.

It is interesting to note that the President did take this occasion to urge these improvements in the Social Security Act, as recommended by the Social Security Board, although the Declaration of War had intervened since these recommendations were made to him. This was in spite of his announcement at his very first press conference following the attack on Pearl Harbor that "old Dr. New Deal" had to be replaced by "Dr. Win-the-War."

The state unemployment insurance administrators naturally felt that the President's recommendation of a "uniform national system" might be followed by legislation to achieve this result. However, the only specific legislative proposal in 1942 relating to unemployment insurance was for what the President called "temporary and emergency legislation concerning at most the balance of the present year." This proposal was made by the President in a letter to Speaker Rayburn, dated January 19, 1942. In that letter the President requested that Congress appropriate $300 million to finance war displacement benefits which would supplement and extend the protection afforded by the state and territorial unemployment compensation laws. He suggested that the appropriation be made in such a way that the expenditures would be controlled by plans approved by the President and that the administration be by the Social Security Board.*

Neither this proposal nor the various recommendations that the President had made in his January 5, 1942, Budget Message for improving and expanding the social security program received

---

* The suggestion for this legislation was made by Sidney Hillman, Associate Director-General of the Office of Production Management, upon the recommendation of his Labor Supply Policy Committee consisting of representatives of management and labor. Nevertheless, some of the state unemployment insurance administrators alleged that it represented an attempt by the Social Security Board to bring about "federalization."

The proposal began as a measure designed primarily to provide training wages to workers who would take training while they were idle during the conversion of industry to war production. It was to be administered by the Office of Production Management. Lack of training facilities caused a shift in plans, and it then became a proposal for a "withholding wage" to be paid to those workers who would refrain from seeking jobs elsewhere and would hold themselves in readiness for re-employment when conversion was completed.

The Social Security Board pointed out the necessity of relating the proposed "withholding wage" to any benefits payable under the state unemployment insurance laws, and suggested that, therefore, the plan should be administered by the Board. The state administrators indicated that they would accept the proposal if the proposed benefit were fixed at 20 per cent of the weekly benefit otherwise payable under a state unemployment insurance law. This would have meant that in a state with a maximum of $15 the war displacement benefit could not exceed $3 additional, or $18 in all. However, Mr. Hillman insisted that existing state maximums should be disregarded so as to permit the payment of a $24 maximum in all states. The result was that no agreement was reached, and the state administrators were able to prevent the passage of the proposed legislation.

any consideration by the Congress. This was undoubtedly because the Administration did not prepare or support any bills to
implement these recommendations.

Actually, the only substantive social security legislation considered by the Congress in 1942 was contrary to the Administration's wishes. This was in the form of a rider to a pending general
revenue bill which became the Revenue Act of 1942. This rider
postponed until January 1, 1944, the increase in the contribution
rate under the old age and survivors' insurance system which
would otherwise have become effective January 1, 1943.

The President himself had written a letter to the Chairman of
the House Ways and Means Committee and to the Chairman of
the Senate Finance Committee, urging that this rider, which had
been proposed by Senator Arthur H. Vandenberg, be eliminated.
He sent this letter (which I had prepared) at the combined
request of the Secretary of the Treasury, the Secretary of Labor,
the Director of the Bureau of the Budget, the Federal Security
Administrator, and myself.

It must be admitted that the argument presented in this
letter—that failure to permit the automatic increase in the rate to
become effective would imperil the self-sufficiency of this social
insurance system—was blunted by the fact that actual expenditures had been less and actual receipts more than estimated in
1939. However, Senator Vandenberg was sufficiently impressed
that a year later in 1943, when he again proposed a postponement
of the scheduled increase, he agreed to the following amendent to
the Social Security Act, proposed by Senator Murray: "There is
also authorized to be appropriated to the Trust Fund such
additional sums [i.e., in addition to contributions] as may be
required to finance the benefits and payments provided under
this title."

In his letter, dated October 3, 1942, the President had pointed
out that the increase was "not only in accord with the necessities
of the social security system itself, but at the same time would
contribute to the non-inflationary financing of the rapidly mounting war expenditures." He added that, "As soon as the Congress
has disposed of the pending tax bill I am planning to submit a
comprehensive program for expanding and extending the whole
social security system along the lines laid down in my Budget

Message last January. This program would involve substantial further increases in rates of contribution."

While this rider constituted the only social security legislation enacted in 1942, there were several significant administrative developments during the year. One occurred at the height of the Pearl Harbor crisis. It involved the continuing practice in Pennsylvania of making large numbers of "temporary appointments" on a political basis, instead of making permanent appointments from registers established as a result of competitive examinations. This occurred in both the state public assistance department and the state labor department (which administered the unemployment insurance law) but was particularly notorious in the labor department. Moreover, the Pennsylvania Secretary of Labor publicly defied the Social Security Board in its attempts to correct this practice.

The Governor of Pennsylvania, being the person responsible for the practice of political patronage, naturally supported his Cabinet officers. He sought the help of the members of Congress from Pennsylvania who belonged to his political party and also telegraphed the President requesting him to intervene.

The 1939 amendments to the Social Security Act specifically authorized the Social Security Board to require the establishment and maintenance of personnel standards on a merit basis, as a condition for the receipt of federal grants. Moreover, in the case of federal grants for the administration of unemployment compensation, it was not necessary to hold a formal hearing before making a finding that the state agency was not complying with this requirement. Therefore, after giving the Pennsylvania Secretary of Labor an opportunity to defend his actions, the Board notified him that no further grants would be made until he complied with the federal law.

Fortunately, the press supported the action of the Board, as did the President in his reply to the Governor's telegram. When the Governor then wrote the President a long letter advising him of his "capitulation under duress," the President simply sent the letter to me with a note saying: "For preparation of reply for my signature if necessary. However, I think the whole thing might be dropped."

This Pennsylvania episode was important in that it accelerated action by state agencies in establishing effective merit systems.

However, the most important administrative development during 1942 occurred in the administration of the United States Employment Service. After Pearl Harbor, manpower shortages, which had been developing in some areas where defense plants were located, became quite general. The Selective Service Administration was unable to bring about effective allocation of manpower between the armed forces and essential industries. Therefore, the President created the War Manpower Commission by Executive Order 9139, dated April 18, 1942. This commission consisted of representatives of the War, Navy, and Labor Departments, the Selective Service Administration, and several other federal agencies concerned with manpower, with the Federal Security Administrator as Chairman.

The appointment of the Federal Security Administrator was logical because he already had under his jurisdiction not only the United States Employment Service but also the training activities of the National Youth Administration and the Office of Education. Likewise, I was made Executive Director since the United States Employment Service was under the immediate direction of the Social Security Board. I remained Executive Director from May to December 1942, when I resigned to become a member of the War Manpower Commission itself.

The War Manpower Commission was both a policy-making and an operating agency. Because the United States Employment Service was its principal operating arm, it was transferred to the commission by Executive Order 9247 on September 17, 1942.*

---

* The War Manpower Commission did not function at peak efficiency either as a policy-making agency or as an operating agency. It was always regarded by the government procurement agencies as subordinate to them, and each one of these procurement agencies felt that the War Manpower Commission should furnish the manpower needed, regardless of other countervailing considerations. Moreover, there were unresolved conflicts between the military and civilian manpower needs since the Selective Service Administration, in actuality, continued to function as an independent agency to the very end. The Presendent did transfer it to the War Manpower Commission on December 5, 1942, but Congress exactly a year later legalized its independent functioning by Public Law 197.

In its internal operations, the commission also functioned on a pluralistic instead of a straight-line basis. That is to say, there were several points where directives originated. The Excutive Director and the Director of Field Operations both issued directives. In addition, the National Management-Labor Policy Committee actually assumed some operating responsibilities.

Moreover, the operations of the War Manpower Commission were highly

There were some other administrative developments in 1942 as a result of the war. The President in September 1941 had appointed the Federal Security Administrator to be the Director of the Office of Defense, Health, and Welfare. He, in turn, used the regional directors of the Social Security Board to coordinate federal and state activities. In February 1942 the Administrator made the Social Security Board responsible for three wartime welfare programs. One was called Civilian War Assistance and consisted of providing temporary assistance to civilians disabled by enemy action and dependents of civilians killed, interned, or reported missing; to civilian defense workers injured or killed and their dependents; to shipwrecked persons or their dependents; to persons repatriated to the United States; to stranded persons from war-stricken areas; and to civilians evacuated from danger points. This program was administered through the Bureau of Public Assistance.

Another more permanent program was called Civilian War Benefits. This program provided monthly cash benefits ranging from $10 to $85 for wage loss sustained as a result of enemy action. These benefits were paid for temporary total disability or permanent disability of at least 30 per cent of total disability. They were also payable to specified dependents of civilians who died as a result of enemy action. This program was administered through the Bureau of Old Age and Survivors Insurance.

The third program consisted of cooperating with the Depart-

---

decentralized and subject to the direction of local employer-employee advisory groups, as was inevitable in view of the nature of the labor market and the largely voluntary character of the controls exercised over employers and workers. Thus, the War Manpower Commission had no direct authority to compel the transfer of workers from nonessential to essential undertakings. The only sanctions available to induce this transfer consisted of the use of the Selective Service Administration's authority to defer workers in essential activities and the withholding of material priorities by government procurement officers in the case of nonessential undertakings. However, employers with government contracts could be compelled to avoid "labor hoarding" and "labor pirating." This was accomplished by requiring personnel recruitment through the United States Employment Service, which furnished only the number and kinds of workers considered necessary. But, in spite of all these difficulties, the War Manpower Commission was successful enough in facilitating the allocation of manpower that it was not necessary to resort to conscription of civilian as well as military manpower, as was the case in Great Britain.

ment of Justice and the War Relocation Authority in providing assistance to enemy aliens who were interned and to American citizens of Japanese ancestry on the West Coast who were placed in war relocation centers. The assistance included rehousing, transportation, and financial aid to dependents who lived outside the internment camps and war relocation centers. It also included similar help in reuniting families in internment camps and aid to families permitted to leave war relocation centers. The Board used chiefly the Bureau of Public Assistance and the Bureau of Employment Security in carrying out this program.

Discussion of developments in 1942 would not be complete without mentioning the famous report made by Sir William Beveridge in Great Britain, while the bombs were still falling. This report was dated November 20, 1942, and entitled "Social Insurance and Allied Services." It made a great impression on federal officials and persons outside the government concerned with various phases of social welfare. It also made some impression on congressional leaders concerned with social legislation. The President's reaction was mixed. He felt that he himself had originated the idea of a comprehensive social insurance system protecting everybody against all major personal economic hazards throughout a lifetime. Moreover, he was completely immersed in the prosecution of the war and may have considered it inadvisable to press for legislative action on a domestic program, especially since the Democratic majority in Congress had been considerably reduced in the November election.

In any event, the President did not seize upon the Beveridge report as an occasion to dramatize the immediate need for sweeping congressional action. Instead, the President informed me in December of 1942 that he did not intend to send a special message on social security to Congress. He said he wanted to stress full employment as a goal in his annual Message on the State of the Union to Congress and wanted to tie in social security with that objective. He also stated that he wished to paint goals rather than cross *t*'s and dot *i*'s.

I was naturally disappointed that the President had changed his mind about sending a special message, as he had indicated in his letter of October 3, 1942, that he would do. However, I prepared some draft material along the lines indicated by the President and sent it to him on December 29, 1942.

In this draft I included a sentence reading as follows: "A comprehensive contributory insurance system would mean in effect that the citizens of this country would be purchasing from their government an insurance policy to provide a minimum basic protection extending literally from the cradle to the grave." In his message delivered in person on January 7, 1943, the President expressed the same thought as follows: "When you talk with our young men and women you will find that with the opportunity for employment they want assurance against the evils of all major economic hazards—assurance that will extend from the cradle to the grave. This great Government can and must provide this assurance."

It is interesting to note that this expression, "from the cradle to the grave," was not used by Beveridge in his report although it was immediately seized upon to describe his plan. Thus, the phrase was used by *Time Magazine* in its issue of December 7, 1942, and by *The Nation* in its issue of December 12, 1942. And Mr. Churchill used it in a radio broadcast in March 1943, saying, "You must rank me and all my colleagues as strong partisans of compulsory insurance for all classes for all purposes from the cradle to the grave.

I do not recall whether I used the phrase in the draft I prepared for the President because I had heard the President use it. However, Frances Perkins in her book, *The Roosevelt I Knew,* states definitely that the President did use the phrase in discussions with her in 1934 when the Committee on Economic Security was developing its recommendations. It was also used by Republican Congressman Eaton in attacking the social security bill when it was being debated in 1935.

The Social Security Board, in its annual report for the fiscal year ended June 30, 1942, which it submitted to the President through the Federal Security Administrator on December 15, 1942, used a less colorful expression, saying that, "Such a program must necessarily give full recognition to needs at all ages from infancy to the ages when earnings dwindle or cease." While the Board's report used less colorful language, it did devote ten pages to making very specific and comprehensive recommendations for extending the social security program. It recommended a unified social insurance system which would include a straight federal system of unemployment insurance, extension of coverage of the old age and survivors' insurance system to all employees and self-employed persons, protection against wage loss due to temporary or permanent disability, and hospital benefits. It also recommended that federal aid to the states in meeting the cost of public assistance be made more adequate by extending it to all needy persons and by providing special aid to low-income states.

The Board was hopeful that the Beveridge report would be helpful in securing congressional consideration of its recommendations. The National Resources Planning Board was also hopeful that its report, "Security, Work, and Relief Policies," would be regarded as the American Beveridge plan. It had submitted its report to the President on December 4, 1941, more than a year previously, but the President had not seen fit to transmit it to Congress.

I felt that continued general public discussion of social security would be helpful and therefore wrote the President on December 4, 1942, recommending that he forward the National Resources Planning Board's report to Congress before he transmitted the Social Security Board's annual report with its very specific and sweeping recommendations. The Board had cooperated in providing extensive data for inclusion in the "Security, Work, and Relief Policies" report and preferred that this report be sent to Congress first because it was largely historical, descriptive, and analytical in character. While it comprised 550 pages, telephone book size, only five pages were devoted to specific recommendations. Dean J. Douglas Brown of Princeton, in a paper included in the *Proceedings of the Academy of Political Science* (Vol. XXI, No. 2) for January 1945, characterized the report as follows: "It was, I believe, this contrast between the emotional content of the relief approach and the rational content of the social insurance approach which caused the elaborate report of the National Resources Planning Board on social security to receive so little attention in this country at the very time that the Beveridge report on the same subject aroused widespread interest in Great Britain and throughout the world. Beveridge emphasized social insurance, something in which all could participate, all the time.

The N.R.P.B. report discussed, at length, direct relief and work relief, about which in 1942 neither the future recipients nor the future supporters were emotionally concerned."

The National Resources Planning Board's report was transmitted to Congress by the President on March 10, 1943, and the Social Security Board's report shortly thereafter. Actually, as it turned out, neither report ever did attract widespread attention, probably because the President did not clearly demonstrate that he expected immediate congressional action.

Prior to the transmittal of these two reports, the former Chairman of the Social Security Board, John G. Winant, who had become Ambassador to Great Britain, cabled me that Sir William Beveridge had requested a visa so that he could come to the United States in April 1943 for a lecture tour. He inquired whether that would be satisfactory. I replied that Sir William's visit would be very helpful but urged that it be delayed until May. The reason I desired this delay was that I was hopeful this would give me time enough to arrange for congressional hearings at which Sir William could testify.

The Ambassador induced Sir William to delay his trip. Unfortunately, the month of May turned out to be exceptionally hot, and Sir William had brought along only heavy tweed suits. When I called at his hotel to greet him, I was severely upbraided by Sir William's bride of a few weeks for causing them to be subjected to the unbearable heat. To make amends I offered to loan Sir William one of my "Palm Beach" suits. Although it was accepted with suspicion, Sir William later came to look upon it as a lifesaver. The only drawback was that it was white and Sir William made one-night stops across the United States, so that he could not have it laundered. When he returned to Washington several weeks later, he looked like a chimney-sweep. His bride, and former secretary, was a sister of Richard Tawney, author of *The Acquisitive Society*. Being already a grandmother and a strong-minded woman, she was not completely mollified by the loan of the suit.

However, it so happened that Winston Churchill was to address a joint session of Congress, and Sir William expressed a keen desire to hear "Winston." Inquiry revealed that no seats were available. I thereupon took Sir William to call upon Speaker

Rayburn, to whom he expressed his disappointment. The Speaker said that he would solve the difficulty by appointing Sir William a deputy Sergeant-at-Arms. So Sir William was presented with an official badge which he proudly displayed, not only the day of Churchill's address but on subsequent occasions. It was only after this incident occurred that I felt Lady Beveridge had fully forgiven me.

I was unable to arrange for Sir William to appear before congressional committees largely because there was no bill pending which could be labeled as an Administration bill. However, I did arrange for the Chairman of the Senate Finance Committee to give a luncheon for Sir William which was attended by congressional leaders. Sir William was thus able to discuss his plan with the most influential members of Congress.

The President, in a radio address on July 28, 1943, dealing with the necessity of planning for the return to civilian life of men and women in the armed services, stated that members of the armed forces should be given credit under the unemployment insurance laws and the old age and survivors' insurance law for their period of military service. On August 14, in a press statement which I drafted, the President pointed out that this was the anniversary of the signing of both the Social Security Act and the Atlantic Charter. In that statement he urged that the old age and survivors' insurance law be extended to cover all employees and self-employed persons. He also urged that the Social Security Act "provide protection against the serious economic hazard of ill health." On September 17, 1943, he sent a message to Congress, reiterating the need for "greater economic protection of our returning men and women in the armed forces" and "a further measure of social security" for all our citizens.

On November 23, 1943, he sent a very lengthy message to Congress reciting the veterans' legislation that had already been enacted and urging the following further steps: (1) to provide mustering out pay which should not be in a lump sum but on a monthly installment basis; (2) to establish a uniform system of allowances for unemployed service men and women; (3) to allow credit under the old age and survivors' insurance system for military service.

But, while the President made these various statements, he still did not indicate that he wanted to press for general social security legislation. Neither did he indicate that the Administration was supporting the comprehensive bill introduced on June 3, 1943, by Senator James Murray, Senator Robert Wagner, and Congressman John Dingell, which came to be well known as the Wagner-Murray-Dingell bill.

This bill had been drafted by Social Security Board officials at the request of its sponsors. It went beyond the recommendations of the Board by including a comprehensive federal health insurance system instead of only hospital benefits. The bill died in committee, although it was strongly supported by organized labor.*

The strongest opposition to the bill came from the American Medical Association. This manifested itself in the activities of an organization known as the National Physicians Committee for the Extension of Medical Service. The public generally appeared to favor government health insurance. Thus, a *Fortune Magazine* poll taken in 1942 showed 74 per cent in favor, and a Gallup poll taken in 1943 showed 59 per cent in favor.

It is interesting to note that a federal health insurance program providing infant and maternity benefits was begun in March 1943 and continued in existence until July 1947. This program was administered by the Children's Bureau through state health agencies. The service, provided to wives and infants of enlisted men in the lower four pay grades, included maternity care (prenatal, delivery, postnatal), care of any illnesses of the mother during this period, and care of infants to the age of one year. The program apparently functioned very successfully. Services were

---

* William F. Green, President of the American Federation of Labor, wrote the President on September 24: "Labor wants more adequate social insurance to carry workers through reconversion and readjustments after the war and to protect us against dependency in the future. We propose to raise the rate of taxation on payrolls to 12 percent—half to be paid by employees and half by employers. . . . Our bill for this purpose which is already before Congress, would increase revenues from social insurance taxes to eight or nine billion dollars. On behalf of wage earners I appeal to you for the opportunity to make this investment in insurance to provide against loss of income through unemployment, old age, permanent disability and sickness. This is the only fiscal proposal that will serve the double purpose of providing the Government with war credit and meeting the insurance needs of Labor."

provided for more than 1,200,000 maternity cases and 230,000 infants. At its peak, births under the program comprised about one-seventh of the total births in the United States.

It is also interesting to note that one state, Rhode Island, proceeded to pass a temporary-disability insurance law without any financial inducement from the federal government. However, this law was administered by the same state agency that administered the state unemployment insurance law. Its employee coverage and benefit formula were the same as those under the state unemployment insurance law. Benefits were payable out of a state fund consisting of employee contributions of one per cent of wages up to $3,000 per annum.

So the year 1943 came to a close with no important permanent legislation having been enacted. Wartime coverage under the old age and survivors' insurance system was provided for seamen employed by the War Shipping Administration, and there was another postponement until March 1, 1944, of the increase in contribution rate which would otherwise have occurred on January 1, 1944.

There was included in the Federal Security Agency appropriation for the fiscal year 1943–44 (contrary to the rules of the House) a proviso which has an important bearing on the federal-state relations established under the Social Security Act. This proviso has been included in all subsequent appropriation acts. It provides that none of the moneys appropriated for grants-in-aid for state agencies to cover the cost of their operations can be withheld because of federal disapproval of their personnel, the manner of their selection, or their rates of pay.

The Social Security Board disagreed with the General Counsel of the Federal Security Agency who expressed the opinion that the Board could not take fiscal exception to individual salary payments even when in violation of state law. This disagreement illustrates what I believe is the proper relationship which should exist between the official who is responsible for deciding policy questions and the staff members who furnish advice. The wise policy-maker will weigh carefully the advice he receives, but must accept the responsibility and have the authority to make the final decision.

In this instance the question was not simply a narrow legal

question involving legal principles and precedents. It was really a policy question involving the interpretation of a certain sentence in an appropriation act in such a way as to reconcile it with the basic language of the Social Security Act and in the light of the general purpose to be achieved. This included a consideration of the effect on the maintenance of a satisfactory federal-state working relationship.

The withdrawal of all federal funds, upon a finding that a state plan no longer provided "methods of administration necessary for the efficient operation of the plan," is so drastic that, if the Board were obliged to rely solely upon that method for securing efficient administration, it would be confronted with two undesirable alternatives: continue to tolerate improper administration or impose great hardship on the innocent beneficiaries for whom the program was created. In contrast, a lesser sanction, involving only the refusal to provide federal funds for the payment of salaries to persons employed in violation of the merit system, could be effective in securing compliance with federal requirements without imposing hardship on the beneficiaries. The effect on the federal-state working relationship also was not so adverse because there was less bitterness than would naturally arise from a highly publicized rupture of relations.

While the President had not proposed or supported any specific bill, he had indicated that the Social Security Board was free to make any recommendations it considered proper. Therefore, the Board, in its annual report for the fiscal year ended June 30, 1943, which it submitted on October 31, 1943, recommended what it called "A Basic Minimum Program of Social Security." This program included all of its previous years' recommendations in more specific and stronger terms. In addition, it included not only hospital benefits but medical services as well. The Board also permitted its Bureau of Research and Statistics to prepare a 39-page pamphlet, "Need for Medical Care Insurance," which was issued in April 1944.

In his Budget Message submitted on January 10, 1944, the President included a section entitled "Veterans Legislation and Social Security." In that section the President said that the "framework of unemployment insurance and retirement benefits must be reinforced and extended." Specifically, he said that the old age and survivors' insurance system should be extended to cover many groups then uncovered and expanded to include disability benefits. He also said that members of the armed forces should be given credit under this system for the period of their military service.

Concerning unemployment insurance, he said he preferred extension of coverage and liberalized benefits to any special legislation, such as providing dismissal payments through war contractors. He also recommended again a program of federal unemployment allowances for members of the armed forces.

The President in this message also urged the Congress to permit the January 1, 1944, increase in the old age and survivors' insurance contribution rate (which had been postponed to March 1, 1944) to go into effect. However, in the Revenue Act of 1943, which went into effect on February 25, 1944, Congress again postponed the increase to January 1, 1945.*

The President, in his Message on the State of the Union, sent to Congress the day following his Budget Message, included what he called a "second Bill of Rights." This declaration has been called the keynote for his postwar plans to raise the American standard of living. It is true that in his Chicago speech of October 28, 1944, made during the presidential campaign, he repeated what he then called an "economic Bill of Rights."

In these rights the President included:

The right to adequate medical care and the opportunity to achieve and enjoy good health;
The right to adequate protection from the economic fears of old age, sickness, accident, and unemployment.

On June 22 the President signed the Servicemen's Readjustment Act of 1944 (G.I. Bill of Rights), which included "readjustment allowances" for unemployed and self-employed veterans. These amounted to $20 a week for a maximum of 52 weeks of involuntary unemployment. In the case of "self-employed" veterans endeavoring to establish a business or profession, the allowance amounted to $100 a month less any net profit during any one month. These readjustment allowances were adminis-

---

* This was the Revenue Act which the Congress passed over the President's veto, although he had charged that it provided relief "not for the needy but for the greedy."

tered by the state unemployment insurance agencies acting for the federal government.

The President, at the time he signed the Servicemen's Readjustment Act, expressed the hope that Congress would take prompt action to develop a program for demobilized civilian war workers which would include appropriate unemployment benefits. The only congressional response to the President's request was to include in the War Mobilization and Reconversion Act a provision establishing an account within the unemployment trust fund from which, up to July 1947, the states might borrow if their own unemployment funds dropped to a certain level. When the President signed this bill on October 3, 1944, he said it was not adequate, pointing out that it did not provide for transportation of war workers to their homes or new place of employment, did not provide for unemployment compensation for federal workers, and did not prescribe minimum standards to govern the amount and duration of unemployment benefits to be paid by the states under their unemployment insurance laws.

On December 16, 1944, the President signed into law a bill which postponed from January 1, 1945, to January 1, 1946, the scheduled increase in the contribution rate under the old age and survivors' insurance system. At the same time he issued a statement deploring the successive postponements that had occurrred, saying that, "The Congress should realize that this bill deferring a statutory increase in contributions toward existing social security merely defers until next year the necessary fiscal receipts to pay the benefits." He concluded by saying, "At an early date I plan to submit to the Congress a comprehensive plan for broadening and improving the social security system."

In his Budget Message of January 3, 1945, he expressed the hope that the Congress would give early consideration to extension and improvement of our social security system and would examine its financial basis. It is interesting that he urged the establishment, through permanent legislation, of an effective *national* employment service. He also said, "Our program should include provision for extended social security, including medical care."

Then in his annual Message on the State of the Union, dated January 6, 1945, he said, "An expanded social security program, and adequate health and education programs, must play essential roles in a program designed to support individual productivity and mass purchasing power. I shall communicate further with the Congress on these subjects at a later date."

It is possible that these many statements by the President merely indicated that he thought it desirable to test public interest in an expanded social security program and to accustom Congress to the idea that he intended to press for such a program. In any event I formed the impression that the President did not consider that the time was ripe for action. Perhaps he would have waited to act until the war had come to an end. We shall never know because the President died suddenly on April 12, 1945, and the war in Europe ended suddenly on May 8, 1945.

6.

Social Security

During the Postwar Years,

1945–48

When the war in Europe ended on May 8, 1945, a sense of urgency developed over methods to cope with postwar problems. However, as events turned out, this postwar period was disappointing with regard to both social security legislation and administration.

On March 26, shortly before President Roosevelt died, the Ways and Means Committee secured the passage of a resolution, authorizing it to spend $50,000 for a study of the need to expand the Social Security Act. President Truman did not await the results of that study but sent a special message to Congress on May 28, 1945, pointing out the failure of the unemployment insurance system to cover all employed persons and its failure to provide adequate benefits to those who were covered. He recommended that the Congress immediately enact a temporary emergency supplementary system, financed by the federal government but administered by the state unemployment insurance agencies. This supplementary system would cover workers not insured under the state systems and would provide supplementary benefits to all workers for 26 weeks up to a weekly maximum of $25 (for workers whose previous wages were high enough so that the percentage of wage loss compensated would yield this maximum amount). It should be noted that the President did not suggest in this message or in any subsequent message that Congress consider federalization of unemployment insurance.*

_____
* I had no occasion to consult with President Truman directly relative to social security matters after he took office. This was partly because he was in general accord with the recommendations I had made during the New

The war with Japan ended on August 14 (which, interestingly enough, was the anniversary of the Social Security Act). The President repeated this recommendation in a special message he sent to the Congress on September 6, 1945. This message covered many other aspects of reconversion from a war to a peace economy. Judge Samuel Rosenman, who assisted in writing it, has stated that it signaled the beginning of the Fair Deal.

The reaction of Congress was disappointing. The Senate passed a bill which would have financed additional duration of benefits up to 26 weeks. However, when the bill reached the House, the Ways and Means Committee voted to postpone action indefinitely.

President Truman, in his September 6, 1945, message, stated that, "This recommendation should not be confused with the broader question of extending, expanding, and improving our entire social security program, of which unemployment insurance is only a part. I expect to communicate with the Congress on this subject at a later date." In a statement which he had issued on the tenth anniversary of the signing of the Social Security Act (August 14, 1945), he had also said that he expected to present to the Congress specific recommendations for improving the Social Security Act.

However, the only subsequent message relating to social security which he sent to Congress during 1945 was one on November 19, outlining a national health program, which had been prepared by Judge Rosenman, assisted by experts from the U.S. Public Health Service and the Social Security Administration. This program included federal aid to the states for hospital construction, expanded public health and maternal and child health services, federal aid to public and nonprofit private institutions for medical education and research, a federal health insurance system cover-

---

Deal days and partly because he relied more upon formal administrative channels than had President Roosevelt (and, technically, the Social Security Board was under the supervision of the Federal Security Administrator). However, I was a neighbor and friend of the Director of the Budget, Harold Smith, whose duty it was to advise the President not only on administrative matters but also on all legislation proposed by administrative officials. I had also worked with Judge Samuel Rosenman, who had been a close adviser and speech-writer for President Roosevelt and continued in that role for President Truman. Judge Rosenman was thoroughly in favor of social security, including health insurance, and President Truman accepted his recommendations completely.

ing the cost of medical care, and a system covering wage loss coordinated with the other cash benefits under existing social insurance systems. The President emphasized that his recommendation regarding health insurance did not constitute "socialized medicine." He also said he would bring up the subject of cash benefits to offset wage loss in a later message on social security.

Senators Wagner and Murray and Congressman Dingell immediately introduced bills to give effect to the President's program. However, no hearings were held until 1946.

Besides issuing these various statements and messages to Congress, the President made an important administrative decision during 1945 affecting social security. That was issuing an executive order on September 18 which abolished the War Manpower Commission and placed the United States Employment Service in the Department of Labor, instead of returning it to the Social Security Board.

The only social security legislation passed by Congress during 1945 was to include in the Revenue Act of 1945 a provision postponing until January 1, 1947, the increase in the old age and survivors' insurance contribution rate which would otherwise have occurred on January 1, 1946.

The Social Security Board submitted its annual report for the fiscal year ended June 30, 1945, on November 1, 1945. It was transmitted to the Congress when it convened in January 1946. Part I of the report was entitled "Facing Forward to Peace." This part covered 77 of the 117 pages of the report and consisted of an appraisal of the adequacy of the existing Social Security Act and detailed recommendations to improve it. The Board recommended a comprehensive, basic national system of social insurance, emphasizing particularly the need for health insurance and protection against wage loss due to temporary as well as permanent disability.

The President, in a radio address on January 3, 1946, entitled "Radio Report to the American People on the Status of the Reconversion Program," called attention to the fact that the House Ways and Means Committee had failed to act on the Senate bill to provide federal supplementation of unemployment benefits payable under state laws, saying, "It will remain locked up in that committee unless the people of the United States insist that it be reported out and passed." However, the bill never was reported out.

The President, in his Message on the State of the Union and in his Budget Message, dated January 14, 1946, enumerated all of the recommendations regarding social security which he had made in 1945 and which the Congress had failed to adopt. He then stated that, "Even without these proposed major additions, it would now be time to undertake a thorough reconsideration of our social security laws."

The study of the need to expand the Social Security Act, which the Ways and Means Committee had been authorized to undertake, was completed in early 1946. It was called "Issues in Social Security" and comprised 742 printed pages. The report did not contain specific legislative recommendations, but did point out alternative ways of improving the existing law.

The study had been made under the direction of Leonard Calhoun, a former Assistant General Counsel of the Social Security Board. Apparently the Ways and Means Committee wanted to make an independent study and probably felt that any study made by the Board would reflect recommendations the Board had already made. However, the Board cooperated fully with Mr. Calhoun and furnished him most of the factual material contained in the report.

The Ways and Means Committee held public hearings from February 25 to June 7, and the printed report of the hearings was 1,510 pages in length. However, the committee stated in its report that, while the Congress now had available a body of information essential to making needed changes in the various social security programs, it was reporting out a bill limited in scope and dealing only with noncontroversial legislative changes. The committee explained that other pressing matters had made it impossible to

The chief changes recommended by the committee were as consider adequately various proposed basic changes. follows:

(1) Postponement until January 1, 1948, of the increase in the contribution rate which was scheduled to go into effect on January 1, 1947.

(2) Guaranteeing survivors of veterans who die within three years after discharge the same benefits they would have received

if the veteran had been fully insured under the old age and survivors' insurance system and had earned $160 per month in covered employment during his military service.

(3) Covering all maritime employment under the Federal Unemployment Tax Act (and paying benefits financed by the federal government to unemployed seamen who had been employed by the Maritime Commission).

(4) Temporarily increasing the maximum amount of public assistance to an individual, which the federal government would help finance on a 50–50 basis.

One of the committee members, Congressman Eberharter of Pennsylvania, was so disturbed by these meager improvements that he submitted a minority report. He stated that he was deeply disappointed at the bill's inadequacies. He also pointed out that only two weeks previously the committee had approved a bill which increased the old age and survivors' insurance contribution rate and provided a graduated federal matching scale for public assistance ranging from 50 per cent to 66⅔ per cent in inverse proportion to a state's per capita income. This minority report further pointed out that the committee was also proposing to repeal the provision which authorized appropriations to the old age and survivors' insurance trust fund out of general revenues if the payroll contributions proved to be insufficient. This second bill did indeed constitute a sudden and strange reversal. Apparently the Democratic majority members were shaken by the minority report on the previous bill which alleged (1) that no increase in the contribution rate was necessary and (2) that a graduated federal matching scale for public assistance will mean "that the aged, the blind, and dependent children will become mere wards of the Federal Government."

When the bill reached the Senate, the Senate Finance Committee agreed with two of the criticisms made in the Ways and Means Committee minority report. It recommended a graduated federal matching scale for public assistance related to the per capita income of the individual states. Although it accepted the proposal to postpone the scheduled increase in the contribution rate under the old age and survivors' insurance system, it refused to repeal the provision which authorized appropriations to the trust fund if the payroll contributions proved to be insufficient.

The recommendation of the Senate committee to include a graduated federal matching scale related to per capita income of the states is especially interesting because the Republican members of the committee joined with the Democratic members in making this recommendation. In fact, Senator Taft, one of the members of the committee, himself included such a provision in a bill he introduced on May 3, 1946, providing for the coordination and expansion of federal government health activities. Moreover, the Republican members of the Senate as well as the Democratic members supported the Hospital Survey and Construction Act of 1946 (better known as the Hill-Burton Act) which also had such a provision. This attitude on the part of Republican Senators was indeed in marked contrast to the attitude of the Republican members of the House Ways and Means Committee as previously mentioned.

The Senate committee also added an amendment to the Federal Unemployment Tax Act, permitting a state to withdraw from its account in the federal unemployment trust fund any employee contributions for the purpose of paying disability benefits. Nine state laws provided for employee contributions, and some now wanted to use these for paying disability benefits as well as benefits for unemployment due to lack of work.

When the bill went to conference to reconcile the differences between the House and Senate, the House conferees receded from the proposal to repeal the general revenue authorization. On the federal matching ratio under public assistance, a compromise was reached which had an indirect effect in increasing the federal matching ratio for the lower income states. This compromise stated that the federal government would pay 66⅔ per cent of the cost of public assistance up to a specified amount (i.e., $15 for an individual recipient of old age assistance) and 50 per cent above that amount up to the specified maximum. Since low-income states usually made lower assistance payments than high-income states, this "two-step" formula had the effect of reimbursing them for a higher proportion of their costs. But this effect was achieved only at the expense of paying to the high-income states a somewhat higher proportion of their costs.

The only other social security legislation enacted in 1946 was an amendment to the Railroad Retirement Act. This amendment provided that, in the case of the death of an individual who had both railroad employment and employment covered under the old age and survivors' insurance system, the wages earned in both types of employment would be combined in determining the eligibility of his survivors for benefits and the amount of the benefits. However, benefits would be payable under only one system—under the railroad system if the deceased employee had had at least ten years' employment covered by that system, and if not, under the other system.

As already stated, at the same time, in November 1945, when President Truman sent to Congress his message outlining a national health program, Senators Wagner and Murray and Congressman Dingell had introduced bills to give it effect. No hearings were ever held in the House. However, the Senate Committee on Education and Labor, of which Senator Murray was chairman, did hold hearings in April through June in 1946 on the Wagner-Murray bill (S. 1606). About 100 witnesses testified, and the final record covered more than 3,000 pages. The Bureau of Research and Statistics submitted an extensive report to the committee on July 6, 1946, captioned "Medical Care Insurance: A Social Insurance Program for Personal Health Services." But the bill was never reported out of committee.

At the very outset of the hearings a bitter exchange of charges and countercharges occurred between Chairman Murray and Senator Taft, who was a member of the committee and who stated he would not participate further in the hearings.

Apparently all this Administration activity did stimulate Senators Taft, Smith of New Jersey, and Ball of the Republican minority to introduce a health bill, S. 2143, on May 3, 1946. This bill provided for the creation of a National Health Agency which would administer all the health activities of the federal government. This agency would make grants to the states to assist them in providing health, hospital, medical, and dental services for persons unable to pay the whole cost. The states would be required to submit a statewide plan and would be permitted to utilize voluntary nonprofit organizations. The grants would be on a matching basis, varying between 33⅓ per cent and 75 per cent inversely with each state's per capita income. The authors of this bill, all of whom were members of the Committee on Education and Labor, never requested that a hearing be held on the bill, and none was ever held.

An administrative change—the return to state agencies of the local United States Employment Service offices—was brought about by the Appropriation Act of 1947. This act provided funds to the Department of Labor and the Federal Security Agency for the fiscal year ending June 30, 1947. It provided that on November 15, 1946, the Secretary of Labor transfer to the state agencies the personnel and equipment in these offices.

Another administrative change was made by presidential order. The President abolished the Social Security Board as of July 16, 1946, and created in its place the office of Commissioner for Social Security, a position to which I was appointed by the Federal Security Administrator. At the same time, the Children's Bureau was transferred from the Department of Labor to the Federal Security Agency and placed within the Social Security Administration.

The immediate effect of this change was negligible since I had been serving as Chairman of the Social Security Board for a number of years and, consequently, made no changes in policy or personnel. But the abolition of the Social Security Board emphasized the fundamental change which took place in 1939 when the Social Security Board was made subordinate to the Federal Security Administrator. Eventually it had very important consequences which will be discussed later.

During 1947 President Truman sent several messages to Congress relative to social security. In his Budget Message on January 3, his Message on the State of the Union on January 6, and his Economic Report on January 8, he included passages repeating his previous recommendations for making more adequate both the social insurance provisions and the public assistance provisions of the Social Security Act. Besides recommending more adequate benefits and extended coverage under existing forms of social insurance and public assistance, he recommended the addition of health and disability insurance and the extension of public assistance to all needy persons.

On May 19 he sent a special message to Congress recommending the enactment of a "national health and disability program." In this message he pointed out that "important advances were made by the last Congress toward realization of some of the goals" which he had set forth in his November 19, 1945, message outlining a national health program. But he emphasized that national health insurance was necessary so that patients could pay for needed medical services and was therefore the "heart" of the total health program he had proposed. He took pains to point out that "a national health insurance plan can and should provide for administration through State and local agencies," because his 1945 proposal and the bills introduced to implement it had been criticized in this regard.

As in 1945, Senators Wagner and Murray (joined by several other senators) and Congressman Dingell introduced bills to implement the President's recommendations. Senators Taft, Smith of New Jersey, and Ball also introduced a health bill in February similar to the bill that Senator Taft, joined by these other Republican senators, had introduced in 1946. Again, the major difference between the Republican bill and the Administration bill was that the Republican bill provided only for grants-in-aid to the states to assist them in providing medical care for needy persons instead of a national health insurance system covering the cost of medical care without applying a means test.

Extensive hearings before the Senate Committee on Labor and Public Welfare were held on both the Republican and the Administration bills during May, June, and July 1947, and January, February, May, and June 1948. However, neither bill was ever reported out. No hearings were held in the House on the Dingell bill.

Actually the only social security legislation enacted in 1947 was Public Law 379 which did three things. One was to postpone again the increase in the old age and survivors' contribution rate scheduled to occur on January 1, 1948. This time the postponement was to January 1, 1950. Another was to extend until January 1, 1950, the 1944 provision for federal loans to states whose unemployment reserves became depleted. And the third was to extend until July 1, 1950, the previous year's temporary increase in the federal matching ratio under the public assistance titles, scheduled to end December 31, 1947.

There was some other legislative activity which did not result in legislation but which, nevertheless, was significant. The Congress rejected the President's Reorganization Plan No. 2. This plan would have made permanent the transfer of the United States Employment Service to the Department of Labor. The transfer had been made by executive order under authority granted by the first War Powers Act. Under the terms of that act, the transfer was effective only until six months after the official termination of the war, in the absence of further legislation.

The other legislative activity of significance was the appointment by the Senate Finance Committee of an Advisory Council on Social Security. This council was appointed on September 17, 1947. It consisted of distinguished and representative persons, many of whom had considerable experience with the operation of the Social Security Act. However, of seventeen members, only two were representatives of organized labor. The council began its deliberations immediately. It had a very small staff, so relied to a considerable extent on the Social Security Administration and the Treasury Department for material on which to base a series of recommendations. These recommendations were made on various dates from April to December 1948.

The President, in his messages to Congress on the budget and in his Message on the State of the Union in January 1948, repeated his recommendations regarding the expansion of the Social Security Act and stated that he would later send a special message to Congress on the subject. This he did on May 24. In that message he said, "On several occasions during the past 3 years I have recommended to the Congress the type of legislation which I believe should be enacted to strengthen our present social-security system. The Congress has not acted on these recommendations. Instead, it is considering legislation which would actually remove the protection of our social-security system from many persons now entitled to its benefits."

The President repeated his previous recommendations in somewhat more specific terms. He urged more adequate benefits and extended coverage under both the federal old age and survivors' insurance system and the federal-state unemployment insurance system. However, it is significant that he, unlike President Roosevelt, did not recommend in this message or at any previous or subsequent time, that the unemployment insurance system become a straight federal system.

It was for this reason that annual reports of the Social Security Board, and later the reports of the Social Security Administration, always discussed at considerable length how the existing federal-state unemployment insurance system should be improved if the recommendation of a single, comprehensive, national system of contributory social insurance was not accepted. The annual reports, beginning with the one for the fiscal year 1944–45, also recommended that, if the federal-state system were continued, the federal unemployment tax should be reduced and the tax-offset provision should be eliminated. Instead, it was proposed that the proceeds of the reduced federal tax then be used to make grants to the states for half the total cost of unemployment insurance—both benefit disbursements and administrative expenses.

The President recommended insurance against loss of earnings due to temporary or permanent disability. His recommendation concerning temporary disability insurance was that "the Federal Government should provide a strong financial inducement to all States to provide such insurance." On the subject of permanent disability he said, "In the case of disability extending for 6 months or more, I recommend that insurance against loss of earnings be established in connection with the present old-age and survivors insurance program."

The President also recommended that the public assistance provisions of the Social Security Act be strengthened by the federal government's matching the expenditures of the state up to a higher maximum amount for each individual recipient, that the federal matching should be related to the financial resources and needs of each state, and that the federal grants help cover the cost of aid to needy persons not included in the existing categories and the cost of preventive welfare services.

The President did not mention health insurance. This was undoubtedly because he had previously sent two special messages dealing with health and because on January 30 he had sent a letter to the Federal Security Administrator directing him to "undertake a comprehensive study of the possibilities for raising health levels." This letter had been prepared by the Administrator himself (Oscar R. Ewing), who had been appointed to office only five months earlier but who took much more aggressive action

Taking the oath of office as Assistant Secretary of Labor (June 8, 1934). From left to right: Secretary of Labor Frances Perkins, Arthur J. Altmeyer, and Samuel Gompers, Chief Clerk (a son of the famous President of the American Federation of Labor)

The first meeting of the Social Security Board (August 23, 1935). From left to right: Arthur J. Altmeyer, John G. Winant, Chairman (former Governor of New Hampshire), and Vincent M. Miles (attorney from Little Rock, Arkansas, and Democratic National Committeeman)

Sir William Beveridge, author of the British "cradle to the grave" social security plan, and Arthur J. Altmeyer, Chairman of the Social Security Board, in New York (June 5, 1943)

*Arthur J. Altmeyer in front of the Social Security Adminis-
tration's central office building in Baltimore (May 1963)*

concerning legislative and administrative matters than had his predecessors.

The Federal Security Administrator had accordingly called a "National Health Assembly" on May 1 to 4, attended by 800 professional and community leaders to advise him. He submitted his report to the President on September 2. The President immediately acknowledged the report and issued a statement pointing out that the National Health Assembly's conclusions supported all of his previous recommendations, except a national health insurance system although it did endorse the principle of contributory insurance as the basic method of financing medical care.

Congress took no action in 1948 on the President's recommendations or on the recommendations of the Advisory Council on Social Security appointed by the Senate Finance Committee. On the contrary, the Congress passed a bill excluding newspaper and magazine vendors from coverage under both old age and survivors' insurance and the Federal Unemployment Tax Act. It also passed a bill narrowing the definition of "employee" in the Social Security Act so that at least a half-million persons who had been covered under previous administrative decisions and United States Supreme Court decisions were excluded.

One reason why the bill narrowing the definition of employee in the social insurance provisions of the Social Security Act was passed rather easily was that this bill also provided for increasing the federal matching ratio and the individual maximum amount which would be matched under the public assistance provisions.

Both Houses had become Republican as a result of the 1946 elections, and both bills were passed over the President's veto. He, therefore, made this legislative action reducing the coverage under the social insurance provisions of the Social Security Act a major issue in the 1948 presidential campaign. During that campaign he repeatedly attacked "the terrible 80th Congress" for this action and other actions.

Besides passing the foregoing substantive legislation, the same Congress brought about important administrative changes. In January 1948, Congress rejected the reorganization plan which would have placed the United States Employment Service permanently in the Department of Labor and would have transferred the Bureau of Employment Security to that department. Instead, Congress included a provision in the Federal Security Agency Appropriation Act, transferring the United States Employment Service back to the Social Security Administration as of July 1, 1948. The President vetoed the bill which was then passed over his veto.

However, Congress did approve of the transfer of the Bureau of Federal Credit Unions from the Federal Deposit Insurance Corporation to the Federal Security Agency where it was placed within the Social Security Administration. This transfer was made because it was believed that there was a closer relationship of the functions of the bureau with those of the Social Security Administration than there was with those of the Federal Deposit Insurance Corporation. At first thought this might seem strange, but actually, cooperative savings and credit institutions have the same goal as social security—providing protection against economic insecurity.

Curiously enough, at the same time that the Social Security Administration was being given those additional administrative responsibilities, the Appropriations Committee of the House of Representatives was taking action to make it impossible for the Social Security Administration to function effectively. This was to make an 80 per cent reduction in the appropriation to the Social Security Administration for centralized functions performed by the office of the Commissioner and not by the individual bureaus or the office of the Federal Security Administrator. These services included supervision and coordination of the work of the bureaus, as well as overall planning and research, and certain services, such as an information program and a basic training program. The previous year the Congress had reduced the appropriation for these activities by 30 per cent. The effect of the two successive reductions was catastrophic, coming as they did after years of consistent reduction in personnel engaged in these activities. There had already been a reduction from 2,130 on June 30, 1938, to 361 on June 30, 1948, in the number of persons in such centralized functions. After June 30, 1948, it was necessary to reduce the number to 59. This number included both clerical and professional personnel in Washington and outside Washington.

The reasons for this unfortunate congressional action were

varied. The Chairman of the appropriations subcommittee in charge of the appropriation bill, Frank Keefe, a Republican, was a suspicious man with strong prejudices (although, ironically enough, he was from Wisconsin and had often complimented me in the course of hearings). It also happened that the clerk of this subcommittee had been on the staff of the Federal Security Administrator for a short time and formed the impression that the Social Security Administration personnel had not been "cooperative." The possibility that a clerk of a committee of Congress might have been a controlling factor in the making of an important decision may surprise persons not familiar with the congressional scene. Actually, in a great many instances, particularly when there is no publicized issue involved, the clerk in charge of the preparation of a committee report is the person who makes the decision.

In this case it is probable that the clerk's feeling was shared by the Administrator's staff generally and perhaps by the Administrator personally. If such a feeling existed, the most likely cause was that the Social Security Board had begun as an independent agency, antedating the Federal Security Agency. As a consequence, it had developed an effective headquarters and field organization which the Federal Security Agency understandably wanted to use for the entire agency. Actually, about one-half of the reduction in personnel from 1938 to 1948, mentioned above, was due to the transfer of such personnel and their functions to the office of the Administrator or to the individual bureaus, in order to achieve maximum economy and efficiency.

But, unfortunately, neither the disgruntled clerk nor the appropriations committee members understood the continuing need in the case of social security for an intermediate organization between the individual bureaus and the Federal Security Administrator in order to achieve maximum economy and effectiveness. This was understood in the case of health, as evidenced by the fact that, at the very same time this drastic reduction was being made in the centralized functions performed by the Social Security Administration, a 33⅓ per cent increase was made in the appropriation of the Public Health Service for carrying on similar functions. This, in spite of the fact that, while the Public Health Service had only about one-third more total employees than the

Social Security Administration, the number of its employees performing these centralized functions was already three times as many.

The fact is that the Federal Security Agency was (and its successor agency, the Department of Health, Education, and Welfare, continues to be) a heterogeneous agency. It included three rather distinct fields of activity—health, education, and welfare. The operations within each of these general fields are closely related. The three general fields are related to each other in some degree. Certainly they share a common fundamental goal of promoting the "good life." Likewise, some general aspects of their activities, such as federal-state relations, are similar. However, so far as specific day-to-day activities are concerned, there is actually very little interchange or relationship among these general fields.

Because of the heterogeneous character and magnitude of the activities carried on by the many bureaus, it is imperative from an administrative standpoint to assemble these bureaus into a number of homogeneous groups having close interrelationships. The activities of each group need to be supervised by an official directly responsible to the overall agency head. In this way the span of control of the head of the agency is kept within a manageable limit, a clear chain of command is established, and the interrelated activities of the various bureaus can be properly coordinated and focused to achieve their common objective.

There are also a number of common services which the official in charge of a particular grouping can perform more efficiently than either the agency head or the individual bureaus. Thus, some research needs to be centralized because it covers more than one major field. But since most of the research is confined to one of the major fields of health, education, or welfare, it needs to be carried on by research units responsible to the administrator in charge of the particular field. Furthermore, much of the research needs to be carried on by units within the operating bureaus, since it is closely concerned with the day-to-day operations of a bureau and obtains much of the necessary data as a result of these operations. But there is need for a research director responsible to the administrator in charge of the major field in which these bureaus operate. The research director should have the responsibility of coordinating the research carried on by the bureaus and also of carrying on research himself on subjects of concern to the entire field.

In the case of social security, which affects so intimately the lives of all Americans, it is necessary to have a sustained and comprehensive information program so that everybody will know about his rights and duties. Likewise, as in any large organization, it is necessary to have an effective personnel training program in order to achieve maximum efficiency of operations. This employee training is especially necessary in social security operations since the social security personnel comes into direct contact with the millions of persons affected by the program and must understand its affirmative responsibility to serve these millions.

As in the case of research, most of the personnel training and information program is related to only one major field and should, therefore, be conducted as closely as possible to day-to-day operations in that field. Basic training for personnel, which needs to be familiar with the entire field, should be carried on by a supervisor of training on the immediate staff of the administrator in charge of that field. Training in the operations of a particular bureau should, of course, be carried on by that bureau.

In my opinion the adverse appropriation reduction by Congress was not only the result of personal prejudice and lack of administrative understanding but more fundamentally the lack of understanding of the need for an integrated system of social security, requiring a focused and integrated administration. As stated in Chapter 1, we in this country have come to think of "social security" as consisting only of the federal old age, survivors', and disability insurance. But, as I already indicated, I believe the concept of social security should embrace a governmental program providing protection against all hazards which would otherwise cause widespread destitution. Such a program would include comprehensive social insurance, public assistance, and services designed to prevent or ameliorate the hazards causing economic insecurity. The Social Security Board from the very beginning had emphasized the interrelated character of the various segments of social security. In its annual reports, recommending a comprehensive social security system, it had pointed out that such a system would provide protection against major economic risks on a consistent basis—that is to say, on a basis that would eliminate gaps, overlaps, and inconsistencies. It had also pointed out that such a system would be the simplest and most economical to administer.

I believe that this lack of understanding of the need for an integrated system of social security, requiring a focused and integrated administration, was caused to a considerable extent by the 1939 change making the Social Security Board subordinate to the Federal Security Administrator and the 1946 change abolishing the Board. Much can be said for the necessity of reducing the number of independent agencies reporting directly to the President, and much can be said for the administrative advantages of a single administrator as contrasted with a multi-member board. No good purpose would be served if I attempted to make a case for the continuance of an independent Social Security Board, since I probably cannot be completely objective. However, I do wish to suggest that if the Board was not going to be maintained as an independent agency, it would have been far simpler, understandable, and effective to recognize clearly the three relatively homogeneous areas included in the heterogeneous overall agency, by creating three deputy administrators in the Federal Security Agency. Now, of course, they would be undersecretaries within the Department of Health, Education, and Welfare: one responsible for health activities, one responsible for educational activities, and one responsible for social security. This would have achieved the twin objectives of emphasizing the importance and integrated character of each of these fields and of establishing a close relationship to the Secretary of the department. I believe it would also have prevented the unfortunate separation in 1963 of the administration of the old age, survivors', and disability insurance system from the administration of the public assistance titles.

7.

The Crucial Years,
1948–52

Political events in 1948 seemed to portend that at long last the need for a more adequate and integrated social security system was coming to be recognized. As already mentioned, President Truman made the action of the Republican Congress, reducing the social insurance coverage, a major issue in his 1948 campaign, along with his continued advocacy of a national health insurance system. Therefore, his election and the election of a Democratic Congress constituted something of a mandate for social security legislation. The likelihood of such legislation was increased by the fact that the Advisory Council on Social Security appointed by the Senate Finance Committee when the Republicans were in control had completed its work and on December 28, 1948, submitted the last of a series of reports recommending extensive changes in the Social Security Act. To a considerable extent its recommendations coincided with those that the Social Security Board and I, as Commissioner for Social Security, had been making year after year.

To me it seemed that the events of 1949 would be decisive as to whether the old age and survivors' insurance system would survive as a contributory, wage-related system. An entire decade had passed during which the only change had been to reduce its coverage. The result had been that the number of persons receiving old age assistance had continued to grow year by year. Thus it was that in 1949 more than twice as many persons were receiving old age assistance as were receiving retirement benefits under this insurance system. Moreover, the average monthly assistance payment had more than doubled since 1939. It was $42 as compared with the average monthly retirement benefit of $25, which was only 10 per cent higher than in 1939. This was far less than the increase in the cost of living and the increase in the wage level.

I felt that, if the old age and survivors' insurance system failed, any hope for a comprehensive contributory social insurance covering all major economic hazards was remote, indeed.

The year started out much as usual. Immediately upon the convening of Congress in January 1949, the President transmitted his Budget Message and his Message on the State of the Union, in which he repeated all of his previous recommendations for improving social security, including a national health insurance system. There was only one significant change from his May 24, 1948, message. In that message he had recommended that "the Federal Government should provide a strong financial inducement to all States" to provide protection against loss of income because of temporary disability. In his 1949 Budget Message he urged that such protection be provided under a straight federal system.

The President followed up the foregoing messages by sending a letter to the Chairman of the House Ways and Means Committee on February 21. With that letter he transmitted drafts of bills to "serve as a basis for consideration and discussion when your Committee begins its hearings." One of the two bills which the President sent dealt with improvements in the public assistance and child welfare provisions of the Social Security Act. The other bill dealt with improvements in the old age and survivors' insurance and its extension to include protection against loss of income due to temporary or permanent disability.

It was felt that it would be less confusing and more convenient for witnesses to have these two aspects of social security covered by separate bills. Both bills were in accordance with the recommendations that had been made many times by the Social Security Board and by me as Commissioner for Social Security.

The President did not include either unemployment insurance or health insurance in his letter or in the bills which he transmitted. The omissions were intentional. These bills had been prepared under my direction, and I felt that it was essential to deal with health insurance and unemployment insurance separately because both were extremely controversial and would therefore delay, if not imperil, favorable consideration of the less controversial recommendations.

Subsequently, on April 22, the President did send a special message on health. In that message he pointed out that subsequent to his November 19, 1945, message, considerable legislation had been enacted, including federal grants for hospital construction, for medical research, and for public health services. He said that the main problem remaining was "to make available enough medical services to go around, and to see that everybody has a chance to obtain these services." The President made four specific recommendations: establishment of a nationwide system of health insurance; federal aid for medical education; increased federal aid for the construction of hospitals and other local health facilities; and increased federal aid for public health and maternal and child health services.

Hearings were held during May, June, and July on bills to implement the President's recommendations, not only by a subcommittee of the Senate Committee on Labor and Public Welfare but by a subcommittee of the House Committee on Interstate and Foreign Commerce. This was the first time that a House committee had ever considered the subject of national health insurance. However, Congress took no action on the first two recommendations. This was due largely to the bitter campaign waged by the American Medical Association, a campaign financed by assessing its members $25 each and directed by a high-powered public relations firm. This firm claimed credit for having previously defeated Governor Warren's health insurance proposal in California. But Congress did make more funds available to finance the activities covered by the second two recommendations.

Senators Taft, Donnell, and Smith of New Jersey introduced the same type of bill they had introduced in previous sessions of Congress. There was also another bill introduced concurrently in the Senate by Republican Senators Flanders and Ives and in the House by then Congressman Richard Nixon and a number of other Republican congressmen. Hearings were held on these bills at the same time and by the same committees that held hearings on the Administration bill.

The so-called Flanders-Ives-Nixon bill requires some discussion since the same type of bill was introduced by Republican members of Congress in many subsequent sessions of Congress. The purpose of this bill was to make it possible for low-income persons to purchase adequate health insurance protection from voluntary, nonprofit organizations by the federal government's paying a proportionate part of the premium, depending on the income of the person insured. The federal government would provide this subsidy under state-operated plans. A state would be required to share in the cost of this subsidy, the federal government's share ranging from one-third to three-fourths, depending upon the state's per capita income.

There would be a national "yardstick" in the form of a comprehensive range of benefits. The cost would be estimated for various health regions, and the insured person would have to subscribe at least 3 per cent of his income under $5,000 (but not less than $6 per year). This minimum subscription could be paid in whole or in part by the state if the person was receiving public assistance or unemployment compensation. If a state plan provided more or less benefits than those specified in the national yardstick, the 3 per cent minimum subscription could be varied accordingly.

Under a state plan the state agency would deal with voluntary, nonprofit, prepayment health service organizations which would issue the policies to the insured persons and pay for the medical services rendered. The state agency would make reimbursement for any deficit between the aggregate income from subscription charges (which would have to be based on the income of the subscriber) and the actual cost to the organization of the medical services rendered. The state would then be partly reimbursed by the federal government, as already stated.

Besides the federal subsidy to help pay the cost of health insurance protection for low-income persons, the Flanders-Ives-Nixon bill provided for federal grants for the construction of hospitals and health centers, federal aid to medical schools, and increased federal aid to the states for the development of local public health units. Neither this bill nor the Taft-Donnell-Smith bill was ever reported out of the Senate committee.

No Administration bill was introduced concerning unemployment insurance in 1949. So the main concern of Congress regarding social security was directed to the consideration of the two bills transmitted by the President on February 21.

The Ways and Means Committee began hearings on the public welfare bill February 28. The hearings on this bill lasted until March 23. On March 24 the committee began its hearings on the old age and survivors' insurance bill, and these lasted until April 27. These hearings resulted in 2,500 pages of testimony. After their conclusion, the committee held executive sessions over a period of 16 weeks. It was not until August 22 that the committee made its report and introduced a bill, H.R. 6000, including all its recommendations.

There were both a majority report and a minority report submitted by the committee. All Democratic members joined in the majority report and all Republican members joined in the minority report. The majority report included the following main recommendations:

I. Changes in the old age and survivors' insurance system
    1. Extension of coverage
        a. Broadening of definition of "employee"
        b. Inclusion of domestic workers
        c. Inclusion of state employees and of local employees by state compact
        d. Inclusion of employees of nonprofit organizations on a compulsory basis for employees and voluntary basis for employers
        e. Inclusion of Puerto Rico and the Virgin Islands for first time
        f. Provision of wage credit of $160 a month for World War II military service
    2. Increase in level of benefits of about 66⅔ per cent
    3. Slight liberalization of eligibility requirements
    4. Liberalization of retirement test to permit a worker to earn $50 a month instead of $14.99 without retirement benefit loss for that month
    5. Inclusion of benefits for permanent total disability
    6. Elimination of 1943 authorization to meet any deficit by appropriation from general revenues
II. Changes in public assistance and welfare

1. A new category for assistance to the permanently and totally disabled
2. Liberalization of federal grant for aid to dependent children by including caretaker
3. Liberalization of federal matching ratio in all categories
4. Authorization of federal matching of payments to public medical institutions (except in aid to dependent children)
5. Authorization of federal matching of direct payments for medical care in addition to cash assistance
6. Inclusion of abolition of waiting lists as a condition for federal matching
7. Extension of federal public assistance matching to Puerto Rico and Virgin Islands (but on a less liberal basis than to the states)

The important differences between the foregoing changes and the recommendations of the Administration were as follows:

I. Old age and survivors' insurance
1. Farm operators and farm workers not included
2. Eligibility requirements liberalized only slightly
3. The annual increment of 1 per cent in the monthly benefit payable for each year of coverage reduced to ½ per cent
4. Benefits for temporary disability not included
5. Maximum annual wage base for benefits and contributions increased from $3,000 to $3,600 instead of $4,800
6. Elimination of 1943 authorization to meet any deficit by appropriation from general revenues
II. Public assistance and welfare
1. Extension of federal matching to include public assistance to all needy individuals, regardless of category, rejected
2. Liberalization of federal matching ratio not related to financial ability of each state
3. Federal matching of cost of welfare services, in addition to matching of public assistance administrative costs, not included. However, the committee's report did say that there was already "ample authorization for Federal sharing in the cost of welfare services to applicants for and recipients of State-Federal assistance." But, unfortunately, this authorization would not extend to services to persons who might, as a result, not need to apply for financial assistance. Actually, explicit language to make clear that the cost of administration included welfare services to applicants for as well as recipients of public assistance was not included in the public assistance titles until 1956. Language to provide 75 per cent federal matching, instead of 50 per cent, for such services and to extend them to persons "likely to become applicants for or recipients of assistance" was not included until 1962.

4. Failure to include as a condition for federal matching that a state plan of public assistance must contain standards assuring similar treatment of persons in similar circumstances throughout the state

5. Elimination of residence and citizenship requirements under state public assistance laws as a condition for federal matching rejected

The majority report explained the elimination of the 1943 authorization to meet any deficit by appropriation from general revenues by saying that "your committee is firmly of the belief that the old-age, survivors, and disability insurance program should be on a completely self-supporting basis." The minority report of the committee opposed a number of the majority's recommendations, such as the increase in the maximum wage base, the annual increment of ½ per cent in the benefit amount, the expanded definition of "employee," the inclusion of permanent total disability benefits under the old age and survivors' insurance system, and the liberalized federal matching formula under public assistance.

In addition, three minority members attacked the old age and survivors' insurance system as "totally unmoral" and advocated uniform benefits to aged persons, widows, and orphans, without a needs test or work clause, financed by a flat percentage income tax. These three members also advocated the abolition of federal grants for old age assistance and aid to dependent children.

On October 2 and 3 the House debated the bill reported by the majority of the Ways and Means Committee. A motion to recommit the bill was lost on a strictly party vote of 113 to 232. It was then passed by a vote of 333 to 14. The Congress adjourned *sine die* on October 19 so the Senate Finance Committee could not consider the bill until after Congress reconvened in January 1950. However, it was obvious from the overwhelming vote in the House that the Senate would take some action to improve the Social Security Act. What that action actually was is discussed later.

Offsetting the foregoing favorable legislative activity, there was a very important unfavorable administrative development. On June 20, 1949, the President signed the Reorganization Act of 1949 under which he could reorganize agencies of government unless either house rejected within 60 days a specific plan submitted to it. Accordingly, the President, on the same day, submitted a number of plans. Reorganization Plan No. 1 would have created a Department of Welfare to replace the Federal Security Agency. This plan was rejected, largely because of opposition to Oscar R. Ewing, the Federal Security Administrator. This opposition was spearheaded by the American Medical Association, which attacked him because of his advocacy of national health insurance.

Reorganization Plan No. 2 transferred the employment service and unemployment insurance activities of the Social Security Administration to the Department of Labor. As already stated, the United States Employment Service had been transferred the previous year from the Department of Labor to the Federal Security Agency by an appropriation bill passed over the President's veto. At that time the Social Security Administration, with the approval of the Federal Security Administrator, placed the service in the Bureau of Employment Security. It was made a division of that bureau coordinate with the Unemployment Insurance Service.

In 1948 the Director of the United States Employment Service was made Director of the Bureau of Employment Security. However, I now believe it would have been better to have maintained the United States Employment Service as a separate bureau.

There has always been a fear on the part of those interested in the successful operation of a public employment office system that its close relationship with the administration of unemployment insurance is detrimental. This fear existed at the very outset of the unemployment insurance program, although, as the 1938 annual report of the Secretary of Labor stated, this close link had resulted in "building up the active files of local employment offices both in quality and quantity" and in "an increased motivation for the use of employment offices by employers."

So far as I can determine, the fear is based on two main arguments, both of which have considerable validity. One is that employment service personnel in the local offices is likely to be diverted from the basic worker-finding and job-finding activities to claims-taking activities. Specifically, it is contended that, when there is an increase in unemployment, the local staff, instead of intensifying its efforts to find jobs and provide placement services, is put to work processing the increased claims load. The other argument is that, even if this diversion of personnel does not occur, the mere physical proximity of unemployment insurance activities to employment service activities causes the local employment office to be stigmatized as an "unemployment office." Thus, highly qualified workers and employers interested in employing such workers are discouraged from patronizing the office.

Proper administrative organization and procedures can and have solved the problem in many states of diversion of local employment service personnel. Likewise, proper location and layout of the local office, coupled with sustained promotional activities, can and have solved the problem of the undesirable image of an "unemployment office."

However, I now believe that more rapid and general progress might have been made in simultaneously relating and strengthening the respective employment service functions and unemployment insurance functions if two separate bureaus had been maintained. Moreover, it might have made it feasible in 1949 to transfer only the United States Employment Service to the Department of Labor, leaving the unemployment insurance program with the Social Security Administration.

I was, and still am, deeply disturbed about the separation of the unemployment insurance program from old age, survivors', and disability insurance and from the other programs administered by the Social Security Administration prior to January 1963. It seems to me to constitute clear evidence of the same lack of understanding of the need for an integrated system of social security and integrated administration as that which has already been discussed in connection with the 1948 drastic reduction in the appropriation for centralized services.

Stated in more specific terms, it was my opinion that there existed a much closer relationship between unemployment insurance and the other social insurance programs than there was between the United States Employment Service and other programs administered by the Department of Labor. This feeling may have been due to bias on my part. However, it should be recalled that, prior to my 14 years devoted to administering the

Social Security Act, I had devoted the same length of time to administering state and federal labor legislation.

In 1949 I did not believe that the solution of this dilemma would be to return the United States Employment Service to the Department of Labor and leave the Unemployment Insurance Division with the Social Security Administration. I believed this would re-create the same administrative difficulty as had been experienced in the past when they had been separated, arising out of the fact that the administration of the employment service and of unemployment insurance were so closely interrelated. In all the states the same agency administered both functions and naturally desired to deal with a single federal agency on its budget, use of personnel, and other administrative matters.

It is my present belief that policy questions and administrative procedures involved in the federal-state relationship have become sufficiently clarified that the administrative disadvantages of separating the employment service and unemployment insurance functions at the federal level no longer outweigh the advantages of doing so.

As a matter of fact, there are now several states where the two are in separate agencies and a considerable number of states where the two functions are in separate divisions of the same agency and operate quite independently of each other. In Great Britain the two functions have always been administered by separate ministries. Apparently this arrangement has operated successfully, even though the two administrative lines do not come together in a single agency at the local level as they do in most of our states.

The reorganization plan to transfer the Bureau of Employment Security became effective on August 20, 1949, since neither house had rejected it within 60 days. Organized labor groups supported the transfer but employers' groups opposed. The Federal Security Administrator, as a presidential appointee, of course also supported the President's plan. The Interstate Conference of Employment Security Agencies did not take a position either in favor of or against the transfer.*

---

* Ironically enough, the lobbyist for an employer group, who had previously been a state employment security official and had led the attack on me in 1941 regarding the transfer of the state employment services to the

In President Truman's messages to Congress at the beginning of 1950, he made brief references to social security. He urged that Congress complete action on the bill to improve the old age and survivors' insurance system. He also urged that Congress "strengthen our unemployment compensation law." In the field of health he called attention to his message of April 22, 1949, and emphasized the need to fill in a major gap in our social security system by providing for a comprehensive system of prepaid medical care insurance financed predominantly by employer and employee contributions. The Social Security Administration repeated its recommendations of previous years.

On seven separate occasions since the Social Security Act had been passed, the scheduled increase in the contribution rate from 1 per cent to 1½ per cent (payable each by the employee and by the employer) had been postponed. However, on January 1, 1950, the scheduled increase in the contribution rate under the old age and survivors' insurance system was permitted to go into effect. This was encouraging evidence that the Congress intended to liberalize the law.

As further evidence of this intention, the Senate Committee on Finance began its hearings January 17 on the bill passed by the House just before the adjournment of Congress. The hearings started with four days of testimony by me. They continued for

---

federal government, offered to organize opposition to the President's plan if I desired him to do so. I declined the offer, which I considered decidedly improper. However, I claim no particular virtue in having done this.

This lobbyist for an employer's group actually has served all these years as the unofficial representative of the state employment security administrators. Indeed, his chief value to the employer group was and still is the great influence he has with these administrators who, in turn, have great influence with members of Congress. I had no doubt that this lobbyist hoped for some quid pro quo, perhaps a more favorable attitude toward employer experience rating, which I had continued to criticize for its adverse effect on adequate unemployment benefits.

I also had no doubt that this lobbyist would do his utmost to defeat the plan anyway. This would not be because the lobbyist had any great regard for or confidence in me. Rather, it would be because he considered the Social Security Administration the lesser evil, as compared with the U.S. Department of Labor. His employer-constituents expressed great fear that the Department of Labor would be susceptible to the influence of organized labor in the operation of the employment service and in its attitude toward employer experience rating. I wish to make it clear that I consider this a mistaken view.

more than two months and resulted in 2,400 pages of testimony, practically matching the record set by the House Ways and Means Committee.

The Chairman, at the very outset, placed in the record a tabular comparison of the recommendations of the advisory council to the Senate Committee on Finance and the provisions of the social security bill as it was passed by the House. I was asked to outline my recommendations and to indicate how they differed from the recommendations of the advisory council and from the provisions of the House bill.

I stated that I was in general agreement with the recommendations of the advisory council concerning the old age and survivors' insurance system, except that I strongly favored the retention of the annual increment of 1 per cent in the benefit amount for every year the worker was covered. The advisory council had recommended that this be eliminated so that higher benefits could be paid in the early years without increasing the long-range cost.

Concerning public assistance, I reiterated my recommendation that the federal grant be related to the fiscal capacity of a state as measured by its per capita income and that the federal government share in the cost of "general assistance." The advisory council, strangely enough, had expressed fear that relating the federal grants to fiscal capacity might result in the low-income states' getting so much federal reimbursement that they might be tempted to fix too high a level of assistance payments. Also strangely enough, the advisory council had made a strong case for federal grants to help the states in meeting the cost of "general assistance," but proposed that the federal matching be fixed at a far lower percentage than for old age assistance, blind assistance, and aid to dependent children.

The advisory council had also made rather sweeping recommendations to improve the unemployment insurance system. These included extension of coverage, an increase in the maximum wage for the calculation of contributions and benefits, contributions by employees as well as employers, a 1½ per cent minimum combined contribution rate, and federal standards for disqualifications. Five of the seventeen advisory council members recommended nationalization of the unemployment insurance system.

Since the Administration had not had an unemployment insurance bill introduced during either the previous session or the current session, neither the House Ways and Means Committee nor the Senate Committee on Finance made any substantive changes in the Unemployment Tax Act except to modify the definition of "wages" and "employment" in that act to conform in minor respects to the changes that were being made in the old age and survivors' insurance system. However, the maximum annual wage subject to the federal unemployment tax was left at $3,000, and the exclusion of agriculture and domestic workers and, of course, the self-employed was continued.

During the course of the hearings I was asked the following question by Senator Taft: "What would you think of the suggestion that we simply put everybody under the Federal old-age and survivors insurance at a minimum rate? They get a minimum. With no wage credit, they get a minimum, $25. or $30., separated entirely from the States. Give no further assistance to the States. The State could add to that whatever it wanted in the case of each State. In other words, if we are going to give an old age pension to a man who has 1-year credit, why not give it to him when he has not had any credit? We will never get to the old-age insurance plan under this thing. The old-age assistance is growing still and is something that is going to grow for some time. Why do you not put the whole thing under the old-age insurance and give everybody a flat figure and simply say to the States, if this is not enough, and it would not be enough probably for a lot of them, it is up to the States to provide the addition to it."

My reply was, "First, you have a political question. It really is not a technical question. It is a political question of what this flat amount is going to be. You suggest $25. Somebody else may suggest $50. Somebody else might suggest $100."

Senator Millikin, who had been Chairman of the committee in the previous Congress, entered the discussion to say, "Let us say everybody got $25. and that the States had nothing to do with the $25. The States would immediately set a pressure here for everybody to get $75. . . . I want to make clear I am against setting a flat amount. . . ."

I went on to say, "You cannot, to my mind, develop anything along the lines that you have suggested unless you decide first and foremost whether you are going to have universal coverage and universal contribution to finance the future. . . ."

It is interesting to note that Republican Senator Hugh Butler of Nebraska submitted a minority report recommending that the Senate reject the bill in the form recommended by the Senate Finance Committee. He suggested that a research body be set up consisting largely of actuaries, saying, "Let the most careful examination be made of the possibilities of a universal flat-rate pension system which may be financed on a strictly pay-as-you-go basis." Senator Butler was from the same state as Congressman Curtis (now Senator), the member of the Ways and Means Committee who had written the separate minority report, advocating a system of uniform benefits financed by a flat percentage income tax.

The Senate Committee on Finance submitted its report to the Senate on May 17. It was concurred in by all members except Senator Butler. However, two Democratic members reserved the right to support "additional liberalizing amendments" on the floor of the Senate.

The recommendations of the Senate Committee on Finance differed from the House bill in the following major respects:

I. Old age and survivors' insurance
   1. The definition of the term "employee" made more restrictive
   2. Regularly employed agricultural workers covered, with minor exceptions
   3. Employees of nonprofit organizations covered on a compulsory basis, but employers on a voluntary basis. If the employer did not elect to be covered, the wages credited were cut in half.
   4. Benefits increased somewhat more
   5. Annual increment for each year of covered employment completely eliminated
   6. Eligibility conditions greatly liberalized for older workers with as few as six quarters of coverage since January 1, 1937, to become eligible. However, with the passage of time this minimum requirement would automatically increase to roughly one-half of the elapsed time since January 1, 1951.
   7. Inclusion of benefits for permanent total disability eliminated
II. Public assistance and welfare

1. Inclusion of a new category of assistance to needy persons permanently and totally disabled eliminated
2. Liberalization of the federal grant for aid to dependent children by including the caretaker eliminated
3. Liberalization of the federal matching formula eliminated
4. Existing federal matching ratio of 75 per cent for old age assistance reduced to 50 per cent if the needy person became eligible for old age insurance benefits after the passage of this bill

The Senate debated this social security bill from June 13 to June 20. Ranking Republican Senators Millikin and Taft supported the bill. The only strong opposition came from Senator Butler of Nebraska and Senator Cain of Washington, who both favored a uniform universal old age pension not related to income loss or need.

On the floor of the Senate only two important substantive changes were made in the recommendations of the committee. One was to raise the maximum annual earnings for calculating contributions and benefits from $3,000 to $3,600 to correspond with the amount in the bill as it came from the House. The other was to include the caretaker as a person eligible under aid to dependent children. However, there was added to the recommendations of the Committee on Finance an amendment to the unemployment compensation provisions in the federal statutes which affected the authority of the Secretary of Labor to find that a state unemployment insurance law failed to meet federal standards for administrative grants and for tax credit. This amendment provided that the Secretary could not find that a state agency had denied unemployment compensation to individuals entitled thereto until the question of entitlement had been decided by the state's highest judicial authority. It further provided that a finding of the Secretary that the state law (as interpreted by the highest judicial authority) violated any of the requirements of the Federal Unemployment Tax Act could not become effective until 90 days after the governor of the state had been notified of such finding.

This change in the federal law was made because of a disagreement which had arisen between the federal Bureau of Employment Security and the California unemployment compensation agency as to whether the state agency was violating the section of the federal law prohibiting the denial of compensation to any otherwise eligible individual for refusing to accept a job involved in a labor dispute.

The final vote on the bill was 81 to 2. However, because of the criticisms and doubts expressed during the course of the Senate debate, both the Democratic and the Republican members of the Senate Committee on Finance agreed to Senate Resolution 300 directing the committee to make a further study of the social security program.

When the bill, as passed by the Senate, was returned to the House on June 20, the House did not agree to the changes but sent the bill to conference. Actually it was not until August 1 that the House and Senate conferees reached agreement. The major points at issue were resolved as follows:

I. Old age and survivors' insurance
　1. Agreement by House conferees to the inclusion of regularly employed agricultural workers
　2. Coverage of employees of nonprofit organizations on a voluntary basis, provided the employer elected to be covered and two-thirds of his employees agreed. Present employees who did not agree were not covered but all new employees would be.
　3. Modification of definition of the term "employee" to correspond more closely to the House definition
　4. Acceptance of the more liberal benefit formula adopted by the Senate
　5. Acceptance of Senate's elimination of the annual increment
　6. Acceptance of the more liberal eligibility conditions adopted by the Senate
　7. Acceptance of Senate's exclusion of benefits for permanent total disability
　8. Rescheduling of the next increase in the contribution rate, from 1½ per cent to 2 per cent (each by employer and employee), to January 1, 1953, instead of January 1, 1951, as proposed by House, or January 1, 1956, as proposed by Senate
II. Public assistance and welfare
　1. Acceptance of the inclusion in the House bill of a new category of public assistance to needy persons permanently and totally disabled
　2. Acceptance of Senate's elimination of the increased federal matching ratio contained in the House bill
　3. Elimination of Senate's reduction in the federal matching ratio for old age assistance if the needy person was eligible for old age insurance benefits

The conference report was accepted by both the House and the Senate, and the bill was sent to the President, who signed it on August 28, 1950. Thus, after a year and a half of congressional consideration, the first major revision of the Social Security Act since 1939 became law. Seldom has a single piece of legislation received such long and intensive consideration.

The 1950 amendments unquestionably represented a major advance in the strengthening of our social security system. About 8 million more workers were brought under the protection of the old age and survivors' insurance system on a compulsory basis. Of these more than one-half were self-employed. In addition, another 2½ million could be covered on an optional basis. The benefits were increased by about 80 per cent on the average, and eligibility conditions were greatly liberalized. This was a little more than the increase in the price level since 1937 but only two-thirds of the increase in the wage level since then. Federal matching under the public assistance provisions was liberalized to include assistance to the permanently and totally disabled, assistance to the caretaker of a dependent child, cash assistance to persons otherwise eligible but located in public medical institutions, and the cost of medical care not covered by the cash assistance grant.

However, the amendments fell short of the recommendations made by the President and by me in several important respects. The extension of coverage of the old age and survivors' insurance system included only "regularly employed" agricultural employees and none of the farm operators. Likewise, professional persons were not included in the self-employed persons who were covered. The failure to include benefits for disabled persons, at least those permanently and totally disabled, was most unfortunate.

The chief reason for the exclusion of insurance benefits for disabled persons was the opposition of the American Medical Association, plus the opposition of employers' organizations and casualty insurance companies. The representative of the American Medical Association testified that, "To initiate a Federal disability program would represent another step toward wholesale nationalization of medical care and the socialization of the practice of medicine." The opponents all emphasized the great administrative difficulties and the high cost of such benefits.

The opposition of the American Medical Association represented a change in the position it had taken throughout the years, even as late as 1947 when its House of Delegates adopted a report saying, "Social security measures to maintain income such as disability insurance, old age insurance, and public assistance are likewise of vital importance."

Similarly, the opposition of the U.S. Chamber of Commerce represented a change in its position since 1944 when it adopted by an overwhelming vote a proposal recommended by its Committee on Social Security that, "For workers totally and permanently disabled at or after age 55 a system of benefit payments, calculated on a basis consistent with that for Old Age and Survivors Insurance, should be provided. . . . Such a plan for premature superannuation would also reduce possible pressure for a reduction of the retirement age for those who are able to work until 65.

I was also concerned about the elimination of the annual increment in the monthly benefit for every year of coverage. I recognized that it was desirable to increase the benefits payable in the early years without increasing unduly the long-range cost. However, I was concerned about the criticism that young workers paying contributions over a long period of years would not "get their money's worth" in benefits.

The effect on public opinion of this criticism is probably not so serious today since it is largely offset by the fact that more than 10 per cent of the entire population are now receiving monthly benefits—and these are old people, widows, orphans, and seriously disabled persons.

It is true that for the next ten to fifteen years even high-wage earners will continue to receive far more protection than they could purchase from a private insurance company with the contributions they have made. By that time it is possible that, because of the almost universal coverage of this social insurance system, the desirability of financing a part of the cost from general revenues will be recognized, so that the individual contribution rate will not need to rise above the level justified by the protection afforded long-term contributors. Another way to prevent this from happening would be to increase the proportion of the cost financed by employers and decrease the proportion financed by employees and self-employed persons.

Regarding public assistance, the major respects in which the 1950 amendments fell short of the Administration's recommendations were failure to provide federal matching for assistance rendered all needy persons; failure to provide this matching in accordance with a ratio directly related to an individual state's fiscal ability to meet its share of the total cost; failure to require statewide standards assuring similar treatment of persons in similar circumstances; and failure to eliminate residence and citizenship requirements.

Of course, the 1950 amendments also did nothing to improve the unemployment insurance system. Neither did they do anything to fill the major gap still remaining in our social insurance system, the failure to provide any protection against the cost of medical care.

Nevertheless, the effect of the old age and survivors' insurance amendments on public assistance was impressive. The greatly liberalized eligibility requirements meant that many thousands of persons already retired and receiving old age assistance, as well as those retiring after the amendments became effective, could qualify for insurance benefits. Moreover, the increased monthly insurance benefits payable to persons already retired and to those retiring in the future meant they would not be in need of supplementary old age assistance. The result was that the old age assistance rolls immediately began to decrease after September 1950, the first month that the old age and survivors' insurance amendments were in effect. By February 1951 the number of persons receiving retirement insurance benefits exceeded, for the first time, the number receiving old age assistance. The number of recipients of old age assistance has continued to decrease ever since, in spite of the continued increase in the number and proportion of aged persons in our population.

The number of recipients of aid to dependent children also decreased temporarily but the interruption of the upward trend was only temporary, because the great majority of dependent children were dependent from causes other than the death of the breadwinner. Some were dependent because of the disability of the breadwinner. But most were dependent because of the "absence from the home" of the breadwinner. "Absence from the home" includes the situation of illegitimate children who have been deprived of parental support as well as children who have been deprived of such support because of the breakup of the marriage relationship. Of course, no social insurance system can provide protection against destitution due to such causes, which have continued to grow in seriousness.

The main administrative impact of the 1950 amendments was, of course, upon the Bureau of Old Age and Survivors Insurance. Its claims load immediately doubled, and at its peak was four times higher than before the amendments. Its total work-load increased 47 per cent during the fiscal year which began July 1, 1950, as a result of the liberalized eligibility requirements and extended coverage. However, the man-hours required to handle this increased work-load increased only 20 per cent. The bureau was able to recalculate and process the benefits payable to the three million beneficiaries on the rolls so that their September checks were mailed out on time, October 3, only 36 days after the law was signed.

The Bureau of Public Assistance had the task of interpreting the amendments and assisting the state agencies in the development of their plans to put them into effect. One of its problems was to explain to the state agencies how far the new category of aid to the permanently and totally disabled could be extended to include persons not completely bedridden and unable to help themselves. The bureau indicated that persons would be eligible if their impairment was sufficiently severe to prevent them from engaging in a useful occupation (including homemaking). The bureau also urged each state to establish a close relationship with the state rehabilitation agency. These relationships have proved to be very rewarding throughout the years. The bureau also assisted the state agencies to define the extent to which they would pay for medical care.

There were two other amendments to the public assistance provisions of the act which the bureau assisted the state agencies in administering. One required that a state plan for aid to dependent children must provide for notifying law-enforcement officials regarding children deserted by a parent. The other required that a state plan for old age assistance, aid to the blind, or aid to the permanently and totally disabled must provide for a state authority to be responsible for establishing and maintaining standards for medical institutions in which recipients reside. Both amendments required interpretation and the development of appropriate administrative procedures.

The President, in his Message on the State of the Union, January 8, 1951, and in his Budget Message, January 15, 1951, mentioned the need for improving our social security system. In these messages he emphasized that social insurance rather than public assistance was "the primary vehicle for providing social security." He stressed particularly the need to provide "insurance against loss of earnings through sickness, and against the high costs of modern medical care." He proposed specifically that since a period of preparation would be required to set up the health insurance system, "a small payroll tax of one-fourth of 1 percent each on employees and employers be levied to provide for initial expenses.

The annual report of the Social Security Administration for the fiscal year ended June 30, 1950, was sent to the Congress shortly thereafter. It reiterated the recommendations made in previous years for a comprehensive contributory federal social insurance system and a comprehensive federal-state system of public assistance and welfare services. It continued to emphasize that the major gap in the social insurance provisions of the Social Security Act was failure to provide protection against wage loss due to disability and failure to provide protection against the cost of medical care. It continued to recommend that protection against unemployment should be included in the federal social insurance system but did not make any specific recommendations about unemployment insurance provisions, since the Bureau of Employment Security had been transferred to the U.S. Department of Labor.

While there was no legislation in 1951 primarily concerned with the social insurance provisions of the Social Security Act, there was a very important amendment to the Railroad Retirement Act, effective October 30. This amendment provided, in effect, for joint coverage of railroad employees by the Railroad Retirement Act and the old age and survivors' insurance system.

It will be recalled that according to a 1946 amendment wages earned under both systems would be combined in determining survivors' benefits. The 1951 amendment went further and provided for coordination with respect to retirement benefits as well. If the worker had less than ten years of railroad employment at the time of his death or retirement, his railroad wages were credited under the old age and survivors' insurance system for benefit purposes. If he had more than ten years of railroad employment, his retirement benefits were calculated separately under each system. However, survivors' benefits were always to be calculated on the combined wages, benefits being paid under the Railroad Retirement Act if there had been more than ten years' railroad employment, and under the old age and survivors' insurance system if there had been less than ten years' railroad employment.

The only other social security legislation passed in 1951 was in the form of a rider to the Revenue Act of 1951. This was the so-called Jenner amendment, which became effective October 20, 1951, and has remained in effect. It provides that no state shall be deprived of any grant-in-aid under the four public assistance titles of the Social Security Act because of state legislation permitting public access to public assistance financial records so long as such legislation prohibits the use of any list of names for commercial or political purposes.

This rider was attached because the Federal Security Administrator had made a finding in July 1951, following my recommendation, that the Indiana law permitting such access was in conflict with a provision of the Social Security Act requiring safeguards which "restrict the use of disclosure of information concerning applicants and recipients to purposes directly connected with the administration of the State plan." The United States District Court of the District of Columbia had upheld this finding.

The proponents of the Jenner amendment contended that there were large numbers of recipients of public assistance who were not in need. They believed that such persons or their relatives would be frightened or shamed by publicity so that they would leave the assistance rolls. The opponents of the Jenner amendment, including myself, believed that it was contrary to the basic purpose of the public assistance provisions of the Social Security Act, namely, to provide financial aid to needy persons in a humane and constructive manner. The opponents believed that the injury done to eligible persons by this public invasion of their private lives would far outweigh any saving of public funds due to the elimination of ineligible persons from the assistance rolls.

The Social Security Administration interpreted the Jenner amendment to permit public access only to the rolls showing the names of recipients and the amount of public assistance they received, but not to permit access to the case records themselves which usually contained private and confidential information received from not only the recipients but others familiar with their circumstances. Actually, few persons other than newspaper reporters inspected the rolls, and these only in the first few months after the Jenner amendment became law. Moreover, during the year following, the decline in public assistance rolls in the seven states that permitted public access was no greater than in the states that did not. Clearly, the general decline throughout the country was due to the expansion of the old age and survivors' insurance system and the higher level of employment.

A serious situation developed during the closing months of 1950 and the early part of 1951 because of the failure of the State of New York to adopt statewide standards for determining eligibility for public assistance and the extent of need. From the very beginning the Social Security Board had interpreted the public assistance provisions of the Social Security Act to require that a state plan must assure that persons in similar circumstances were treated similarly throughout the state. However, it was not until February 1949 that the Bureau of Public Assistance issued a statement of principles for the use of state agencies in the determination of eligibility and amount of assistance.

States that had direct state administration, and not administration through local governmental units, rather readily recognized the necessity of statewide standards for the guidance of their field employees. However, many states that administered the plans through local governmental units were reluctant to impose statewide standards because of the opposition of the local officials who insisted upon establishing their own standards. Ironically enough, my home state, Wisconsin, was one of these, contending that there was a long tradition of "home rule."

Unfortunately, there was not (and there still is not) an explicit provision in the law requiring equitable treatment of needy individuals in similar circumstances wherever they may live in the state. The 1949 bill prepared by the Social Security Administration contained such a requirement but it was eliminated by the House Ways and Means Committee. However, the Social Security Board and I, as Commissioner for Social Security, believed it was basic to the purpose of the public assistance provisions and clearly implicit in all of the other specific requirements, such as "the plan shall be in effect in all political subdivisions, and, if administered by them, be mandatory on them"; and "granting an opportunity for a fair hearing before the State agency to any individual whose claim under the plan is denied."

The Commissioner of Welfare of the State of New York contended that each county could establish its own standards for the determination of eligibility and the extent of need—in effect, that a state plan could consist of a collection of county plans with varying standards.

In November 1950 the state's Commissioner of Welfare was notified that the federal government would be obliged to cease making further grants unless statewide standards were established. Several heated conferences were held at which the state's Commissioner of Welfare contended that the federal law did not require statewide standards and that it would not be possible to establish such standards because of the varying conditions throughout the state. It was not entirely clear whether it was being contended that the standard of living or the cost of a given standard of living varied throughout the state. In either event it would not justify the existing wide variation in the amount of property an applicant could possess and still be eligible.

It was finally agreed that a joint group of home economists would make a study of the actual cost of the family budgets of recipients in typical urban and rural areas of the state. To the surprise of the state officials, it was found that there was very little difference between New York City and upstate New York, except for rent. This facilitated an agreement between the federal and state officials, which was consummated in May 1951.*

In the early part of January 1952 President Truman sent to the Congress his Message on the State of the Union, his Economic Report, and his Budget Message. He also announced the appointment of a Commission on the Health Needs of the Nation. The 16-member commission consisted of doctors, dentists, labor leaders, employers, and others, none of whom was in the government.

The chief recommendations regarding social security which the President made in these messages were more adequate retirement and survivors' benefits, further extension of coverage, and inclusion of benefits for permanent and total disability under the federal old age and survivors' insurance system; strengthening the federal-state unemployment insurance system; and "additional help on a matching basis" to assist the states to bear the costs of public assistance.

The annual report of the Social Security Administration for the fiscal year ended June 30, 1951, was sent to the Congress in April 1952. The recommendations which it contained were in some respects more detailed than the President's had been but were, of course, in accord with his. Thus, while emphasizing again that the great gap was failure to provide protection against wage loss due to disability and protection against the cost of medical care, the report specifically recommended that hospitalization benefits be provided for workers and their dependents who had already become eligible for monthly cash benefits under the old age and survivors' insurance system.

It will be recalled that in 1942 the Social Security Board had recommended hospital benefits for persons insured under the old age and survivors' insurance system. This was a year before it recommended a comprehensive health insurance system. The 1951 proposal, it should be noted, was even more limited than the

---

* A circumstance which had complicated reaching an agreement was the fact that Governor Dewey and Federal Security Administrator Ewing (who came from New York) were political adversaries. Therefore, I was surprised and gratified that at the Governors' Conference in October 1951 Governor Dewey came up to me and thanked me for my help in reaching an agreement. I am also happy to record that, with the settlement of the disagreement with New York, the establishment of statewide standards ceased to be an issue between the federal government and the states.

1942 proposal because it applied only to persons already entitled to monthly cash benefits, i.e., workers at least 65 years old, widows, orphans, and elderly dependent parents.

But even this very limited proposal failed to receive much congressional attention. This may have been because, before the report containing the proposal reached Congress, the President had appointed the commission on health needs. Indeed, the President said in his Economic Report, "Looking further ahead, other improvements are needed to provide protection to meet costs of medical care and loss of earnings due to illness; these and other health problems will be studied by the President's Commission on the Health Needs of the Nation."

While three bills providing for hospitalization benefits for beneficiaries under the old age and survivors' insurance system were introduced, no hearings were held on them. In every subsequent session of Congress similar bills have been introduced. The more recent ones have been limited to aged persons entitled to retirement benefits

While the Social Security Administration report continued to recommend protection against income loss due to permanent total disability as a part of the federal old age and survivors' insurance system, the recommendation concerning protection against income loss due to temporary disability was couched in more general terms. It read as follows: "The Administration recommends a nation-wide program of temporary disability insurance appropriately related to permanent and total disability insurance, old age and survivors insurance, and unemployment insurance." The reason for the report's not being more specific was that unemployment insurance was no longer administered by the Social Security Administration but by the U.S. Department of Labor.

In the area of public assistance, the Commissioner's annual report for the first time recommended that federal matching of the cost of public assistance should be based entirely upon the average payment per recipient and should no longer exclude individual payments in excess of specified individual maximums in arriving at the maximum average payment. This would result in some increased federal matching because payments above the average, in some individual cases, would be offset by payments below the average in other cases. However, the great advantage would be that it would facilitate federal matching of the cost of medical care, which is highly unpredictable and varied in the individual case but not so when averaged.

On May 16 the Ways and Means Committee reported out a bill without having held hearings. The committee explained in its report that all of its recommendations were within areas which had been intensively studied. It also stated that, "Your committee recognizes that there are other amendments to the old-age and survivors insurance program which are needed, but these six have been selected because of their urgency and because of the widespread agreement on their desirability." There was no formal vote taken by the committee but a voice vote indicated that, with the exception of perhaps one or two Republican members, the committee was in agreement. Consequently there was no minority report.

The six "urgently needed changes in the old-age and survivors insurance program" which the committee listed in its report were (1) benefit increases; (2) liberalization of the retirement test; (3) wage credits for military service during emergency period; (4) preservation of insurance rights for those permanently and totally disabled, (5) removal of bar to coverage for certain persons under state and local retirement systems; (6) correction of defects in benefit computation provisions.

The proposed increase in benefits averaged 12½ per cent. The liberalization of the retirement test consisted of permitting a beneficiary to earn $70 a month instead of $50 without having his retirement benefit suspended. The existing provision granting a wage credit of $160 a month for World War II service was extended to include war service thereafter until January 1, 1954. The earlier opportunity given the states to cover, under old age and survivors' insurance, state and local employees not covered by other retirement systems was extended to permit coverage of such employees if two-thirds of these employees voted in favor of being covered.

The most important change recommended was the proposal to preserve the already acquired rights of persons who became permanently and totally disabled. This proposal would not result in payment of benefits for a period of disability but would maintain the eligibility for retirement and survivors' insurance benefits and the monthly amount of such benefits calculated as of the date of onset of the disability. This was important because under existing law eligibility was dependent upon the proportion of elapsed time since a person had been engaged in insured employment. A period of disability was counted as part of the elapsed time but not as a part of the time under insured employment. Moreover, the average monthly wage upon which the monthly benefit was dependent was calculated by using the total elapsed time as the divisor, including the period of disability in the divisor.

The Chairman of the Ways and Means Committee on May 19 made a motion to suspend the rules and pass the bill, which required a two-thirds vote. To his amazement the Republican members of his committee, with one exception, failed to support his motion, and 70 per cent of the Republican members of the House voted against the motion. This surprising development was due to telegrams sent by the Washington representative of the American Medical Association to members of the House of Representatives opposing this so-called disability freeze provision. The telegram called this provision "socialized medicine," contending that "it gives the Federal Security Administrator absolute power over certain medical activities."

The ranking Republican member of the Ways and Means Committee, Daniel Reed of New York, called the provision a "sneak attack," the expression which had been in current use to describe the Pearl Harbor attack. He went on to say that, "The great issue presented by H.R. 7800 is whether we in the legislative branch of the Government are now to surrender our prerogatives and our duty under the Constitution to the Federal Security Agency, headed by Mr. Oscar Ewing." The Chairman of the Ways and Means Committee countered by asserting that there was "no more socialized medicine in [this provision] than there is frost in the sun."

The bill was sent back to the Ways and Means Committee, which struck out the language of the provision that made specific reference to the Federal Security Administrator. However, the opponents of the bill, led by Congressman Reed, contended that the Federal Security Administrator still had full authority under section 205 (which had been in the old age and survivors' title of the act since 1939) to issue rules and regulations for establishing the right to benefits. This authority, it was argued, would still enable the Federal Security Administrator, a known advocate of health insurance, to introduce socialized medicine into the social insurance program. Congressman Reed complained bitterly that this change in the bill was made by the Democratic members of the Ways and Means Committee in a "secret political conclave" from which the Republican members had been excluded.

Chairman Doughton of the Ways and Means Committee replied by pointing out that the entire provision, section 3, relative to the "disability freeze" had been taken from a bill introduced by a Republican member of the committee. He also pointed out that Congressman Reed himself had apparently favored this provision until the American Medical Association had sent its avalanche of telegrams to members of Congress on May 19. As evidence, he pointed out that on that very day Congressman Reed had announced (as reported on page 3,066 of the *Congressional Record*) that he would introduce a "Republican Social Security Bill" and had said that "section 3 of the bill is a very important improvement which preserves the insurance rights of persons permanently and totally disabled."

The Chairman of the Ways and Means Committee concluded by saying, "This is probably the last social security bill which I will ever introduce for, as you know, I am going out of Congress and what political motives could I have?" An immediate vote was not taken because of objection that a quorum was not present.

The next day, without further debate, the House voted to suspend the rules and passed the bill by a vote of 361 yeas and 22 nays on June 17. This large vote was in part a tribute to the Chairman of the Ways and Means Committee and a repudiation of the attack that had been made upon him.

When the bill reached the Senate, it was referred to the Committee on Finance, which proceeded immediately to consider it in executive session. The committee reported the bill favorably to the Senate on June 23, with the following major changes: (1) increasing the maximum earnings permitted under the "retirement test" from $70 to $100; (2) deleting the provision to preserve the insurance rights for persons permanently and totally disabled; (3) deleting the provision which removed the bar to coverage for state and local employees already under existing retirement systems. The committee explained that there was insufficient time for the hearings which would have been necessary for proper consideration of these two provisions.

Senator McFarland, who had succeeded at a previous session of Congress in having the federal matching ratio for public assistance payments raised above the original 50 per cent, again submitted an amendment to increase the ratio further. This successive increase in the matching ratio seems to support President Roosevelt's 1939 prediction that, "Once you get off the 50–50 matching basis, the sky's the limit and before you know it, we'll be paying the whole bill." All that I can say in defense of my continued advocacy of a matching ratio related to a state's per capita income is that it is based on an objective and rational standard which might have prevented the matching ratio from becoming a political football.

The bill as reported by the Senate Committee on Finance, with the addition of the McFarland amendment, was passed by the Senate and sent back to the House, which disagreed; whereupon it was sent to conference. The House conferees recommended that the House accept the Senate's deletion of the provision which removed the bar to coverage of state and local employees already under existing retirement systems. The conferees recommended that the maximum earnings permitted without loss of monthly benefits be compromised at $75 a month. They also recommended that the McFarland amendment be accepted for a temporary period, expiring September 30, 1954.

On the so-called disability freeze provision, the conferees recommended a strange compromise. It was that the provision would specify that no application for preserving already acquired insurance rights could be accepted prior to July 1, 1953, and that the entire amendment itself would cease to be effective the day before, i.e., June 30, 1953! The amendment also specified that the determination of whether a disability existed and the length of time it existed must be made by a state agency; that the Federal Security Administrator must enter into such an agreement with a state agency; and that he could only reverse a state agency's determination to make it less favorable to the applicant. That is to say, he could decide that an applicant was not disabled or had a disability which had lasted for a shorter period of time, but he could not decide that an applicant was disabled or had a disability which had lasted for a longer time.

The conference report contained the following explanation of this abortive "disability freeze" provision:

> The action recommended by the conferees will permit appropriate steps to be taken for the working out of tentative agreements with the States for possible administration of these provisions. It is the intent of the conferees that hearings will be held on this entire matter early in 1953 and at that time the congressional committees will go into the administrative and other provisions. It is intended to obtain the views at that time of interested groups on the methods of obtaining evidence of disability, under what circumstances and by whom determinations should be made, and whether or not these provisions or any modifications thereof should be enacted into permanent law.

The bill as amended in accordance with the conferees' recommendation was passed by both houses on Saturday, July 5, and Congress adjourned on July 7. The bill was signed by President Truman on July 18.

In a statement the President issued at the time he signed the bill, he said:

> The provision thus nullified by this extraordinary arrangement is analogous to the waiver of premiums in private insurance policies. This provision would permit aged persons whose disability has forced them into early retirement to have their benefits recomputed so that lost time due to their disability would not count against them. . . .

The net result of the medical lobby's maneuvering was the impairment of insurance protection for millions of disabled Americans. What the lobby could not engineer outright, it won by delay. And be it noted that this victory for the lobby, at the people's expense, was accomplished by a great majority of the Republicans in the House.

The only other legislation passed in 1952 which was related to social security was contained in the Veterans' Readjustment Assistance Act of 1952 (known as the G.I. Bill of Rights for Korean Veterans). Title IV of that act provided payments of $26 a week for each week of involuntary unemployment, up to a maximum of $676, for veterans with military service between June 27, 1950, and January 31, 1955. If a veteran qualified for unemployment insurance under any other law, he was entitled to receive only the difference between $26 and the amount of weekly benefit to which he was entitled under the other law if such amount was less. This program, like the previous Servicemen's Readjustment Act of 1944, was administered by the state unemployment insurance agencies and in accordance with the unemployment compensation law of the state where the veteran was located, "insofar as such law is applicable."

This act differed materially from the Servicemen's Readjustment Act of 1944. That act provided a uniform amount of $20 a week for involuntary unemployment (up to 52 weeks). It also provided benefits to "self-employed veterans endeavoring to establish businesses or professions." It permitted a veteran to choose whether he would make a claim for a federal readjustment allowance or for state unemployment insurance, if he had acquired any rights thereunder. Since $20 was usually in excess of the amount payable under a state law, the result was that in the peak year of 1946 the total federal readjustment allowances amounted to $1,553,407,000 as compared with state unemployment insurance benefits of $1,094,850,000.

The 1944 act had its own eligibility and disqualification requirements, whereas the 1952 act utilized the individual state's eligibility and disqualification requirements (except for outright cancellation of benefits). Thus, whether or not an unemployed veteran actually was entitled to benefits depended upon where he applied for benefits. This may have been necessary to protect the federal government, since otherwise the state agencies would have the opportunity as well as the financial incentive to declare applicants ineligible or disqualified under the state law but entitled to veterans' benefits. However, it illustrates the anomaly of relying upon state administration and state laws to implement a national law providing benefits to persons who have served the national government. This served as a precedent for legislation two years later providing unemployment compensation for federal civil employees.

The 1952 changes in the old age and survivors' insurance system were not substantial, the increase in benefits barely keeping pace with the increase in the price and wage level; and there was no extension of coverage. However, the inconclusive legislative action taken to preserve the rights of permanently and totally disabled persons was very significant from a long-range point of view. The reason was that at the same time it revealed the problem of providing some protection to permanently and totally disabled persons, it also made the failure to find a solution inescapably obvious. This created a situation which future Congresses could hardly avoid resolving, especially since a number of its leading members had become deeply concerned about it.

In fact, Senator George, the Chairman of the Finance Committee, stated on the floor of the Senate that, "Speaking for myself, and not for the Committee, I would be disposed to go further than the House Committee went in the question of permanent and total disability. . . . We must try to bring the permanent and totally disabled cases under old-age and survivors' insurance at an earlier age than 65." He also stated that the Finance Committee, when it met in January 1953, would take up both the question of permanent and total disability and the further voluntary extension of the old age and survivors' insurance to state and local government employees.

There were no important administrative developments in 1952. However, the work-load of the Bureau of Old Age and Survivors Insurance increased 17 per cent over the previous year. The new claims load increased 39 per cent because many potential claimants delayed filing their claims until July 1, 1952, in order to take full advantage of the more liberal benefit computation provided by the 1950 amendments. In addition, as a result of the 1952 amendments, changes had to be made in the benefit amounts of 4,600,000 beneficiaries already on the rolls. These changes had to be made between July 18 and the date the benefit checks for September were issued, because, just as in 1950, the congressmen desired the checks to be received before the November elections.*

The Bureau of Old Age and Survivors Insurance also was obliged to follow out the congressional desire that preliminary work be done in developing policies and methods for evaluating

---

* It is interesting to note that, in the face of the increased work-load, the new Republican Administration, taking office in January 1953, sharply curtailed the budget of the bureau for the second half of the fiscal year which had begun on July 1, 1952. This resulted in a 100 per cent increase in the backlog of pending claims, a delay in their processing, a decline in the quality of administration, and a reduction in service to the public.

permanent and total disabilities. The bureau obtained the advice of technical consultants from a number of state agencies on the administrative problems that would be involved in the type of federal-state agreements called for under the terms of the "freeze" provision.

It is possible that Congress might have found a less anomalous solution to the "disability freeze" problem had it not been necessary to adjourn to enable members to attend the national political conventions being held in July 1952. The platforms adopted at these conventions made no reference to this particular phase of social security, but did contain other planks that require mention.

On financing the cost of medical care, the Democratic Platform did not go further than to say, "We commend President Truman for establishing the non-partisan commission on the Health Needs of the Nation to seek an acceptable solution of this urgent problem." The Republican Platform was very specific, saying, "We are opposed to Federal compulsory health insurance with its crushing cost, wasteful inefficiency, bureaucratic dead weight, and debased standards of medical care."

The two presidential candidates followed these approaches in their respective campaign speeches. The Democratic candidate indicated his opposition to "socialized medicine" (just as President Truman had always done in advocating health insurance) and stated he looked forward to the report of the President's commission in December. The Republican candidate issued a statement that he was opposed to a national health insurance plan because it would be a "federally operated and controlled system of medical care." Instead he advocated voluntary insurance plans, together with locally administered indigent medical care programs for those unable to participate.

The Democratic Platform also contained a sentence which had been inserted without any discussion and which gave me considerable concern. It read, "We favor the complete elimination of the work clause for the reason that those contributing to the Social Security program should be permitted to draw benefits upon reaching the age of eligibility and still continue to work."

The Republican Platform did favor extension of coverage of the old age and survivors' insurance system, but also included a sentence which gave me still more concern than the sentence in the Democratic Platform. It read, "We shall make a thorough study of universal pay-as-we-go pension plans."

Concerning the proposal to eliminate the so-called retirement test or work-clause, I have always felt that this proposal ran counter to the basic purpose of social insurance—to compensate in part for loss of income actually sustained. To pay retirement benefits to persons who do not retire increases the cost of the social insurance system without providing commensurately increased protection to those who need it most, i.e., those who have retired. Thus, it fails to provide maximum protection at minimum cost. Moreover, to the extent that the minimum retirement age were to be reduced, as often proposed, the cost of eliminating the retirement test would be further increased.

The argument that those who have contributed have paid for a pension payable at the minimum retirement age is, of course, not correct. They would have been obliged to pay far more for the privilege of drawing a benefit upon reaching the minimum retirement age although continuing to work.

The argument that compelling a worker to retire in order to draw a retirement benefit discourages him from continuing to lead a personally satisfying and socially useful life is not supported by the facts. Many surveys of beneficiaries have established that at least 74 per cent of workers have retired because of ill health or retirement policies of their employers, or because they cannot find jobs. A very small percentage of those who voluntarily retired indicated they would have continued to work full time if they could have drawn both their wages and a retirement benefit as well.

While the increased cost of paying retirement benefits to those who continue to work at their regular jobs would be considerable, perhaps about one per cent of payroll, my main concern was that, by violating the principle of relating benefits to loss of income, it increased the support for universal pensions payable regardless of loss of income or established need. As again evidenced by the provision in the Republican Platform, there was still considerable agitation for such a proposal.

Because of these circumstances I felt it desirable to develop a plan which would have some chance of satisfying the demand for elimination of the "retirement test" and reduction in the minimum retirement age, without violating the principle of relating benefits to income loss. I, therefore, took every suitable occasion to propose what I called a "flexible retirement" system. I suggested (1) increasing the monthly retirement benefit amount for each year that a person deferred retiring after reaching the minimum retirement age; and (2) paying monthly benefits to persons becoming permanently and totally disabled prior to reaching the minimum retirement age.

The Democratic candidate for President, Adlai Stevenson, did not advocate the repeal of the "work clause" as did the Democratic Platform. Instead he said, "The present law should be changed to encourage people who are still alert, able-bodied and eager, to keep on working even after they are 65." I have reason to believe he had in mind the plan just outlined, since I had explained it to the persons helping him with his speech-writing.

The Republican statement relative to making a study of "universal pay-as-we-go pension plans" was disturbing because it seemed to indicate that the Republican Party was preparing to support the flat-pension approach which was still being advocated by a number of leading Republicans, including Senator Hugh Butler, a member of the Senate Finance Committee. However, the Social Security Administration was prepared to submit to the next Congress a proposal which, it hoped, would satisfy the flat-pension advocates and also preserve the advantages of the existing system. This was because immediately after the passage of the 1950 amendments the Social Security Administration had again undertaken an intensive study of the so-called double-decker approach.

It will be recalled that this approach had been under consideration prior to our entry into World War II. It consisted essentially of paying a minimum uniform pension to all aged persons plus a supplementary pension related to length of insured employment and income from such employment.

The extension of coverage and the liberalization of eligibility requirements brought about by the 1950 amendments had helped in meeting the problem of providing social insurance protection to more aged persons. It was estimated that ultimately the old age and survivors' insurance system would be paying benefits to 80 or 90 per cent of the retired aged, even without any further extension of coverage. However, in 1952 only 40 per cent of retired persons over 65 were actually receiving benefits under this system. Even though another 11 per cent of those not working were receiving benefits under some other public retirement, a sizable proportion of the aged was still not protected by any retirement system.

The Social Security Administration in its 1950, 1951, and 1952 annual reports recognized this problem of providing immediate social insurance protection to persons already retired or about to retire who could not meet even the liberalized eligibility requirements regarding length of employment in a covered occupation. The following quotation from its 1950 report is typical:

> If any such proposal for "blanketing in" the present aged is adopted, the cost of the resulting noncontributory benefits should be met out of general taxation rather than from the contributions of covered workers and their employers. In order that the cost of payment to noncontributors be kept within bounds, it is absolutely essential that any plan to bring in the present aged be accompanied by extension of coverage under the insurance system to all gainful employment. If this is done, those retiring in the future would have eligibility based on contributions and the need to pay benefits to noncontributors would be confined largely to the present aged. Only with universal coverage could a plan for "blanketing in" the present aged be considered as a transitional device which would not substantially increase the long-run cost of the system or threaten the contributory principle upon which the insurance program is founded.

We in the Social Security Administration were quite aware of the social need for protection of those already aged. We were also keenly aware of the anomaly of paying benefits far in excess of contributions to those who just met the minimum eligibility while excluding those who had had no opportunity to do so. However, we were concerned that "blanketing in" the presently aged might weaken the incentive for uncovered groups to want to be covered under a contributory social insurance system. Uncovered groups, such as farm operators, might feel that "free" benefits payable out of general taxes made it unnecessary to do so.

We were even more concerned about the effect the payment of a uniform amount would have upon a system which paid differential benefits related to differentials in earnings. If this "free" benefit amount were fixed too high in relation to the supplemental benefit based on past earnings, there would be resistance to paying contributions related to past earnings because the contributors would not be getting their "money's worth" in additional benefits. On the other hand, if this basic benefit amount were fixed too low, it would not reduce significantly the need for old age assistance. Thus, this "free" basic benefit could easily become a political football.

It was because of all these considerations that the Social Security Administration never felt justified in actually advocating a "double-decker" system. But immediately after the presidential election, a proposal of this kind became a public issue.

On November 15, 1952, eleven days after the election of a Republican President, the Board of Directors of the U.S. Chamber of Commerce voted to submit to its members a policy declaration on social security reading as follows:

> Experience now demonstrates that adherence to the basic purpose of a sound social security program for the aged requires:
>
> a) Adoption of a reasonable plan in lieu of federal grants for old age assistance, to extend immediate protection under the Old-Age and Survivors' Insurance System to the present unprotected aged; and
>
> b) Periodic adjustment of the equal taxes on employer and employees and the tax on self-employed to support benefit disbursements on a current basis.

This proposed policy declaration was printed on the first page of an explanatory pamphlet and was preceded by a statement that a "yes" vote means, "Your organization favors a single, all-inclusive system, on a pay-as-you-go basis, providing a basic layer of social security benefits to all the retired aged."

It was obvious that the issuance of this policy declaration was timed to follow the presidential election and was related to the statement in the Republican Platform already quoted. This increased its importance and the attention it received.

It was not surprising, in the light of the simple, attractive statement of the meaning of a "yes" vote, that the members of the chamber voted 16 to 1 in favor of the policy declaration. However, examination of the 14-page explanatory pamphlet accompanying the policy declaration convinced me that what was actually being proposed was unsound and would have a disastrous effect on the federal old age and survivors' insurance system as well as on the federal-state old age assistance program.

In fact, I felt that the only virtue the plan had was a negative one, in that it did not propose to repeal outright the existing old age and survivors' system and substitute for it a universal flat pension. But, even so, the proposal did pose a grave threat to the maintenance of a contributory social insurance system providing benefits related to wage loss.

Of course, any proposal to pay the minimum benefit payable under the insurance system, regardless of whether any contributions had been paid, with no other change in the benefits related to past earnings, constitutes something of a threat. Thus, this proposal to pay the minimum benefit of $25 per month to all retired aged persons meant that those who had contributed but were entitled to only this minumum amount would get nothing more in return for their contributions. Those who qualified for more than the minimum would not get all the benefits then specified in addition to the $25 payable to all retired persons, but only the amount in excess of $25. This proposal was all the more indefensible because it was proposed to pay the cost of this minimum benefit to all aged persons out of the payroll contributions of employees and employers.

It was also proposed to abolish federal grants to the states out of general revenues for old age assistance. So, in essence the entire proposal simply meant that the federal cost of old age assistance would be met out of payroll contributions instead of general revenues. This would be true for all time to come. Contributing workers at least, if not their employers, would certainly question both the logic and the equity of such a plan.

Moreover, the suggested "basic layer of social security benefits to all the retired aged" was far too low to justify the chamber's proposal to eliminate all federal grants for the old age relief programs, leaving any residual relief for state and local action. Nor was its statement justified that "relief benefits would be needed only in unusual cases where the individual concerned has extraordinary needs."

The chamber calculated the cost of its proposal upon the assumption of a $25 per month basic benefit, which was the minimum monthly benefit payable under the federal old age and survivors' insurance system. This amount was less than the amount that the states were then paying to 80 per cent of the old age assistance recipients. All the states, with the exception of about a half-dozen, would have been obliged to provide out of their own funds more than they were then appropriating to match federal funds in order to maintain even the existing level of assistance which in many states was inadequate as measured by the state's own standard of adequacy.

It was naive to believe that the states would consent to being left with a larger cost for old age assistance. Thus, there would actually be two political footballs: (1) constant pressure on the federal government to continue making grants to the states for old age assistance, and (2) constant pressure to increase the "free" basic benefit under the federal old age and survivors' insurance system to a higher amount.

Moreover, the proposed "pay-as-you-go" method of financing would have aggravated the foregoing dangers and difficulties of attempting to substitute one system of federal benefits for the two existing systems of social insurance benefits and public assistance grants from the federal government. Every year there would be a congressional debate about the financing of the benefits. This debate would inevitably involve the size of the benefits and the conditions for the receipt of such benefits, as well as the proportion of the cost to be borne out of general revenues and payroll contributions.

8.

The Uncertain Years, 1952–54

In view of the situation as it existed in December 1952, I naturally looked forward with considerable trepidation to what action the new Republican Administration would take in the field of social security regarding both legislation and administrative organization. As far as I personally was concerned, I had stated, prior to the presidential election, that I would resign as Commissioner for Social Security when I reached the minimum retirement age on May 8, 1953. Therefore, I proceeded upon the assumption that my report for the fiscal year ending June 30, 1952, would be my last.

The report, as usual, consisted partly of a recital of administrative activities, partly of an analysis of the operation of the various programs for which I had some responsibility, and partly of recommendations for improving and extending these programs.

These recommendations were similar to those made in previous reports, modified, of course, to take account of legislation that had been put into effect since previous recommendations. First of all, they called for a comprehensive, basic, nationwide system of contributory social insurance as "an orderly and equitable method of assuring continuing income to families whose earnings are interrupted by unemployment, sickness, disability, retirement, or death of the breadwinner, and of insuring families against the cost of medical care." They also called for "a public assistance program able to meet satisfactorily needs that cannot be covered by social insurance." Adequate family and child welfare services in cooperation with nongovernmental agencies were also recommended.

The President's Commission on the Health Needs of the Nation submitted its report on December 18, 1952. It was issued in five volumes, the first volume consisting of its findings and recommendations and the other four covering the material which it had assembled. The members of the commission agreed that "all persons should have access to comprehensive health services of high quality." They also agreed that a financial barrier often prevents the patient from using available health resources and proposed "prepayment as the basic method for meeting the cost of personal health services." However, the members of the commission disagreed as to the best method for promoting prepayment. The majority proposed a "cooperative Federal-State program to assist in the financing of personal health services" and federal grants-in-aid from general revenues for the purpose of assisting the states in making health services available, not only to public assistance recipients but to the general population. The majority also proposed that "the Old Age and Survivors Insurance mechanism be utilized to purchase health service benefits on a prepayment basis for beneficiaries of that insurance program, under a plan which meets Federal standards and which does not involve a means test." A minority of three contended that either "the participation of every State must be assured by Federal statute, or the Federal government must make such health services available in those States which for any reason do not participate." The commission's report received very little attention. This was probably due in part to the fact that the commission had been appointed by an Administration which was going out of office.

President Truman submitted his Message on the State of the Union to Congress on January 7, 1953. He stated in that message that he would not follow his previous custom of including proposals for legislative action but instead discuss "the course we have been following the past eight years and the position at which we have arrived." Most of his message was devoted to international affairs. However, he did include several paragraphs on domestic problems, saying that at the end of the war we were faced with the question of whether we would carry forward the great projects of social welfare that the New Deal had introduced into our national life, or would the progress of the New Deal be halted in the aftermath of war as decisively as the progress of Woodrow Wilson's New Freedom had been halted after World War I. The President then proceeded to point out the progress that had been made after the war in promoting the general welfare.

After his Inauguration, President Eisenhower also decided to submit a Message on the State of the Union, which he delivered in person on February 2, 1953. This message covered the broad field of foreign policy, fiscal and economic policy, loyalty and efficiency of government personnel, natural resources, farm policy, labor policy, and civil and social rights. He mentioned that the individual citizen must have safeguards against personal disaster inflicted by forces beyond his control, that the welfare of the people demands effective and economical performance by the government of certain indispensable social services, and that there was need for assuring the solvency of the entire social security system and for guarding against its exploitation by the irresponsible. He also stated that he would submit specific recommendations for establishing a commission to study the proper relationship among federal, state, and local programs in this whole field, together with a reorganization plan defining new administrative status for all federal activities in health, education, and social security.

The most specific legislative recommendation President Eisenhower made on social security was as follows: "The provisions of the Old Age and Survivors Insurance Law should promptly be extended to cover millions of citizens who have been left out of the Social Security System. No less important is the encouragement of privately sponsored pension plans."

This recommendation did not make it clear whether or not he was supporting the proposal of the U.S. Chamber of Commerce. Unfortunately, I did not have the confidence of the newly appointed Federal Security Administrator, Mrs. Oveta Culp Hobby, and, therefore, was not in a position to ascertain whether the President had reached any conclusion about that proposal.

I realized, of course, that with the change of administration my continuance as an official in a policy-making position was quite unthinkable. However, I did not fully appreciate that it would be quite impossible for me to be of any real assistance in briefing those who would be assuming responsibility after my departure. This was due mainly to the natural suspicion and unwillingness of officials of the incoming administration to rely upon the advice and judgment of any official identified with the New Deal, the Fair Deal, and the "Welfare State," to use the political parlance of those days.*

In an effort to be of assistance to the incoming Federal Security Administrator, I had written her on November 28, 1952, offering to send her any material she might want. On January 7, 1953, I prepared for her use a very brief memorandum, captioned "Major Problems Likely to Require Attention During the Next Six Months." This included a statement relative to the abortive permanent total-disability "freeze" and U.S. Chamber of Commerce referendum. On January 19, 1953, I prepared for her a more extensive memorandum similarly captioned, explaining that the first one dealt only with the few matters which might need attention immediately.

On February 16, I prepared a memorandum for the Federal Security Administrator, at her request, captioned "Personnel,

---

* But the personal characteristics of the new Federal Security Administrator greatly accentuated the difficulty. She gave the impression of glacial calmness, impersonality, objectivity, and decisiveness. However, an aide who worked very closely with her when she headed the Women's Army Auxiliary Corps once remarked to me that she was in reality a sensitive, shy, and uncertain person who found it painful to deal with fellow officers and to make difficult decisions. In any event, I found that the Administrator preferred written communication to oral, said very little herself after calling a general conference, and usually did not make an immediate decision.

I well remember that on one occasion the well-known industrialist, Henry J. Kaiser, asked for a conference with the Administrator to present a plan for federal aid in assisting physicians to establish medical centers where they could practice group medicine on a prepayment insurance basis if they so desired. This, incidentally, had been one of the recommendations of President Truman's Commission on the Health Needs of the Nation. Mr. Kaiser emphasized that the physicians themselves would control the organization of these centers and their functioning.

Mr. Kaiser was flanked by a number of aides who assisted him in making an elaborate exposition of his plan. He elicited such little response from the Administrator that he finally said he would try to get the necessary legislation on the assumption that she had no objection. Whereupon she said very quietly and succinctly, "If you do I shall cut your throat." This response left Mr. Kaiser speechless and terminated the conference.

Terms of Reference and Organization of an Advisory Committee on Extension of Coverage of the Old-Age and Survivors Insurance System." In a previous conference with the Administrator I had learned only that she was concerned primarily about implementing the statement in the President's message. Therefore, in this memorandum I took occasion to include the following paragraphs:

I wish to point out that even though the terms of reference of an Advisory Committee are limited to a consideration of the extension of coverage of the old-age and survivors' insurance system, there are some relationships and effects of such an extension that will need to be considered, as follows:
(1) What benefit amounts should be provided to persons newly covered and what adjustments, if any, should be made as regards benefits payable to long-time contributors;
(2) What adjustments, if any, should be made in the method of financing the benefits provided groups previously covered.
There is also the question of whether this Advisory Committee should give any thought to the significance of extension of coverage as regards Federal grants to the States for public assistance. Likewise, there is a provision in the present old-age and survivors insurance title relating to the "freezing" of benefit rights already acquired by persons who become permanently and totally disabled. This provision expires June 30, 1953.

I included in the memorandum a list of persons who might be considered for appointment to the advisory committee. This list classified the persons in three groups: from employer groups, from employee groups, and from the general public.

In the employer group I was careful to include the Chairman and one other member of the U.S. Chamber of Commerce Committee on Social Legislation, as well as representatives of the three national farmer groups. In the employee group I included representatives of both the American Federation of Labor and the Congress of Industrial Organizations. One of the persons in this group was President of the Agricultural Workers Union.

In view of the foregoing I was much disturbed when the next development was a telephone call to my secretary by an assistant of the Federal Security Administrator on February 27, informing me that the Administrator had appointed an advisory group of five "civilians" to meet with her on March 5 and that three of the five were members of the Chamber of Commerce committee but none was a representative of either organized labor or farmer groups. I was even more concerned when I was informed a few days later that Congressman Curtis, the member of the House Ways and Means Committee who had issued the minority report in 1949 calling the system "totally unmoral," had also been invited. Congressman Curtis had also stated in his 1949 report that "benefits should be uniform in amount and independent of previous wage history.

Congressman Curtis, still a member of the Ways and Means Committee, had just been made Chairman of a special subcommittee to "conduct thorough studies and investigations of all matters pertaining to our Social Security laws." The Chairman of the Ways and Means Committee (which had a Republican majority) in appointing Congressman Curtis had passed over Congressman Kean of New Jersey, a higher-ranking Republican member, although Congressman Kean had taken a very active and favorable interest in social security.

But I was glad to note that the Undersecretary of the Treasury, Marion Folsom, had been invited to attend and that a professor from the New York School of Social Work, Dr. Eveline Burns, was one of the five "civilians" constituting the advisory group. Mr. Folsom had been a member of the advisory council which had assisted the Committee on Economic Security in developing its recommendations in 1935. He had also served as a member of the advisory council appointed by the Senate Special Committee on Social Security and the Social Security Board in 1937. He later became Secretary of Health, Education, and Welfare. Dr. Burns had served as a consultant to the Social Security Board and the Social Security Administration on many occasions.

I was not invited to attend the meeting of this group on March 5 or a subsequent meeting on March 17, although members of my staff were directed to attend. There was no public announcement made of these meetings. However, a radio broadcaster on a program sponsored by the American Federation of Labor learned of them and, because of the predominance of Chamber of Commerce representatives, dubbed the advisory group the "Hobby Lobby."

The fact that the Chamber of Commerce had announced on February 20 that it was calling a national conference, to get its proposed changes "fully explained to the people back home" and to create "strong grass-roots support for the plan," added color to this charge as it was picked up by other news media. The Federal Security Administrator reacted quickly to this unfavorable publicity by adding seven additional members to the advisory group, including representatives of organized labor and two representatives of farm organizations.

When this enlarged advisory group met on April 1, it agreed to issue an interim report at an early date which would be confined to the extension of coverage to additional groups of current workers. This agreement was, of course, satisfactory to the labor representatives because it temporarily excluded consideration of the Chamber of Commerce proposal and was probably acceptable to the employer representatives because they thought that it would facilitate the "blanketing-in" later of persons no longer working.

The Federal Security Administrator, in a news release covering this April 1 meeting, stated, "The consultants will be asked first for their views on the feasibility of various alternative courses for extending coverage to large numbers of additional persons not now covered by the system. Subsequently they will be asked for additional recommendations in respect to other improvements in the social security system.

On April 10, my last day in office, I called upon Undersecretary of the Treasury Folsom to bid him goodbye and to request that he take an active part in the Administration's plans for amending the Social Security Act. I emphasized to the Undersecretary that I considered the Chamber of Commerce plan unsound and a grave danger to the contributory wage-related character of the old age and survivors' insurance system. This startled and disturbed the Undersecretary, who had not been able to give the plan intensive consideration.

Of course, the opposition of organized labor was probably the most important factor in deterring the Administration from endorsing the chamber's plan. However, I believe the Undersecretary's subsequent participation in the Administration's consideration of amendments to the Social Security Act had great influence in preventing any precipitate endorsement of the chamber's plan.

Another influence discouraging the Administration's endorsement of the chamber's plan was the attitude of Senator Byrd, a high-ranking Democratic member of the Finance Committee of the Senate. Senator Byrd addressed the chamber on April 27, 1953, chiding it for advocating the use of contributions under the old age and survivors' insurance system to reduce expenditures from general revenues. He said, "I feel that Social Security funds are a sacred trust of the Government. . . . Payments paid into these funds are not ordinary income that the Government can use to balance the budget.

After five more meetings of the expanded advisory group (which was called "Consultants on Social Security"), it reached agreement on the additional groups of current workers, both employees and self-employed, which the consultants as individuals believed should be covered under old age and survivors' insurance, and submitted its report to the Secretary of Health, Education, and Welfare (formerly the Federal Security Administrator) on June 24, 1953.

The report of the Consultants on Social Security stated:

In actual practice, the various phases and aspects of social insurance such as coverage, benefits, and financing, are not separable. In complying with the request that we make recommendations regarding extension of coverage, it has not been possible for us to make a study of certain other features of the old-age and survivors insurance program, the existence of which means the present plan falls short in certain respects of providing all the various advantages which a contributory old-age and survivors insurance system can have for the country.

The report also stated:

On the other hand, our recommendations for extension of coverage at this time do not include the blanketing-in of persons already age 65 or over who, because they have not become eligible through prior work in covered employment, are not receiving insurance benefits. We have excluded this group from consideration in this report because their inclusion would involve very substantial modifications of the present program which would require careful and prolonged study.

The report further stated that the consultants were not making recommendations with respect to railroad workers or employees of the federal government. The reason stated was that a Joint Congressional Committee on Railroad Retirement was making a study of the railroad retirement program and its relation to old age and survivors' insurance and that a Committee on Retirement Policy for Federal Personnel, appointed by the President, was including in its study the relation of old age and survivors' insurance to the federal employee retirement systems.

The largest group that the consultants recommended should be covered was the 3,000,000 self-employed farm operators. The next largest group consisted of 2,700,000 less regularly employed farm workers who were not covered by the 1950 amendments. Another large group was composed of about 500,000 self-employed professional persons who were specifically excluded by the 1950 amendments. Altogether, it was proposed that about 6,500,000 additional persons would be covered compulsorily. In addition, about 4,000,000 state and local employees (excluded because they were employed in positions covered by other retirement systems) could be covered on a voluntary basis, as could ministers and members of religious orders.

On August 1, the President transmitted the report to the Congress, saying in his message, "This is a specific plan for a specific purpose—the extension of coverage. Other important improvements in the Social Security Act are now under study and will be the subject of further recommendations."

Since the Congress was about to adjourn and did adjourn August 3 without taking any action, it is not clear what purpose was served in sending the report to Congress at that late date. It may have been that the Federal Security Administrator, in submitting the June 24 report, expected the President to transmit it immediately to Congress, not realizing the time required for prior "clearance" with the Bureau of the Budget and other governmental agencies

The Chairman of the Ways and Means Committee, Daniel Reed, although a Republican, apparently was not prepared to endorse the recommendations since he merely introduced "by request" the bill drafted by the Administration (H.R. 6812) to implement its recommendations. However, another Republican member of the Ways and Means Committee, Congressman Kean of New Jersey (who, as already stated, had a long record of favoring social security), introduced an identical bill (H.R. 6846) indicating that he favored the recommendations.

There was one other legislative recommendation regarding old age and survivors' insurance that the Administration made in 1953. That was in a special message from the President on May 20, regarding tax legislation. In that message the President stated that a general reduction in taxes would be unsound since there was a deficit in the general budget. But he did say that, since current receipts were well in excess of current expenditures, "The increase in the old-age insurance tax from 1½ to 2 percent on both employees and employers now scheduled to go into effect next January 1, should be postponed until January 1, 1955." He went on to say that, "From now on the old-age tax and trust account should be handled more nearly on a pay-as-you-go basis."

The Congress had ample time to act on the President's recommendation to "freeze" the old age and survivors' insurance tax rate, if it had been so inclined. However, the Chairman of the Ways and Means Committee showed no desire to act. It was rumored that the reason was the Administration's failure to support his proposal to reduce individual income taxes by 10 per cent on July 1, 1953.

The reason the Chairman of the Ways and Means Committee gave was that he had appointed a Subcommittee on Social Security to report at the next session of Congress and that, "The proper method of financing the system is, of course, one of the subjects of study."

Several months after the adjournment of Congress, on November 7, the Chairman of the Ways and Means Committee and the Chairman of the Subcommittee on Social Security both declared their opposition to an announcement by Congressman Simpson, the ranking Republican member of the committee, that he would sponsor legislation to eliminate the increase in tax rate retroactively when Congress reconvened. Of course, I do not know what reasons prompted the opposition of these two key members of the Ways and Means Committee. It may simply have been that they both accepted the judgment of the Chief Actuary of the Social Security Administration that the scheduled increase in the tax rate was necessary to maintain the old age and survivors' insurance system on a self-sufficient basis.

Actually, there were only two minor pieces of general legislation affecting the old age and survivors' insurance system enacted at the 1953 session of Congress. One extended from January 1, 1953, to July 1, 1955, the period for allowing "free" wage credits of $160 a month for military service. The other permitted the State of Wisconsin to cover, under the old age and survivors' insurance system, public employees already covered by a public retirement system.

With regard to unemployment insurance, the only legislation passed in 1953 consisted of extending the Unemployment Tax Act to include vessels operated by agents of the Secretary of Commerce of the United States. However, hearings were held in April by the Ways and Means Committee on several bills providing for the use of the excess of federal receipts over disbursements under the Federal Unemployment Tax Act.

Identical bills were introduced by two members of the Ways and Means Committee, one a Democrat and the other a Republican, and were supported by state employment security officials, the U.S. Chamber of Commerce, and the National Association of Commerce. Both bills had been drafted by the same lobbyist, operating under the name of Unemployment Benefit Advisors, Inc., who had approached me in 1949 offering his services to prevent the transfer of the Bureau of Employment Security to the U.S. Department of Labor. The main feature of these two bills was the distribution to the states of 80 per cent of the total receipts in excess of the total federal grants made to cover the administrative expenses of state employment security agencies. The retained 20 per cent would be used to make loans to the states whose reserves were becoming exhausted.

There was a third bill, introduced earlier by a Democratic member of the Ways and Means Committee, which was supported by organized labor groups. This bill would have used all of the excess receipts to make grants to states whose unemployment reserves were becoming exhausted.

The Department of Labor opposed the first two bills and supported in part the third bill. Because of this disagreement the Ways and Means Committee, after the public hearings had been concluded, drafted a bill, entitled the "employment security administrative financing bill," which attempted to reconcile these differences.

The Department of Labor, the Treasury Department, and the

Bureau of the Budget joined in opposing this bill. In spite of the opposition of the Administration, a majority of the Ways and Means Committee supported the bill, and it was reported favorably (although three Democratic members submitted a minority report). The House approved the bill (after refusing to recommit it), and it was sent to the Senate on July 18 where it was referred to the Finance Committee. The Finance Committee did not schedule hearings until March 1954.

The action of the Ways and Means Committee and of the House indicated that the Congress regarded the excess collections under the Federal Unemployment Tax Act primarily as taxes collected from the individual states rather than from individual employers, wherever they happened to be located. It is unfortunate that the Administration did not support affirmatively the basic principle contained in the third bill which was before the Ways and Means Committee. In essence, this was to use the excess collections to establish a reinsurance fund out of which grants would be made to states whose reserves were being depleted because of unusually large unemployment benefit costs. This would have strengthened the financial base of the entire federal-state system which the Federal Unemployment Tax Act had brought into existence because it was recognized that mass unemployment was a federal responsibility. The Social Security Administration had recommended this in its annual report for 1949, the last year that it had responsibility for the administration of unemployment insurance.

I ceased to be Commissioner for Social Security on April 10. This termination occurred automatically in accordance with the provisions of Reorganization Plan 1 of 1953. This plan abolished my position as Commissioner *for* Social Security and created a new position of Commissioner *of* Social Security.

The plan had been sent to the Congress on March 12 and would have gone into effect automatically in 60 days, i.e., May 11, if the Congress had not advanced its effective date to April 11. This created an embarrassing situation since valuable survivors' benefit rights would be lost merely because I would not still be in active service on May 8, 1953, when I reached the minimum retirement age (and, as already stated, had planned to retire).

The newspapers learned of this situation, and as a result the

Federal Security Administrator was subjected to considerable adverse publicity. She then sent me a memorandum, offering to employ me as a "consultant" for the four weeks elapsing between April 10 and May 8. I sent a memorandum in reply, stating that I would not feel justified in accepting any remuneration as a consultant, since I had already fully presented my views and recommendations in my annual reports to the Congress and in detailed memoranda to her. I did say that, "I would, of course, have been glad to continue to serve as Commissioner until my successor takes office."

As it turned out, my departure from my position as a government official did not prevent my becoming involved in very important and significant developments immediately thereafter. These developments concerned my relations with the Subcommittee on Social Security of the Ways and Means Committee.

The Chairman of this subcommittee, Congressman Curtis, was scheduled to speak on the opening night of the National Conference of Social Work, May 31. I did not arrive until the next day. When I did, I found that the chief topic of conversation was this speech. In the words of one of the participants who was delegated to assemble some of the extemporaneous and prepared speeches dealing with social security, "Representative Curtis' ringing challenge to Old Age and Survivors Insurance was perhaps the most significant paper presented at the Conference. Presented to a large audience on the opening night of the Annual meeting, this paper challenged, alarmed, and saddened many of the listeners. Many interpreted it as a preview of the subcommittee's report to the Congress."

The character of Congressman Curtis' speech may be judged from the following excerpts:

Why is it that the man or the woman who because of lack of education or opportunity or because of physical handicaps or other shortcomings is unable to earn but a pittance through his best years receives the smallest amount of benefit in his old age. . . .

Who are now eligible to receive the maximum benefits under our social security law? They are those people with dollar incomes in their productive years substantially greater than the income of others around them. Included are the corporation executive, the successful business proprietors, the higher paid employees—and even a large number of wage earners—who might be described as being in the middle and upper income brackets.

In promoting its program, why has this Federal Agency said that checks would come as a matter of right? Does the person who is paying Old Age Survivor's [sic] Insurance taxes acquire a right that is legally enforceable against the government? Does the law so provide? If not, why did the agency say that?

Probably the most significant passages in the Congressman's speech were the following:

> The question I wish to ask is: "Is this the best possible social security system that we can devise? Is it necessary to tie eligibility for benefits to the question as to where or for whom the individual has worked? Is there a better way? . . ."
>
> Isn't there something wrong with the basis of tying OASI coverage and eligibility to employment or income from certain sources?

I was called up out of the audience to reply to the speech. The following excerpts from my remarks indicate my general reaction:

> I do not think it would be particularly profitable to undertake to answer all of the rhetorical and loaded questions which comprised most of Congressman Curtis' speech. They are all calculated to discredit contributory social insurance in general and the Federal Old Age and Survivors Insurance System in particular, without the necessity of assuming any responsibility for proposing specific changes to cure alleged defects or proposing outright repeal. . . .
>
> Congressman Curtis has a perfect record since he has been in Congress of opposing social insurance. . .
>
> Congressman Curtis now happens to be Chairman of a Subcommittee of the Committee on Ways and Means which is studying old age security. As such he has appointed as staff director one who is also on record as opposed to social insurance and in favor of flat pensions subject to a means test. It is, therefore, important that we clarify the fundamental issues at stake in the differences between those like Congressman Curtis and his staff director who do not believe in social insurance and those like myself who do.

I then went on to explain why I believed that a system of contributory social insurance best achieves the twin goals of social adequacy and individual equity. I also pointed out some misstatements and inconsistencies in the Congressman's speech.

The most serious misconception of the Congressman was that he did not consider that the old age and survivors' insurance system was truly "insurance" since it was not based on a contractual right. He failed to recognize that it was based upon a statutory right enforceable in the courts. Therefore, I was obliged to say that, "Apparently he does not know that the beneficiaries may and do sue in the Federal courts to enforce their rights. Indeed, that is one of the great virtues of social insurance since it means that the specific benefits provided by statute must be paid and cannot be withheld or reduced in the discretion of any administrative official."

Before the National Conference of Social Work adjourned, it was kind enough to select me to be its President for the year 1954–55. I am inclined to believe that this action was due largely to the unfortunate circumstances surrounding the termination of my career as a government official and to the character of Congressman Curtis' speech.

On June 9 I received a letter from the Chairman of the Subcommittee on Social Security inviting me to prepare a "statement of the principles underlying the present programs of Old Age and Survivors Insurance and Old Age Assistance."

I declined this invitation, stating that I believed that compliance with this request would be not only pointless but misleading. I heard nothing further from the Chairman of the subcommittee until September 24 when I was served with a subpoena, directing me to appear before his subcommittee. Whereupon I wrote a letter, requesting the Chairman to furnish a list of questions he wished to ask or at least specific items he wished to discuss, so that the necessary material could be assembled.*

While the Chairman of the Ways and Means Committee had announced his appointment of this subcommittee on February 20, the Ways and Means Committee did not pass a resolution specifying its terms of reference until May 21. This resolution directed the subcommittee to conduct studies and investigations of "all matters pertaining to our social security laws." Among the various items to be included were "suggested amendments, changes, and improvements." On May 27 the House of Representatives adopted House Resolution 243, authorizing the expenditure of $100,000 by the subcommittee.

---

* The texts of these letters will be found in Appendix IV.

The Chairman proceeded to appoint as staff director the co-author of a book which advocated that the old age and survivors' insurance system be abandoned and that a flat uniform benefit be paid on the basis of need. In addition the Chairman appointed a "Chief Counsel" at $20,000 a year, a magazine writer at a similar rate, and seven other staff members at salaries in excess of the maximum salary paid staff members of regular congressional committees.

Some of these persons had previously been employed by a state Chamber of Commerce or the Council of State Chambers of Commerce, or a Republican political group. Therefore, the labor organizations particularly, and some other organizations as well, began to attack the subcommittee as being biased, reactionary, and political.

The first public hearings were held on July 24 and 25 and were devoted entirely to taking testimony regarding population trends and tax treatment of individuals under private pension plans. It was not until November that hearings were held relating directly to social security.

In the interval between the first and second series of hearings, the Chairman of the subcommittee issued two amazing press releases, one on August 24 and the other on August 25, attacking the Department of Health, Education, and Welfare and the Secretary personally. In the first press release he stated, "Now there has come clear evidence that the Department of Health, Education and Welfare, the source of much essential information, is unwilling to cooperate with the investigation. It is hard for one to believe that Mrs. Hobby has been insincere in her statements about improving social security, but the fact remains that her Department is not cooperating with the House Subcommittee." In the second press release he said, "All we want are the facts. We intend to get them. I will not tolerate delays, evasive answers, or anything that falls short of full cooperation."

Of course I know nothing about the relations between the Department of Health, Education, and Welfare and the sub-committee. It may have been that these outbursts merely repre-sented superficial irritation at the length of time required to assemble the large amount of data requested. But it may have been deep-seated resentment that the Administration had not indicated whether it would support the Congressman's 1949 proposal of a universal uniform old age pension, which he had indicated at the National Conference on Social Work he still favored.

At the hearings in November considerable attention was given to the increasing proportion of children dependent because of the father's absence from the home (rather than because of his death or incapacity); to the great variation among the states in the number of aged persons receiving public assistance and in the average amount received; and to the fact that I had stated on many occasions that a needy person had a statutory right to assistance although that right was conditioned on need. Concerning old age and survivors' insurance, much attention was given to the number of beneficiaries living abroad; to the fact that in the early years of the system aged workers would draw retirement benefits, the value of which would be far in excess of the contributions they had paid in; to the fact that current and future beneficiaries would have to be paid largely out of contributions being paid by younger people still working and their employers; to the alleged discrimination against married women workers because they would not be allowed to draw dual benefits; and to the failure to protect all the aged population.

The final day of the public hearings, November 27, was devoted entirely to taking my testimony. I had received a letter from the Chairman of the subcommittee, in reply to my letter of September 25, notifying me that the subcommittee wanted me to testify on Friday, November 27, as well as Saturday, the 28th, and Monday, the 30th. However, the Chairman did not furnish me with a list of the questions to be asked or the specific items to be discussed, as requested, although he had done so for previous witnesses.

In addition to the Chairman there were one Republican member and two Democratic members present. The hearing started fairly peacefully. I was shown the brief filed by the Department of Justice in the 1935 Supreme Court case involving the constitutionality of Titles II and VIII of the Social Security Act. The Chief Counsel stated that, "One of the things which the committee is interested in going into, Mr. Altmeyer, is whether the arrangements provided in title II of the Social Security Act are, in fact, insurance.

The Chief Counsel asked me whether I recalled the statement in the brief reading, "The act cannot be said to constitute a plan for compulsory insurance within the accepted meaning of the term 'insurance.'

I was next asked to read statements I had made the day following the Supreme Court's decision, in which I had referred to the "Federal old-age insurance program" contained in the Social Security Act. This I did and then stated, "Titles II and VIII were inseparable and formed a single plan. It [i.e., the Court] rejected in effect the arguments made by Government counsel and to my mind clearly established that in the opinion of the Court both the contributions and the benefit titles made a single whole which, in my humble judgment, can be properly described as an insurance system."

The Chief Counsel than proceeded to ask me to read excerpts from subsequent statements I had made referring to the "old age insurance" system. I did so, commenting, "I certainly appreciate your calling my attention to these earlier statements. They mean exactly what I intended them to mean and they mean just what I mean today and believe in today."

At this point one of the Democratic members interrupted the questioning to ask me whether I had "a pair of Oregon boots on." I was not aware that "Oregon boots" were used to prevent prisoners from running away, so I replied, "I have a pair of 3-year old shoes that I have had resoled twice."

The Democratic member then proceeded to ask whether I had chains and wristlets on and shouted, "Bringing a man like you here under subpoena! Mr. Chairman, you ought to be ashamed of yourself." A long, angry exchange of words then ensued, the Democratic member demanding that the Chairman cease pounding "that damned gavel." In the transcript the word "damned" was discreetly omitted.

The questioning then continued for some time, I being asked to confirm excerpts from statements I had made. I finally stated I objected not only to my being obliged to read isolated excerpts but to the Chief Counsel's doing so. I stated my position as follows:

Maybe it would be helpful to you if I said to you, in the interest of saving time, money, and keeping the volume of the record to a minimum, that I stand on my statement that I made at the very beginning, that I consider that titles II and VIII together constitute an insurance program. This is merely repetitious, I submit. If you want to establish that I have taken that position since 1935, I admit it and I am proud of it, and I insist it is the correct position in keeping with the legislation which I was charged with administering, so I see no point in continuing to read comments that I have made through the years emphasizing that fundamental principle. . . .

Mr. Chairman, I want to make it clear, either you accept my statement, which I am prepared to stand on, that this is a contributory social insurance system, and forego this meticulous, long-drawn-out, dreary quotation of speeches and statements made over the years, or you incorporate all of the material from which you quote. I have no objection to either one. I would prefer the first because I think it saves time, money, and reduces the hearings to a minimum, so that the full committee may have some chance to determine what was done by the subcommittee."

But the same sort of questioning continued for about an hour and a half. Some of the differences between private insurance and social insurance, as stated in a 1947 pamphlet of the Social Security Administration, were brought out.

At last the Chief Counsel asserted, "Now, Mr. Altmeyer, from these addresses, brochures, radio scripts, and booklets, it is apparent that, beginning with May 24, 1937, you and your associates have continuously referred to title II benefits and the related tax statute as insurance; sometimes as providing insurance protection; as an insurance contract to be distinguished from a handout."

I interrupted the Chief Counsel to ask whether he had used the term "contract" inadvertently, and asked him, when he replied he had not, to document his statement. It developed that he was basing it entirely upon a single sentence appearing in a long statement made by Professor Witte in 1939 when he appeared as a private citizen before the Committee on Finance of the Senate.

I then stated that I thought what Professor Witte meant was that social insurance created a definite statutory right enforceable by law. I went on to say, "The point I wish to make, Mr. Chairman, is that a statutory right which is enforceable by law is the important element in this insurance system, this old-age and survivors insurance system, and under the State unemployment insurance laws, and under workmen's compensation, and other types of social insurance. Now, the question of whether it is a contractual right or a noncontractual right is immaterial and unimportant, so long as it is a statutory right, enforceable by law, and not subject to the whim or caprice of any political body or administrative official."

I agreed with the Chairman that persons covered under social insurance "do not have a contract that cannot be changed by the one party, the Government," whereupon the following colloquy occurred:

MR. ALTMEYER. Of course, I am amazed, Mr. Chairman, that it took all this time for us to have a meeting of minds, because a simple inquiry of the Attorney General or of the General Counsel or of any attorney on your staff, I think, would have cleared up this question of what was meant by "right" under the old-age and survivors insurance system. There has never been any confusion so far as that.

MR. DINGELL. He did not have to be brought in on the end of a chain to admit that, did he?

MR. ALTMEYER. Let me add, Mr. Chairman, that I think that the statutory right is far stronger than a contractual right under some private insurance companies, for the very reason that you have a responsible legislative body, the Congress of the United States of America. You have at the present time about 90 million people who have accumulated wage credits. Now, it is inconceivable to me that the Congress of the United States would ever think of taking action to prejudice their rights that have developed under existing legislation. On the contrary, the Congress of the United States has continually improved, increased their rights.

When the subcommittee reconvened in the afternoon, the Chairman informed me that I could proceed to make my prepared statement. I told the Chairman that he had misunderstood me and that I did not have a prepared statement since I did not know that I would be permitted to make any statement. I stated that I had some rough notes to guide me in any connected statement I was permitted to make. I went on to say, "I do not know whether you want me to discuss principles as you call them, or philosophy, or whether you want me to give a history of the development of the Social Security Act, or whether you want me to make recommendations for its improvement. I had hoped, of course, that this subcommittee had a purpose which was to develop recommendations for the improvement of the Social Security Act, but now I am at a complete loss as to what your purpose is."

The Chairman responded by saying, "As to what should be in that statement, you will be the judge. I do not want it said that you were not permitted to make a statement that you chose to make. I am granting you that right now."

I then stated that, if it met with the Chairman's approval, I would like first to discuss the history of the Social Security Act to bring out the significant elements that the Congress had in mind, and after that discuss what I hoped would be the future developments of social security in America. So I proceeded to discuss the report of the President's Committee on Economic Security in 1935, the President's message to the Congress transmitting the report, the majority and minority reports of the Ways and Means Committee accompanying the social security bill, and the 1936 presidential campaign. At that point the Chairman pointed out that I had already taken 40 minutes to make my statement. This provoked an exchange of words between the Democratic members and the Chairman. I was asked by a Democratic member whether I was in a hurry to get away, and I replied that I had been told to be available for three days. The Chairman then stated that the hearing would be shortened up, whereupon the Democratic member inquired, "Shortened up? I had not heard that. Have you a porcupine by the tail and don't know what to do with him?"

After the Chairman indicated that I should proceed, I said, "Mr. Chairman, we are down to 1939. I must apologize for taking so much time of the committee, but I thought, since you indicated in your letter to me that you were interested in the philosophy and principles of the Social Security Act, the best place to find that philosophy and principles was in the official records.

After a few more minutes I was asked how much more time I would take, and I replied that I would need about two more hours to present the documentary history and after that some time to present my personal views. But I suggested that I might be able to reduce the time if the Chairman were more precise as to what he wanted.

The Chairman insisted that I had said I had a prepared statement to make, but he told me to proceed, saying a night session would be necessary. Whereupon I quoted from President Roosevelt's message of January 16, 1939, transmitting a report of the Social Security Board on ways and means of improving the Social Security Act, as well as from the report itself. I also quoted from the December 10, 1938, report of the Advisory Council on Social Security. I then quoted from the majority and minority reports of the Ways and Means Committee, accompanying the 1939 bill.

In presenting the historical material, I took occasion to point out its relevance to the questions I had been asked. In doing so I incidentally called attention to the use of the expressions "old-age insurance system" and "contract" in the Republican minority report, since the day's hearing had consisted largely of questions attacking my alleged misuse of such terms.

After finishing with the 1939 material, I proceeded to present excerpts from the Democratic majority report of the Ways and Means Committee on the 1949 bill. Before I could proceed to quote from the minority reports (the longest one of which had been submitted by the Chairman of the subcommittee), another altercation occurred between the Democratic members and the Chairman, revolving around the question of whether I had indicated how much time I would take to make my statement. The Chairman then pointed out that I had already taken an hour and 37 minutes and said, "Wind up your statement as quickly as you can."

The Democratic members protested and argued that if the Chairman was going to limit the presentation, he should specify the amount of time he would allow. When the Chairman refused to do so, a Democratic member commented, "I know you are seasick now. He is not your kind of witness. You should not have asked for the 3 days. . . . You are on the ropes."

I then proceeded to discuss the Republican minority reports of the Ways and Means Committee submitted in 1949. I concluded by saying, "Now, I haven't, Mr. Chairman, expressed my personal views as to what I think could be done to improve the law."

The Chairman stated that the committee was not a legislative committee and asked me what further I wanted "to read from the statement that you said you had." I replied, "Well, I have a statement, Mr. Chairman—it would probably take me an hour and a quarter—as to my views and recommendations regarding improvement of the present social security system. But, if you are not interested in learning about my views, I forego that privilege.

The Chairman then said, "You have used almost 2 hours. If you have something that you want to say in just 2 or 3 minutes, wind it up." Whereupon I concluded my statement as follows:

May I then say, Mr. Chairman, that in the consideration of the development of a social security program, we ought to proceed upon the assumption that we want to develop a social security system based upon a free enterprise system, and designed so as to promote all of the values inherent in a free enterprise system.

May I also say that we must proceed upon the assumption that every effort will be made to make this free enterprise system as productive as possible and as just as possible to the participants thereof.

I believe that a social security system ought to be designed to provide a minimum basic protection upon which the individual may build a further degree of protection as desired by him and his family. I do not look upon that minimum basic protection as simply an animal level of subsistence. I look upon it as a level that permits some degree of gracious living to all of the American people, and I believe that there is no fixed amount that should be established as the limit of a decent, humane, minimum basic protection for all of the American people.

I believe that a system of social security ought to protect all of the people against all of the major economic hazards which lead to destitution. I believe that a contributory social insurance system enabling people to help pay for their own protection ought to be the first line of defense against destitution, and the major element in any system of social security.

I believe that benefits should be related to income loss under this contributory social insurance system.

I believe that we must preserve both the principle of individual equity and the principle of social adequacy.

I believe that we should have a safe system of financing that looks to the future as well as the present and makes certain that we know where we are going and have set up an automatic system of financing so that these benefits that are provided as a matter of statutory right by the Congress of the United States may be preserved and protected and paid when due.

I believe that public assistance should be retained as the second line of defense against destitution.

I believe that every effort should be made to prevent the hazards causing destitution. I believe that there should be industrial accident prevention, that there should be employment offices to reduce the amount of unemployment to a minimum, that we ought to have hiring and firing practices that would permit persons in their fifties and sixties and seventies to continue to work if they want to and are able to do so. I think it is tragic and inhuman to throw them on the scrap heap just when they reach an arbitrary age limit, whether it is 65 or whether it is any other, and I believe that we should have rehabilitation programs of all sorts to enable people to continue to be productive, to restore their productive capacity if it has been lost or impaired.

Now, Mr. Chairman, I have very definite views as to how to accomplish these objectives, but since you have informed me that my time is at an end, I want to thank the committee for the privilege of appearing, and if at any future time I can be of any further assistance to the committee, I shall be glad to.

Since it was then after 4 o'clock, I had assumed that my appearance before the subcommittee was at an end. However, to my surprise, the Chief Counsel resumed his questioning to establish that I had used the expression "insurance" after the 1937 Supreme Court decisions holding that the social insurance titles of the Social Security Act were constitutional.

After still more questioning the Chief Counsel lost his temper when I said I could not hear him, shouting at the top of his voice, "Can you hear me?" The Chairman made a calming gesture. One Democratic member said, "Do not get any rougher than that, Mr. Counsel." Another said, "I do not think the witness can be browbeaten by your yelling at him, Mr. Counsel. He is not the type to be browbeaten. The first thing you learn in studying law is not to attempt to browbeat the witness."

At a later point I was asked whether I subscribed to the statement, "The attitude which people have toward the payment which they will receive and the conditions under which they will receive it is a matter of the first importance; a security system does not give security, even if physical needs are met, unless people know they can count on the payment and feel good."

I replied, "I do, and I think you are doing more to destroy the confidence of the American people in this system than anybody else except the chairman of this committee."

The hearing continued thereafter for another two and a half hours. The Chief Counsel continued to question me in an effort to establish that the old age and survivors' insurance system was not "insurance" because it was not based upon a contract. In doing so, the Chief Counsel quoted definitions from law books and court decisions to the effect that insurance was based on contract. I suggested that these definitions referred to private insurance and that the Chief Counsel would have been "better advised to have examined some texts on social insurance."

Again the Chief Counsel undertook to establish that my associates and I had misled the public in referring to the payment of benefits "as a matter of right," because the payments were not based on a contract. I continued to insist that a statutory right was fully as strong as a contractual right, saying that I was confident Congress would continue to improve and increase the rights of the workers.

When the Chief Counsel undertook to establish that isolated individuals might lose some previous rights even though workers in general benefited by amendments to the law, I replied, "I am saying that you have to look at social insurance as to whether it provides greater or less protection than it did before. In my judgment the 1950 amendments provided greater protection to millions of insured workers. I am sure you will flyspeck the picture until the picture itself becomes obscured, but I suggest that you use a little gasoline or some cleaning fluid and restore the brilliance of the colors in the original picture."

The hearing finally ended at 6:55 P.M. with a statement by the Chairman that "it is apparent that the people of the country have no insurance contract." Thus, as far as the Chairman was concerned, establishing that obvious fact was the main reason for holding the hearing.

What purpose the Chairman had in mind in emphasizing that the old age and survivors' insurance system was not based upon an individual insurance contract, and therefore could be altered by the Congress at any time, can only be a matter of speculation. As I indicated in my testimony, the effect on beneficiaries was bound to be unfortunate because it raised doubts as to the certainty and security of their benefit rights. I cannot help believing that the Chairman and his staff must have realized this would be the effect.

However, I do not believe that was the main purpose. I believe that the Chairman considered it necessary to establish that this social insurance system was not based upon inviolable individual contracts providing specific benefits in return for specific payments, so that he would be justified in proposing what he considered a more equitable, more adequate, and financially sounder system of protection. This probably was also his purpose in pointing up in previous hearings what he considered individual inequities, inadequacy of coverage, and unsound financing.

But this final day of hearing did result in considerable unfavorable publicity and did sharpen the attack of the labor organizations on the Chairman and his activities as well as on the U.S. Chamber of Commerce proposal which was still being publicized by the chamber. Whether all this had any effect on the Chairman of the subcommittee and on the Chairman of the Ways and Means Committee itself I do not know. However, each of these gentlemen two weeks later issued a public statement that he favored the continuance of the contributory principle, the maintenance of the trust fund, and the payment of benefits related to past earnings.

The Chairman of the subcommittee made his statement as a part of a speech he delivered before the Nebraska Association of County Officials. In that speech he also said:

In recent months I have had a lot of work to do in regard to Social Security. I have had a rough time. We have had some rough sessions down at Washington. I have been verbally pounded, harassed and blockaded by the rudest men that the left wing, partisan groups could produce. Lest I be misunderstood, I want to say that not all of the minority members of my committee have performed in this manner.

In my opinion, it was necessary that we have the testimony of Mr. Arthur J. Altmeyer, who for 18 years has been the principal architect and manager of our Social Security program. Because this left-wing, partisan opposition didn't want any questions asked about this multi-billion dollar program that affects the lives of all our citizens, they tried to distract attention. I was forced to proceed with the hearings over the rumble of mutterings, slurring remarks, harassing statements and profanity.

The left-wing chose this course for two reasons. In the first place they did not want the errors of the past to be known, and in the second place, their irrelevant remarks and the trouble that was bound to emanate therefrom provided propaganda material for a few irresponsible radio men and writers who falsely pretend to give the public the news but who in reality are propagandists of the cheapest sort.

. . . .

Without hesitation, I freely admit that I do not now adhere to all I said in my minority report of 1949. . . .

At the close of the last day of hearings at which I testified, the Chairman of the subcommittee told reporters that the subcommittee probably would come up with some "broad, basic recommendations" to the House Ways and Means Committee after the Christmas holidays. This seemed to contradict the statement he had made during the course of the hearing that the subcommittee was not a legislative committee and would not consider proposals for legislation. Moreover, he had on many other occasions referred to it as a fact-finding committee only.

Actually, the Chairman of the subcommittee, in his capacity as Chairman, made only one general comment that might be considered as a recommendation. It was contained in a very brief letter he wrote to the Chairman of the Ways and Means Committee, transmitting an 18-page staff memorandum captioned "Some Major Findings." In that letter, after reporting what he described as "the significance of some findings resulting from the staff's research," he simply stated, "I believe that a single program should serve not the few, but all of our aged, and dependent children. Moreover, I believe that minor adjustments can enable us to achieve this objective and that they are at hand."

Subsequently, on December 31, 1953, the Chairman of the subcommittee, as an individual, issued a press release reading as follows:

Representative Carl T. Curtis of Nebraska today proposed important amendments in the nation's Social Security program which would (1) pay benefits now to five million more of the nation's aged; (2) raise the minimum benefit to $45 per month; (3) extend coverage to occupations now outside Social Security; and, (4) liberalize the eligibility requirements.

The Curtis proposal would retain the present wage-related benefit structure by: (a) continuing monthly payments up to the present maximum of $85; (b) increasing to $45 the monthly benefits for all those now receiving less than $45; (c) maintaining the contributory principle of the present law; and, (d) continuing the present trust fund arrangement.

On January 6, 1954, Congressman Curtis introduced bill H.R. 6863, to give effect to his proposals. This bill differed from the proposal of the U.S. Chamber of Commerce, already discussed, in the following important respects:

(1) It proposed a universal minimum monthly retirement benefit of $45 instead of $25 to all persons 65 years of age and over.

(2) It covered dependents and survivors of all aged persons (as well as those of younger persons already protected).

(3) It would apply the employee's tax rate to the "adjusted gross income" of all individuals (whether employed or self-employed) under 65 years of age. This adjusted gross income would include income from investments, rent, or the like, as well as earnings from employment or self-employment.

(4) It did not propose to eliminate federal grants-in-aid to the states for old age assistance.

My concern about the relation between the universal minimum benefit, payable regardless of past earnings, and the differential benefits, payable on the basis of past earnings, has already been discussed in connection with the U.S. Chamber of Commerce proposal. This concern was even greater regarding the Curtis proposal because the minimum benefit was higher. Thus, a person who had earned an average wage of $82 a month all his life would receive no more when he retired than a person who had no earnings. This was because the differential benefits already specified in the law would not be paid in addition to the minimum benefit. In other words, the universal minimum benefit would always be subtracted from the differential benefits otherwise payable.

The proposal to substitute a gross income tax for the tax on earnings from employment would have more than covered the increased cost of the proposed universal old age pension. However, it would not have solved the problem of properly relating the differential benefits to the minimum benefit. In fact, it would have complicated it. In my opinion, it would have been less confusing and more equitable to pay for the cost of the universal minimum benefit out of general revenues and the cost of the additional differential benefits out of payroll taxes.

The Curtis bill did compare favorably with the U.S. Chamber of Commerce proposal in that it did not propose to eliminate the federal grants-in-aid for old age assistance. It was probably because of this and the higher minimum benefit proposed that the U.S. Chamber of Commerce did not throw its support behind it. In any event, I agreed with the Congressman about the significance of his bill, if not about the soundness he attributed to it when he introduced it: "Mr. Speaker, as the Congress proceeds to make social-security coverage universal, we are faced with our last good opportunity to make the program sound."

Therefore, I looked forward with keen interest to the position the Administration would take in proposing amendments to the Social Security Act. The annual report of the U.S. Department of Health, Education, and Welfare for the fiscal year offered no clue since it made no specific legislative recommendations, in contrast to what had been done in previous years. It merely referred to the President's message of August 1, 1953, and said, "Other problem areas are in process of exploration and legislative proposals in these areas are being developed."

The President's Message on the State of the Union, of January 7, 1954, had a section entitled "Labor and Welfare." In that section he stated that, "Protection against the hazards of temporary unemployment should be extended to some 6½ millions of workers, including civilian Federal workers, who now lack this safeguard."

Concerning the old age and survivors' insurance system, he called attention to and repeated his recommendation for extension of its coverage. He said, "This and other major improvements in the insurance system will bring substantial benefit increases and broaden the membership of the insurance system, thus diminishing the need for Federal grants-in-aid for such purposes. A new formula will therefore be proposed, permitting progressive reduction in such grants as the need for them declines. . . . My more detailed recommendations on this and the other social-insurance problems I have mentioned will be sent to the Congress on January 14."

Concerning health he said, "I am flatly opposed to the socialization of medicine. The great need for hospital and medical services can best be met by the initiative of private plans. . . . A limited Government reinsurance service would permit the private and nonprofit insurance companies to offer broader protection to more of the many families which want and should have it. On January 18 I shall forward to the Congress a special message presenting this administration's health program in detail."

On January 14 the President sent to the Congress his message containing his specific recommendations regarding the old age and survivors' insurance system and the federal grant-in-aid programs for public assistance. This message made it clear that the Republican Administration did not intend to propose a general uniform old age pension or support either the U.S. Chamber of Commerce or the Curtis proposals for "blanketing-in" all aged persons.

The President called the old age and survivors' insurance system "the cornerstone of the Government's programs to promote the economic security of the individual." He further stated, "I am determined to preserve its basic principles." He then proceeded to recommend, in addition to the extended coverage previously recommended, (1) a liberalized "retirement test" so that a retired worker would not suffer as great a reduction in the amount of his monthly benefits when he worked part-time; (2) a more liberal formula for calculating the monthly benefits; (3) raising the maximum earnings to be taken into account in calculating the benefit; (4) elimination of the four lowest years of earnings in computing the worker's average monthly wage upon which the monthly benefit depends; (5) protection of the previously acquired benefit rights of persons who become totally disabled.

As regards public assistance, the President recommended that the federal matching formula should be changed to take into account the fact that a broadened old age and survivors' insurance system would progressively reduce the extent of need for public assistance, and that the formula should be related to the financial capacity of each state as measured by its per capita income. He also recommended that the federal matching be based entirely on the average payment per recipient so that states could offset high payments in individual cases with low payments, instead of being obliged to eliminate any payment in an individual case which exceeded a specified maximum.

All of the recommendations of the President were in accordance with recommendations made in the annual reports of the

Social Security Administration when I was Commissioner. Of course, they did not include such recommendations as social insurance to cover the cost of medical care and loss of earnings due to temporary or permanent disability. Nor did they include federal grants to the states to cover the cost of public assistance to all needy persons. Nevertheless, the President's recommendations represented a complete endorsement of the fundamental principles upon which the social insurance and public assistance provisions of the Social Security Act were based. They also represented a continuation of the course of development charted by the previous Administration. So it can be said that the Social Security Act for the first time became a truly nonpartisan feature of our American way of life.

This acceptance of the basic principles was, of course, due primarily to the fact that experience had demonstrated that the principles were compatible with our economic, social, and political institutions. However, it was also due to the fact that the administration of the act had been efficient and understanding of these principles and of their importance in the lives of individual human beings. The resulting satisfaction with the law and its administration was reflected in widespread public support which the Administration was obliged to recognize.

The readiness of the new Administration to advocate precisely the same course of further development of the law as did the old Administration was due to its early recognition of the fact that it could rely on the expert and nonpartisan advice and judgment of the top officials of the Social Security Administration. Actually, the only change of top personnel that occurred was in the position which I had held. Moreover, my successor was a close friend and a public welfare official in my home state who shared my own views regarding the administration of the law and its improvement.

As I see it, these top officials were really not faced with the dilemma of reconciling their loyalties to the old and new Administrations. While it is probable that a majority were Democrats, it was because the Democratic Party better represented their philosophy that government had an affirmative obligation to promote the welfare of its citizens, and that was the philosophy embedded in the Social Security Act.

The Chairman of the Ways and Means Committee, following the precedent of 1950, introduced two bills embodying the President's social security proposals, immediately following the transmittal of the President's message to Congress. One bill contained the old age and survivors' insurance recommendations and the other contained the public assistance recommendations. The Chairman announced that hearings would be held as soon as the tax bill was out of the way.

It is interesting to note that the Secretary of Health, Education, and Welfare, in developing these recommendations which the President accepted, did not seek the advice of the group of Consultants on Social Security which she had used to consider extension of coverage. When she announced the appointment of that group on April 2, 1953, she had said that, "Subsequently they will be asked for additional recommendations in respect to other improvements in the social security system." Undoubtedly, the reason she did not use them was that she recognized it would be impossible to reconcile their divergent views concerning the "blanketing-in" proposals of the U.S. Chamber of Commerce and Congressman Curtis, and it would also be difficult to obtain a consensus on such other matters as liberalization of the benefit formula, increase in the maximum earnings taken into account for determining benefits and contributions, and the so-called disability freeze.

The Ways and Means Committee began its public hearings on April 1. By that time it had become evident that the committee would not follow the lead of the Chairman of its subcommittee in its attitude toward changes in the Social Security Act. As a matter of fact, the Chairman, in opening the hearings, merely made the following brief mention of the work of the subcommittee:

I appointed a subcommittee to make factual studies of the social security program, as it exists today. That subcommittee held extensive hearings this past summer and fall. Those hearings have been published for some time and are available to the members of the committee as well as to the general public. My understanding is that a factual staff report will also be forthcoming as soon as the final editing is completed. It is my expectation that this report will be available to the committee by the time it begins executive sessions on this bill. However, I understand that most of the staff material consists of a summation of the testimony already published in the hearings, and is therefore, available at this time.

Actually, the staff report was not submitted to the Chairman of the subcommittee until August 20, the day the joint conference committee of the House and Senate reached agreement on the bill which had passed both houses. It was not published until December 20.

The first witness appearing before the committee was the Secretary of Health, Education, and Welfare, Mrs. Oveta Culp Hobby. She stated that she was confining her testimony to the bill covering changes in old age and survivors' insurance. Her only reference to the public assistance bill was to say that it would reduce the federal matching percentage for old age assistance in a particular state as a larger and larger proportion of aged persons in that state became beneficiaries under old age and survivors' insurance. Although the implication seemed to be that she would later testify regarding the public assistance bill, she did not in fact do so.

The Secretary estimated that the old age and survivors' insurance bill would extend coverage to 10½ million additional employees and self-employed persons, of whom 6½ million would be covered immediately and another 4 million would be eligible for coverage under voluntary group arrangements (mostly state and local government employees already under another retirement system and clergymen). The only large groups still excluded would be federal civil servants, military personnel, and railroad workers covered under separate retirement systems.

The major additional groups to be covered compulsorily would be farm operators and farm workers (who were not covered under existing law because of its rigid test of eligibility). Together these two groups totaled 5.8 million. Another important group was self-employed professional persons, such as physicians, dentists, and lawyers.

The major farm organizations, with the exception of the American Farm Bureau, had been in favor of being covered for a number of years. The American Farm Bureau still reiterated its opposition, but rather perfunctorily in the form of a short letter to the Chairman of the committee.

The other important recommendations made by Secretary

Hobby were elimination of four years of lowest earnings in calculating the average monthly earnings on which benefits depend; increase in maximum earnings base from $3,600 to $4,000 for benefit and contribution purposes; increase in the monthly benefit by raising the percentage of average monthly earnings payable and by increasing both the minimum and maximum monthly benefit amounts payable; a more liberal and flexible test of retirement, so that a worker would only have one monthly benefit suspended for each $80 earned over $1,000 per year; preservation of previously acquired benefit rights of persons totally disabled for an extended period.

A complicated Administration recommendation regarding public assistance was incorporated into a separate bill but was never explained to the committee by a representative of the Department of Health, Education, and Welfare. However, it was referred to by several other witnesses. The recommendation was that the federal matching ratio should vary above or below 65 per cent, inversely with the per capita income of each state, within a range of 60 per cent to 80 per cent. The percentage so calculated would be reduced by 1 per cent for each 5 per cent of a state's population over age 65 who received an old age insurance benefit.

The chief opposition to the Administration's proposals was expressed by employer groups, insurance groups, the American Medical Association, the American Dental Association, and supporters of the Townsend plan. The labor groups did not oppose the Administration's proposal, although they favored a more liberal bill introduced by several Democratic congressmen and senators.

The U.S. Chamber of Commerce and the Council of State Chambers of Commerce, of course, supported the proposal of the U.S. Chamber of Commerce. They specifically opposed the increase in the taxable wage base, the general liberalization of benefits, and the "freezing" of the benefit rights of disabled persons. The National Association of Manufacturers opposed all of the changes proposed.

The life insurance companies opposed any liberalization of the benefit formula, except a small increase in the minimum benefit payable; any increase in the maximum earnings taken into account for benefit and tax purposes; and any use of the term "insurance" in the law; they also opposed the "disability freeze." They laid much stress on their belief that the liberalization of benefits violated the original idea of providing only a "floor of protection."

The American Medical Association opposed both the inclusion of self-employed doctors and the "disability freeze." The American Dental Association representative stated his association had reversed its 1948 resolution in 1949 and was opposed to dentists' being covered. However, a number of state dental societies notified the committee that they favored inclusion.

The Townsendites were given respectful attention and considerable time. This was natural since 160 congressmen had signed their names to a petition to bring the Townsend bill out of the committee to the floor for a vote. They, of course, urged their plan for a uniform universal pension as a substitute for the Administration's bill.

The American Federation of Labor endorsed the Administration's bill but urged still greater liberalization of the wage base and the method of computation of benefits as well as payment of benefits for extended total disability. The Congress of Industrial Organizations also endorsed the bill. It made the same recommendations for improvement and in addition recommended the inclusion of benefits for temporary disability.

It should be noted that Congressman Curtis did not press for consideration of the bill which he had introduced. In fact, he did not refer to his bill at any time. He did say once, in questioning Nelson Rockefeller who was then Undersecretary of Health, Education, and Welfare, that, "I personally feel very strongly that you cannot have a Federal system and have it operate properly without universal coverage. But, of course, that is all water over the dam." Apparently, by "universal coverage" he meant "blanketing-in" of all presently aged persons. The ranking Democratic member of the Ways and Means Committee followed Congressman Curtis to inquire of Mr. Rockefeller what the position of the Administration was on "blanketing-in." Mr. Rockefeller replied that, "The Secretary is most concerned with the security of the present aged population, but after studying many types of plans and proposals for blanketing in, it was her conclusion that it could not be done without creating serious inequities and grave dangers for the OASI system itself." He then proceeded to discuss all the dangers.

The House Ways and Means Committee, in executive sessions extending over a period of more than a month, approved of the Administration's old age and survivors' insurance proposals, with the following major modifications: (1) Self-employed physicians would continue to be excluded from coverage (although at one time the committee had decided to include them); (2) The extension of coverage to sporadically employed agricultural workers was made more limited.

With regard to public assistance, the committee merely extended the existing temporary matching provisions for another year. All of the changes made in executive sessions were incorporated into a new bill which was introduced and reported favorably by the committee on May 28. Two Republican members (but not Congressman Curtis) submitted a minority report, protesting that there had been no hearings on "the interrelated assistance system" and that the bill "would violate our basic principles to extend its taxes and benefits beyond the levels required to meet its purpose of providing a minimum floor of protection against destitution."

The bill was debated by the House on June 1 under a "closed rule" which prevented amendment except by the Committee on Ways and Means. It was passed by a vote of 356 to 8.

Congressman Curtis, during the course of the debate, had observed, "I believe all of us look forward to the time when all of our aged people and widowed mothers with dependent children will be eligible for these benefits paid without a means test. . . . Because of this bill, this situation will be corrected in time. I hope some measure will be devised to accelerate this process. While some important improvements remain to be accomplished, I recommend passage of HR 9366." About this time he announced he would not be a candidate for re-election. The probable reason was that labor organizations in his district had carried on a very vigorous campaign attacking his record on social security. However, both the Senators from Nebraska died within three months of each other, one on April 12 and one on July 1. The Congressman then announced his candidacy for the Senate, perhaps because he believed that any labor opposition in his congressional district would be overcome outside his district. He was successful in the November election that year and was re-elected in 1960.

The hearings before the Committee on Finance extended from June 24 to July 9. The Secretary of Health, Education, and Welfare and her associates presented the same recommendations and supporting material that they had submitted to the Ways and Means Committee, with one major exception. The Secretary presented a different proposal for modifying the federal matching of state expenditures for old age assistance. She proposed that in those old age assistance cases added to the rolls after January 1, 1955, where the individual is receiving an old age retirement benefit, the federal matching should be reduced to 50 per cent of the monthly amount paid an individual up to $55. At the time she made this suggestion, the existing federal grant-in-aid was 80 per cent of the first $25, plus 50 per cent of the balance up to $55, paid an individual.

The representatives of the same groups that had appeared before the House Ways and Means Committee presented the same views as previously. The Finance Committee held executive sessions from the close of the public hearings until July 27 when it submitted its report. The main changes the committee made in the bill as it had come from the House, regarding the old age and survivors' insurance system, were (1) exclusion of farmers and all self-employed persons; (2) broadening of the coverage of farm workers to coincide with the Administration's recommendations; (3) further liberalization of the "retirement test."

In public assistance, the committee merely increased the extension of time of the existing temporary federal matching formula from one year to two years.

The elimination of farmers and self-employed professional persons was due largely to the insistence of Senator George, the former Chairman of the committee and its ranking minority member when the Administration changed in 1953. When he was Chairman, he had supported the extension of coverage to non-agricultural self-employed persons in 1950. However, subsequently he developed a very strong feeling that extension of coverage to self-employed persons was contrary to the basic purpose of the old age and survivors' insurance system, which, he argued, was intended to protect only wage-earners who could not provide for their own protection.

On July 13 the committee voted to include these self-employed persons on a voluntary individual basis. This would have been disastrous from both an administrative and a financial standpoint, because of adverse selection. Therefore, a staff member of the Department of Health, Education, and Welfare, who was assisting the committee, telephoned me to discuss the situation. I had, of course, worked closely with Senator George in the past and appreciated his confidence and support. So I decided to telegraph the Senator on July 14 as follows:

Newspaper stories relative to your feeling that extension of coverage to farm operators should be voluntary prompt me to again presume upon our longtime cooperation in development of social security to make alternative suggestions which I believe will meet your basic concern which I share that no major group be covered unless we are certain that overwhelming majority desires coverage. Main reason some farm operators may not desire coverage is because they believe their late retirement makes such coverage less beneficial to them. To meet this objection and assure general acceptance I suggest following two amendments firstly reduction from 75 to 72 or even 70 years of age at which monthly benefits would be payable without retirement test and secondly an increase of 4% in monthly benefit for each year after reaching 65 years of age that a person delays retirement so that a person retiring at age 70 would draw a 20% higher monthly benefit than a person retiring at age 65. Cost of these two amendments which I believe are highly desirable for persons already covered as well as for newly covered groups is surprisingly low less than 1%. I would strongly recommend against permitting individual voluntary election. When we studied this possibility in past we were appalled at increased cost due to adverse selection and also convinced it would result for most part in persons being covered who needed protection the least rather than the most. I estimate additional cost of extension on voluntary basis would amount to between 20 and 30 billion dollars in next 20 years. As always my highest regards and deep appreciation.

Of course, my hope had been that the Senator would withdraw his opposition to compulsory coverage. However, the Senator read the telegram to the committee to reinforce his strong view that these persons should be excluded. The Senator sent me the following telegram on July 20 to explain his position:

Re Urtel July 14. Senate Finance Committee yesterday eliminated professional groups and farm operators from social security. We had no satisfactory evidence of the wishes of any single group eliminated to come under social security. Regards.

The Senate debated the bill on August 13. Nine amendments were adopted, six proposed amendments were defeated, and six other proposed amendments were withdrawn. None of the amendments adopted was of major importance.

The bill was sent back to the House and a joint conference committee was appointed to reconcile the differences brought about by the Senate changes. The conferees reached agreement and made their report on August 20. The conference report made the following main recommendations:

(1) That insurance coverage be extended to farm operators, effective January 1, 1956.

(2) That the coverage of farm workers be broadened more than the House bill had proposed but less than proposed in the Senate change.

(3) That lawyers, dentists, and other medical practitioners continue to be excluded from the insurance system.

(4) That the existing temporary federal matching ratio under public assistance be continued to September 30, 1956.

Senator George, one of the conferees, declined to sign the conference report because of the inclusion of farm operators and certain self-employed professional persons. He made a very impassioned speech when the report was debated, pointing to his long record of active support of the social security program. He called the inclusion "creeping socialism" and predicted dire consequences to the social security program. The Chairman of the Finance Committee, Senator Millikin of Colorado, in an effort to pacify the Senator, pointed out that the effective date had been delayed so that there would be ample time for Congress to reconsider its action if any considerable farmer opposition developed.

Although this explanation did not satisfy the Senator, the Senate proceeded to approve of the conference report, as did the House, on the same day it was submitted. This was August 20, the last day of the session, and on September 1 the President signed the bill into law.

Three out of four of the major farm organizations making their views known to the congressional committees had recommended inclusion. The fourth, the American Farm Bureau Federation, merely registered its opposition in the form of a brief letter, stating that experience to date with coverage of the self-employed was still insufficient to determine the practicability of covering farmers. Actually, no serious opposition developed subsequent to the passage of the bill, and the inclusion became effective on January 1, 1956.

In my judgment the inclusion of farm operators conclusively assured that any future major change in the old age and survivors' insurance would retain its essential character of relating both benefits and contributions to past earnings. The basis of my belief is that the farmer group exercises political power far in excess of its numbers and that, when its attitude coincides with the attitude of organized labor, the combined effect on Congress is decisive. For the same reason I also believe that it is inevitable that the old age, survivors', and disability insurance system will eventually provide protection against the cost of medical care. It is less certain whether this federal social insurance system will include wage loss due to temporary disability, because insurance against that hazard must necessarily be confined to employees whose wage loss is demonstrable. Therefore, farm operators would not have a compelling self-interest in such inclusion. This is also true of insurance against unemployment wherein the farm operator as an employer may have an adverse interest.*

---

* I am happy to record that in 1956, when the inclusion of farm operators became effective in spite of the bitter opposition of Senator George, the Senator demonstrated on the floor of the Senate his abiding devotion to social security. On July 17, 1956, in the course of debate on changes in the Social Security Act, the Senator offered an amendment to pay social insurance benefits to totally and permanently disabled workers at age 50. He stated that he believed such benefits should be paid at any age but was acceding to the wishes of some senators in fixing this age requirement.

In February of 1956, while the Finance Committee of the Senate was holding hearings on the social security bill, I wrote to Senator George and Senator Byrd, supporting the bill. Senator George was still a member of the Finance Committee but had relinquished the Chairmanship when he became Chairman of the Committee on Foreign Affairs. Senator George referred to my "long letter" during the debate as evidence of the administrative feasibility of paying disability benefits. This was to meet the usual negative argument that the administrative problems were insuperable, but the real reason was the opposition of employer groups, insurance companies, and the American Medical Association.

The American Medical Association, insurance companies, and employers'

Other legislative developments during 1954 represented an anticlimax to the events just described. It will be recalled that what was called the "employment security administrative financing bill" passed the House at the end of the 1953 session of Congress, too late to be considered by the Senate. Hearings were held on the bill by the Finance Committee of the Senate in March 1954. Senator John F. Kennedy appeared before this Senate committee to oppose the bill. He urged as an alternative a bill that had been introduced by the Senators from Rhode Island; their bill would have earmarked the receipts by the Federal government under the Federal Unemployment Tax Act in excess of its disbursements to cover the states' administrative expenses. Out of the fund thus created, the federal government would make outright grants to states whose unemployment reserve funds fell below a certain level, provided the state maintained a contribution rate of at least 2.7 per cent of payroll.

The House bill was reported favorably by the Senate Finance Committee without amendment. Senator Kennedy offered an amendment on the floor of the Senate requiring a state, in order

---

groups had continued their opposition and had succeeded in persuading the Finance Committee to eliminate the disability provision which the House Ways and Means Committee had included. Moreover, the Administration strongly opposed the inclusion of disability benefits.

Senator George led the fight for his amendment. In the course of the debate the Senator said, "Senators voted for that provision [referring to disability benefits under the congressional retirement system] but now they haggle and hesitate when they are asked to do something for the poor people of this country who earn their living by the sweat of their brows." It was largely due to the great prestige of the Senator and the desire to do him honor on his pending retirement that the Senate adopted his amendment by the close vote of 47 to 45.

Actually, the effect of the exaggerated costs predicted by the opponents to the disability provision was to induce Congress to set the contribution rate far higher than necessary. Thus it was possible in 1958 to add benefits for dependents of disabled persons and in 1960 to eliminate the age 50 requirement without further increasing the contribution rate (which is ¼ per cent of taxable wages for employees, ¼ per cent for employers, and ⅜ per cent for self-employed persons). Incidentally, when the cost of providing disability benefits was under discussion in 1950, I had made a rough calculation of my own, which turned out to be surprisingly accurate, although it was utterly unscientific. I had merely taken the permanent total disability cost experience under workmen's compensation laws and multiplied it by 3, on the theory that employees were exposed to the hazard of work injuries for only 8 hours of a 24 hour day!

to be eligible for its pro rata redistribution, to incorporate certain minimum benefit standards in its law. The standards that Senator Kennedy proposed were standards which the President had suggested in his Economic Report on January 28, 1954, that the states incorporate into their laws. The Senator's amendment was defeated 56 to 30.

Senator Kennedy also offered an amendment to limit the use of the redistributed funds to the payment of benefit costs, as had been recommended by the Administration. This amendment was also defeated. The final vote on the passage of the bill was 78 to 3, only Senator Kennedy and the two Senators from Rhode Island voting against passage.

As already mentioned, the President's Message on the State of the Union had urged that, "Protection against the hazards of temporary unemployment should be extended to some 6½ millions of workers, including civilian Federal workers, who now lack this safeguard." In his Economic Report of January 28 the President made his recommendations regarding unemployment insurance more explicit. He recommended that the Federal Unemployment Tax Act should include all employers of one or more employees at any time (instead of employers of eight or more employees for twenty or more weeks in a year); that the coverage of workers engaged in processing agricultural products should be extended to coincide with the coverage of the old age and survivors' insurance system; that federal employees should be eligible for unemployment insurance benefits in accordance with the law of the state in which they last worked; and that new employers should be given the benefit of "employer experience rating" after one year in business instead of after three years.

At the hearings on the Administration's bill held by the House Ways and Means Committee and the Senate Finance Committee, the representatives of the U.S. Chamber of Commerce and the National Association of Manufacturers opposed extending the Federal Unemployment Tax Act to smaller employers on the grounds that the states should be left free to decide whether it was desirable to do so and that such extension might create a precedent for the federal government's establishing minimum benefit standards. The representatives of organized labor endorsed the Administration's proposals as far as they went.

However, the representatives of organized labor made it clear that they believed the recent rapid rise in unemployment to 8.5 per cent of the labor force made it imperative for the Congress to go much further. They strongly endorsed a Democratic bill which would have established federal minimum benefit standards and federal reinsurance grants to states in financial difficulty because of high unemployment.

The bill, as reported by the Ways and Means Committee, contained the following major modifications of the Administration's bill: (1) It extended coverage to employers of four or more employees for twenty or more weeks instead of employers of one or more employees at any time; (2) it eliminated the broadening of coverage of workers engaged in processing agricultural products.

The House passed the bill on July 8 by a vote of 309 to 36, after voting down an amendment to include federal minimum benefit standards. Four days later it was also passed in the Senate.

The Secretary of Labor, following the suggestion made by the President in his Economic Report that the states improve their unemployment insurance laws, wrote to the governors on February 16, 1954. He said he was writing at the suggestion of the President and called attention to the two major suggestions the President had made: That maximum weekly benefits be raised so that the payments to the great majority of the beneficiaries may equal at least half their regular earnings; that the potential duration of unemployment benefits be raised to 26 weeks for all workers who meet the minimum requirements.

The President had pointed out in his Economic Report that the average weekly unemployment benefit in 1938 had represented 43 per cent of the average weekly wage but had fallen to 33 per cent since then. He had also pointed out that only four states provided 26 weeks of benefits to all workers who met the minimum requirements.

The suggestions made by the President and repeated by the Secretary of Labor had virtually no effect on state legislation to improve either the level of weekly benefits or the duration of benefits. At the end of the 1955 sessions of state legislatures, the average weekly benefit still represented only one-third of the average weekly wage, and the number of states that provided 26 weeks of benefits to all eligible workers had increased only from four to six.

I find it difficult to understand why the President and his advisers could possibly have believed that mere exhortation would have any effect on state legislatures, most of whom were responsive to the combined opposition of employers and rural constituencies, regarding more adequate unemployment insurance. I find it equally difficult to understand the thinking of the Administration which led to its health reinsurance proposal.

The President sent his Health Message to the Congress on January 18, as he had announced in his Message on the State of the Union that he would do. In the Health Message he recommended continuation of present federal programs, with increased appropriations, and a broadening of the scope of the Hospital Survey and Construction Act. He also repeated his recommendation for the establishment of a "limited government reinsurance service" but gave no details except to say that, "It can be launched with a capital fund of $25 million provided by the Government to be retired from reinsurance fees."

The President's proposal of a "government reinsurance service" was not accompanied by a bill to implement it. In fact, newspaper stories appeared stating that the Administration not only was finding it difficult to frame a bill which would accomplish its avowed purpose of stimulating the extension of voluntary health insurance to cover more people and to provide more adequate protection, but was also finding that the insurance industry saw no need for such a program.

The Secretary of Health, Education, and Welfare thereupon appointed a group of consultants to assist her in revising a draft bill which the department had prepared. The group consisted of eight persons who were officials of commercial insurance companies and nonprofit health insurance groups, serving as individuals and not as representatives of their organizations. They worked for six days on revising the draft bill.

The Administration bill was introduced in both houses on March 11. It provided for a revolving fund of $25 million, out of which the government would reimburse a health insurance organization for 75 per cent of the amount that its benefit costs exceeded its premium income. The objective, as stated in the bill, was encouraging experimentation to extend and adapt the prepayment method to substantive problem areas or geographic areas, such as coverage of classes of individuals which are not now protected, offering of protection in communities or areas in which such protection is not adequately available, and provision of types of benefits or services not widely available.

The Secretary appeared before the Senate and House committees to which the Administration's bill had been referred. When asked by a member of the House Committee on Interstate and Foreign Commerce whether the individuals she had used as consultants were in accord with the provisions of the bill, she replied, "Mr. Dolliver, I have to answer that question, and I do not want you to think that I am evading it, but I am answering it literally as the eight agreed that the question could be answered. There was unanimous agreement that the gentlemen thought that this was the best way to implement the President's re-insurance proposal."

Subsequently, one of the consultants, who spoke for the American Hospital Association and the Blue Cross Association, stated that he thought the bill would encourage experimentation in extending coverage and benefits. However, another consultant, who appeared on behalf of the American Life Convention and the Life Insurance Association of America, stated that, "I have not, myself, been able to see any purpose for which I think that we probably would use it," and still later, "I am not in favor of the bill.

The representative of the commercial health insurance companies stated that, "Reinsurance, therefore, does not provide a means of making insurable what would otherwise be an uninsurable risk. . . . It does not help to sell insurance nor does it reduce the cost of insurance. If our citizens are not to labor under a misunderstanding, it is essential for them to realize that reinsurance is not a panacea, and that it does not provide additional funds to finance the cost of medical care. . . ."

The representative of the U.S. Chamber of Commerce stated the position of that organization as follows: "Reinsurance does not make insurance available to any class of risk or geographic area not now within the capabilities of voluntary insurance to reach. . . . The national chamber believes that it is contrary to the public interest for Government to enter the business field which is being served by private enterprise. For all of the foregoing reasons, Mr. Chairman and gentlemen, the national chamber strongly opposes the passage of this legislation."

The representative of the American Medical Association also opposed the bill, stating, "I think you know the answer, but the reason is that after the Federal Government started giving these insurance companies money, when it got to be a certain amount the Federal Government would start to have some control of the insurance companies, and then in turn it would go down to the control of the doctor, patient and everybody else, and that would be socialized medicine."

The American Federation of Labor representative did not oppose the Administration's bill, but pointed out that "this bill is long on its aspirations and goals but timorous and hesitating in its implementations." He emphasized that it did not cope with the central problem of enabling low-income families to purchase health insurance. The representative of the Congress of Industrial Organizations flatly opposed the bill, saying, "We fail to see how this bill will extend coverage to the so-called difficult sections of our population, the aged, the unemployed, the medically indigent, the chronically ill."

Although the hearings before the congressional committees disclosed the foregoing lack of enthusiasm and even strong opposition to the bill, the Administration made strenuous efforts to arouse public support. On May 17 the President invited 17 life insurance officials to a luncheon conference, concerning which a White House press release said, "There was a general expression on the part of the life insurance company representatives who were present favoring the general objectives of the bill."

On July 9, the day the bill was reported out by the House committee, the Secretary of Health, Education, and Welfare spoke from the White House over radio and television in support of the bill. She was introduced by the President. In her address she said that the President's reinsurance plan would help in extending voluntary health insurance to the 63 million Americans not having such protection and make broader protection possible for the 92 million who already have some protection "so that the payments will cover more of your hospital bills" and "help you get better insurance protection against long-term illness."

She concluded by saying, "This is a new approach toward solving the health problems of the people. It rejects socialized medicine. It protects your right to choose your own doctor. It is a key part of the Eisenhower program for better health."

In spite of this build-up, the bill failed of passage in the House, when it was debated four days later, by a vote of 238 to 134. One Democratic congressman, in the course of the debate, said, ". . . the fires of enthusiasm which have been developed, and which have been kindled in favor of this bill would probably freeze water, would they not?" In the Senate the bill was reported out by the committee which had held hearings, but it was never brought up for debate.

Thus ended what to me is still a most curious and inexplicable episode in the history of social security legislation. However, this is undoubtedly because I was no longer in a position to observe at close range the individuals involved and all the forces at work.

9.

The Years Ahead

I trust that this recital of events surrounding the passage of the Social Security Act and its development during the period I have presumed to call the formative years has thrown at least some light on why we have the sort of social security system we do have today. I also cherish the hope that it may be of some help in appraising that system not only in the light of conditions existing today but also in the light of conditions existing yesterday. In saying this, I am reminded of Santayana's admonition that those who are ignorant of history are doomed to repeat the mistakes of history.

I feel rather strongly that I should let this recital speak for itself, without attempting any overall appraisal of past events. I am afraid that any attempt to make an evaluation would result instead in a self-serving interpretation of all that has happened. However, I cannot forbear indulging in speculation on what the development of social security might have been if different decisions had been made by the President and his advisers, myself included, in situations where, I think, alternatives were possible.

When I call the period 1934–54 the formative years, I mean that the events of those years determined the major characteristics of our social security system as it exists today. I do not mean to assert that there have been no important improvements since 1954 for indeed there have been,* and I most certainly do not

---

* See Appendix I, "Significant Events of Social Security, 1935–65."

rule out the possibility of fundamental changes in the future. Therefore, in addition to speculating about the effect of past decisions, I shall attempt an evaluation of the adequacy of our social security system as it exists today and suggest considerations which, I think, should be kept in mind in revising it.

Of course, the paramount decision made in 1934 was the rejection by President Roosevelt of the thesis that "recovery must precede reform" and his insistence that, in addition to relieving the existing human distress, it was essential to develop a long-range social program to prevent human destitution. If the President had not taken this position, it is very likely that one of the contemporaneous radical proposals would have gained momentum and perhaps been enacted into law. As it was, the President's rejection of any panacea, such as the "Townsend revolving old age pension plan" or Senator Huey Long's "share the wealth" proposal, meant that any program developed would be based upon available experience in this and other countries and would take into account its impact upon our political, economic, and social institutions.

President Roosevelt's desire to place chief reliance on wage-related contributory social insurance meant not only the rejection of uniform old age pensions but also a sharp separation between insurance benefits related to past contributions and assistance benefits payable on the basis of individual need. It is interesting to note that many other countries which started with uniform pensions, including countries behind the Iron Curtain, later adopted supplementary pension plans which related the amount of the pension to wages. Whether this would have been the course of development in this country is questionable, because the extravagant old age pensions proposed would have left no room for a supplementary system.

President Roosevelt's desire to make maximum use of the states, reinforced by the fear that a national contributory social insurance law would be declared unconstitutional, resulted in the present federal-state system of unemployment insurance. This would have happened in old age insurance as well, if the actuarial and administrative difficulties of a state-by-state system had not seemed to be insuperable.

I am convinced that, if it had not been for the strong views held by President Roosevelt and his advisers concerning the advantages of contributory social insurance and maximum reliance on the states, we would probably have today a national noncontributory form of social security in this country. I think it would have been national in character because of the desperate condition of the country and the serious breakdown of state governments during the Great Depression. I think it would have been noncontributory (that is, paid for out of general revenues) because of the doubtful constitutionality of a contributory social insurance system and because of the greater ease of financing.

However, I think the present unemployment insurance system would have become much more adequate in compensating for wage loss if the Administration had made different recommendations in 1935 and 1939, which it could have done without altering the fundamental federal-state character, without increasing the danger of unconstitutionality, and with fair likelihood that its recommendations would have been accepted by Congress.

In 1935 the Business Advisory Council of the Department of Commerce had recommended that there be employee contributions for unemployment insurance, as there were for old age pensions. So did a considerable minority of the advisory council of the Committee on Economic Security. However, the labor representatives particularly and others on this council felt that the cost of unemployment should be borne by employers. If employee contributions had been included in the 1935 bill, I believe that the adverse effect of employer experience rating in keeping benefits low would have been far less. I also believe that the adversary character of existing state laws would have been avoided, as it has been under the old age, survivors', and disability insurance system.

In 1939 the Social Security Board did not support the McCormack amendment, which would have required the maintenance of an average contribution rate of 2.7 per cent unless a state observed specified minimum benefit standards. By that time there was no longer any danger that incorporating benefit standards into the federal law would be unconstitutional. However, the Board believed not only that it would be dangerous to reduce the rate but also that the benefit standards proposed were so low that they might discourage rather than encourage adequate benefit provisions in state laws. In retrospect, I believe the establishment of the principle of minimum benefit standards, regardless of the low level of the initial standards, would have led eventually to incorporation of far more adequate benefit standards in the federal law than now exist in most states. And, of course, the absence of such standards has resulted in average contribution rates far below 2.7 per cent in practically all states.

Another serious mistake that the Social Security Board made in 1939 regarding unemployment insurance was to recommend that the $3,000 maximum wage under the old age insurance system be incorporated into the federal unemployment tax. At the time that seemed to be a perfectly logical recommendation and of no long-range significance. However, it has proved to be a major reason why the level of benefits has not risen commensurately with the rise in the wage level, since it has maintained an unrealistically low maximum wage for calculating benefits. What the Board should have done was to recommend that the $3,000 maximum under the old age insurance system be removed.

In the case of old age insurance, the paramount question, during the years elapsing after the passage of the Social Security Act until 1954, remained essentially what it had been in 1934–35: Would we have a contributory system with both benefits and contributions related to past wages or would we have a uniform old age pension financed either by a general tax of some sort or perhaps simply out of general revenues? In 1940 the Social Security Board and the President were giving serious consideration to recommending a "double-decker" system providing a noncontributory, uniform, universal old age pension plus a contributory variable pension, with both the benefits and the contributions related to wages. The intervention of the war deflected the attention of Congress, and by 1949, when Congress next considered revision of the Social Security Act, interest in a uniform, universal old age pension had considerably subsided. However, some Republican leaders in Congress, notably Senator Taft and several members of the Ways and Means Committee, still supported the idea.

The passage of the 1950 old age and survivors' insurance amendments, which greatly extended the coverage and increased the benefits, removed the danger of outright repeal of the old age insurance but did not eliminate the possibility of the adoption of some form of double-decker system. I think there always was much to be said for the adoption of such a system on the grounds of equity, since the dividing line between a person who barely qualifies for an insurance benefit and one who does not is so fine. However, I still believe we were justified in not advocating such a system because of the danger that the noncontributory uniform pension would be made so large that the superimposed contributory wage-related pension would become insignificant. In any event, I am certain we were justified in opposing the sort of double-decker systems that were proposed by the U.S. Chamber of Commerce and by Congressman (now Senator) Curtis of Nebraska.

As I look back on the ten-year struggle from 1949 to 1958 to incorporate permanent total-disability benefits into the old age, survivors', and disability insurance, I am convinced that struggle could have been avoided and we could have had these benefits 20 years sooner, if the Social Security Board had advocated the immediate inclusion of such benefits when we made our recommendations to the President and Congress in December 1938 and January 1939. In July 1938, following the National Health Conference, the American Medical Association had stated its willingness to support such benefits, although in subsequent years it bitterly opposed them. However, in 1938 the Board was willing to say only that it thought it could solve the administrative problems if benefits were not made payable until one or two years after monthly old age insurance benefits had begun.

In public assistance I think we made two cardinal mistakes in our legislative recommendations. In 1935 we should have recommended federal grants-in-aid to the states for all needy persons, not simply needy persons falling within defined "categories." The number of needy persons not included in these categories was larger than we had realized, and most of the states needed federal aid in providing adequate assistance to these persons. Moreover, this would have saved a great deal of the administrative energy consumed in determining an individual's eligibility and would have facilitated providing constructive assistance on a family basis.

Another major error that was made in public assistance was

President Roosevelt's refusal to accept the Social Security Board's recommendation in 1939 that federal aid to the states be in direct proportion to their need, as measured by their per capita income. The result has been that hundreds of millions of dollars have been funneled into the richer states in order to provide necessary federal aid to the poorer states.

I think our greatest mistakes lay in the decisions we made, or failed to make, concerning protection against the cost of medical care. I believe we were justified in not including this phase of social security in our 1935 recommendations. As it was, the omnibus bill we recommended ran into serious opposition because of the inclusion of old age insurance. If we had included health insurance in the bill, it undoubtedly would have encountered even more opposition. However, after the successful National Health Conference in July 1938, I believe we would have been able to secure favorable congressional action if the President had actively supported Senator Robert F. Wagner's bill, which I had prepared and which incorporated the recommendations of the Interdepartmental Committee to Coordinate Health and Welfare Activities. That bill provided for federal grants to the states to assist them in establishing a state plan of medical care, supported by either contributions from beneficiaries or general taxation, and covering only needy persons or the general population, as a state might choose.

In 1946 I think we may have made a mistake in not seeking to find a common ground with Senator Taft and other Republican senators who had sponsored a bill which would have made grants-in-aid to the states to assist them in establishing plans for paying the cost of health services for persons unable to pay the whole cost. The bill did not confine the plan to the destitute. It also provided that a state could pay premiums to voluntary nonprofit health insurance plans on behalf of such persons. Senator Taft explained that this provision of the bill would "thus encourage those funds, which then, of course, would make available to people in the middle income group who desire health insurance, an opportunity to take out health insurance, if they wish to do so."

The reason we did not seek to find common ground was that we feared any proposal limited to the "medically needy" and dependent upon state action would delay or perhaps prevent the development of a nationwide plan protecting normally self-supporting persons against the unpredictable costs of medical care. However, if we had sought a compromise, it is possible that successful experience in providing protection to low-income persons might have led to progressive extension of this protection to higher-income persons, and eventually to the entire population.

Again, in 1949, I think we may have made a mistake in not seeking to find a common ground with a number of Republican senators and congressmen who introduced an identical bill (including Senators Flanders and Ives and then Congressmen Nixon and Javits) which would have enabled nonprofit health insurance plans to extend their coverage to low-income and high-cost groups. The Blue Cross plans particularly, which undertook to insure persons on a "community rated" basis, have suffered from the competition of commercial insurance carriers that could charge lower premiums to selected individuals and groups. Under the 1949 bill, the federal government would have made grants to the states (varying inversely with their per capita income) to help finance subsidies to nonprofit health insurance organizations. These subsidies would cover the difference between the actual cost of the benefits provided and premiums charged on the basis of the individual income of the insured persons.

The reason we did not look with favor on this proposal was that we felt that the likelihood of many states' adopting plans to subsidize nonprofit organizations was very small because of the natural opposition of commercial insurance companies. Therefore, the only result would be to delay the adoption of a nationwide health insurance program. However, in retrospect that delay could hardly have been longer than the fifteen years that has already elapsed without any nationwide program to cover the cost of medical care.

In addition to these various decisions concerning legislative recommendations which affected the development of social security, there were administrative decisions concerning the interpretation of the legislation on the statute books which also had an important effect on the development of social security. As I have tried to demonstrate throughout this chronicle, administration consists of more than organization, procedures, and personnel, important as these phases of administration are in making social legislation a living reality. Administration also consists of interpreting social legislation in such a manner that it achieves its fundamental purpose most fully.

Thus, the Social Security Board consistently throughout the years called the contributory old age, survivors', and disability benefits system "insurance" and emphasized the statutory right to these benefits. I believe that this interpretation did much to popularize this particular plan, which in 1936 was branded as a "fraud" and a "cruel hoax" by the Republican presidential candidate, but in 1954 was called "the cornerstone of the Government's programs to promote the economic security of the individual" by a Republican President. Moreover, this President went further and stated, "I am determined to preserve its basic principles."

The Social Security Board interpreted the term "employee" (which was not defined in the titles of the Social Security Act establishing this social insurance system) to mean a person who performed service for an individual or organization and was dependent upon the business to which he rendered service, as a matter of economic reality. This was a far broader interpretation than that which existed under the old common-law concept of the master and servant relationship. The Board's interpretation was upheld by the United States Supreme Court. It required an act of Congress to reverse it, and President Truman made this reversal a successful issue in the 1948 presidential campaign.

In unemployment insurance probably the most important interpretation of the law was to decide that the states were required to pay benefits through public employment offices affiliated with the United States Employment Service. If the Social Security Board had not interpreted the Social Security Act in this manner, it is certain that the administration of unemployment insurance in many states would have been a failure. It is also certain that in 1941 we would not have had a nationwide network of public employment offices which was vital in mobilizing the manpower of the country during World War II.

In public assistance the most important interpretation of the law was undoubtedly the Board's decision that state old age assistance plans must provide for the payment of assistance on the basis of individual need. If the Board had interpreted the law as permitting the states to pay uniform monthly allowances to all persons over 65, regardless of need, as some states proposed to do, or even if it had permitted the payment of a uniform monthly allowance to all persons whose income did not exceed a fixed amount, it is probable that the old age insurance system would never have gone into effect.

Other important administrative decisions concerning public assistance included the interpretation of such terms as "state plan," "money payments," and "fair hearing." The Board had interpreted the stipulation of a "state plan" to require a state to establish statewide standards for determining eligibility and individual need, so that persons in equal circumstances would be treated equally throughout the state. If the Board had interpreted the term "state plan" as not necessarily requiring such statewide standards, local administrative units could have done as they pleased, regardless of consistency or equity.

The Board ruled that the term "fair hearing" required that an applicant or recipient of public assistance whose claim was denied must be given the opportunity to have his claim reviewed by someone not involved in making the initial decision. This interpretation helped greatly in assuring consistent and equitable treatment.

The Board interpreted the phrase "money payments" to mean that the recipient must be allowed unrestricted use of those payments. Therefore, a state or county welfare agency, once it had determined the amount necessary to cover a person's need, could not control the actual use made of the money provided. The Board strictly adhered to this interpretation, believing that this was the essential difference between public assistance paid in cash and poor relief provided in kind.

The Social Security Board was confronted with a contradictory mandate from Congress concerning its approval of methods of administration by state public assistance and unemployment compensation agencies. The 1935 Social Security Act required the Board, before authorizing federal grants, to make certain that these agencies had adopted satisfactory methods of administration "other than those relating to selection, tenure of office, and compensation of personnel." The only way the Board could reconcile this contradictory language was to interpret it to mean that, while the Board could require a state to set up a merit system for the selection of personnel, it could not interfere in the case of an individual employee. A national civil service association has credited this interpretation with having greatly stimulated the development of civil service not only for employees of state agencies receiving grants under the Social Security Act but for state employees generally. Naturally I, as an administrator, believe that the Board's interpretation was essential for the success of these federal-state programs. Apparently Congress agreed, because in 1939 it amended the law to make it clear that state and local employees in these programs must be employed in accordance with a merit system.

Upon the basis of this chronological discussion of the development of the Social Security Act, I shall attempt a brief appraisal of the extent to which we have achieved the dream President Roosevelt expressed on one occasion during the war as follows: "When you talk with our young men and women you will find that with the opportunity for employment they want assurance against the evils of all major economic hazards—assurance that will extend from the cradle to the grave. This great Government can and must provide this assurance."

There is no question that President Roosevelt wanted this assurance to consist primarily of contributory social insurance. We do have a nationwide old age, survivors', and disability insurance system and also a nationwide unemployment insurance system. However, the benefits provided are far from being adequate and they do not protect all workers.

The average monthly benefit now being awarded to a retired worker who has been regularly employed in insured employment represents only 30 per cent of his monthly wage loss. If he has a wife who has also reached the minimum retirement age, his monthly benefit is increased by 50 per cent. While benefits have been increased throughout the years to keep pace with the increased cost of living, they have not kept pace with the increased wage level. In my opinion, the benefit level should be raised by at least 33⅓ per cent. I also believe that the remaining 5 per cent of the workers in this country who are not now covered by this social insurance system or some other government insurance system should be given its protection.

The present federal-state unemployment insurance system is quite inadequate both in its benefit provisions and in its coverage. The average weekly benefit paid compensates for only 35 per cent of the average weekly wage loss, and only 12 state laws provide dependents' allowances. Actually, a smaller proportion of the weekly wage loss is compensated today than when these laws were first enacted, because the maximum wage upon which benefits are based has not been increased to keep pace with the increased wage level. One unemployed worker out of four exhausts his benefits before he can find another job. Moreover, 20 per cent of the workers are not insured. The combined result of all these limitations is that only about 20 per cent of the total wage loss resulting from unemployment throughout the country is being compensated. Because of this, Congress was obliged to enact the Temporary Extended Unemployment Compensation Act of 1961, which paid benefits out of the federal Treasury to unemployed workers who had exhausted their benefit rights.

This situation has developed largely because, as has already been explained, the Federal Unemployment Tax Act does not protect employers in states that may desire to have an adequate unemployment insurance law from unfair competition by employers in other states that have inadequate laws, despite the basic intent of the act. I am of the opinion that, if the present federal-state system is continued, the Federal Unemployment Tax Act should be amended: (1) to include minimum benefit standards which would increase the benefit level by 50 per cent; (2) to provide federal grants-in-aid to states whose benefit expenditures exceed a certain percentage of covered payroll; and (3) to require that, if the law continues to give employers credit for contributions they have not made because of favorable experience with unemployment, then experience must be measured by stabilization of employment, not by benefits paid.

I believe the coverage under the Federal Unemployment Tax Act should be extended to include all types of employment covered by the old age, survivors', and disability insurance system. The maximum earnings of $3,000 which are subject to the employers' tax should be raised at least to the level of the maximum subject to the payroll tax under the old age, survivors', and disability insurance system.

The great gap in our present Social Security Act is its failure to include two forms of social insurance which are found in the social security systems of practically all other industrialized countries: insurance to cover wage loss resulting from nonoccupational temporary disability and insurance to cover the cost of medical care. Of course, workmen's compensation laws cover wage loss and medical care for work-connected injuries.

The Railroad Unemployment Insurance Act insures against wage loss due to unemployment caused by disability, as well as by lack of work. Also, four states have temporary-disability laws. It seems to me, however, that a nationwide system of protection against wage loss resulting from nonoccupational disability is essential and might be provided in either of two ways: adding it to the protection provided under the federal-state unemployment insurance system, or incorporating it into the protection provided under the federal old age, survivors', and disability insurance system. I would choose the latter method for several reasons. One is that the states have shown so little interest, the last state temporary-disability insurance law having been passed in 1949. Another is that the states have failed to enact reasonably adequate unemployment insurance laws. A third, very important reason is that it could be related to the protection, under old age, survivors', and disability insurance, for wage loss resulting from permanent total disability: A disabled worker would receive his benefits for temporary disability during the first six months of his disability. Before the end of that time a determination could be made of whether his disability was likely to last twelve months or more from its onset. If so, he would continue to receive benefits without interruption, in accordance with the 1965 liberalization of the definition of disability.

The question of including health insurance in the Social Security Act is far more controversial today than it was when the act was passed. Many people believe that it is no longer necessary to adopt this form of social insurance because of the great growth in private health insurance during the last thirty years. However, only about one-fourth of the nation's expenditures for personal health care are covered by private insurance. Actually, the expenditures by the federal, state, and local governments for personal health care (exclusive of research and public health activities) are almost as much.

Unfortunately, in this country the lower-income groups, which have the most sickness, are the very groups which have the least insurance protection. Moreover, the cost of medical care has been increasing far more rapidly than the costs of other items. Therefore, it is my judgment that the problem of enabling the American people to meet the cost of adequate medical care cannot be completely solved except through a nationwide contributory social insurance system or a nationwide health service system financed out of general revenues.

Since 1960 the Social Security Act has included, under title I, federal grants to the states for providing medical assistance to needy persons over 65 years of age who were not recipients of cash assistance but whose income and resources were not sufficient to meet the costs of necessary medical services. However, it was not until 1965 that the Social Security Act was amended to provide health insurance for persons over 65 years of age, without the imposition of a needs test.

The 1965 legislation provides limited protection against the costs of hospital and related care (not including the cost of physicians' services) to all persons over 65 years of age who are entitled to monthly cash benefits either under the old age, survivors', and disability insurance system or under the Railroad Retirement Act. This protection is also provided persons already 65 years of age or who become 65 years of age before 1968, but who are not entitled to monthly cash benefits under either of these two social insurance systems. Besides providing protection against the costs of hospital and related care, the 1965 legislation also permits all persons over 65 years of age (whether or not they are eligible for monthly cash benefits under the two social insurance systems) to purchase from the federal government protection against the cost of physicians' services, the government paying half of the cost.

This 1965 legislation is very limited in its coverage of persons protected. It is also very complicated in its eligibility, financial, and administrative provisions. However, it will provide valuable experience as a guide to creating a simpler and more universal health insurance system. This is most important, because the problems involved are quite different and much more difficult than those involved in providing cash benefits as a protection against loss of income resulting from unemployment, sickness, permanent disability, old age, and death.

To a considerable extent the inadequacies of our present social insurance system are responsible for the fact that we still have almost nine million destitute persons in this country who are obliged to seek public assistance. However, almost half of this number are receiving aid to dependent children, and two-thirds of these children are in need because of the breakdown of the family, resulting from divorce or separation of the parents, desertion by one parent, or illegitimacy of the child. Only the third who are needy because of the death or disability of a parent could have been protected under social insurance. Moreover, a large number of the adults receiving public assistance are low wage earners or chronically unemployed. Social insurance which provides benefits related to wage loss cannot be adequate when the wage itself is inadequate.

Therefore, even if we had a far more adequate contributory social insurance system, it would still be essential that we have an adequate and humane system of public assistance. Unfortunately, this is not the case. Actually, three-fourths of the states, according to their own standards, do not meet the full needs of recipients in one or more of the federally aided categories. The situation is even worse in "general assistance" which is not federally aided.

As has already been suggested, the federal government should make grants to the states to assist them in providing aid to all needy persons, regardless of whether they fall within circumscribed categories. The states should be required to meet 100 per cent of the need that is established by a state's own standard and certified by the state as sufficient to provide reasonable subsistence compatible with decency and health. I believe this would help to make the public assistance payments more adequate. However, we cannot expect a state to establish a standard of reasonable subsistence any higher than the prevailing minimum standard for self-supporting individuals. If that is too low, the public assistance standard will be too low.

The states should also be required to eliminate all state residence requirements. The reason the federal government is bearing considerably more than half of the total cost of public assistance for the country as a whole is to protect needy Americans, regardless of where they happen to live—and more than five million Americans move from one state to another every year.

Unfortunately, throughout the years the federal government has shared in the cost of administration of public assistance on a far less liberal basis than it has in the cost of the assistance given to needy persons. Apparently, Congress and also state legislatures have looked upon administration as simply overhead expense. The result has been that state welfare agencies have not had sufficient funds to provide constructive social service to help needy persons cope with their many problems and, if possible, become self-supporting. However, at long last, in 1962 Congress did provide for liberal federal sharing in the cost of rehabilitative services not only to recipients but also to applicants for public assistance and to persons likely to become applicants. The long-range results of this change in emphasis can be very great.

I believe that, if our social insurance system were improved in the ways I have suggested, it would prevent most normally self-supporting persons from becoming destitute because of interruption of earnings due to the major personal economic hazards. I also believe that an improved public assistance system would relieve in an effective and humane manner the destitution that does arise, so that all Americans would be able to purchase the necessities of life.

The proportion of the gross national product now used for the social insurances and public assistance in this, the most affluent nation in all history, is 5½ per cent. The proportion that would be needed to provide adequate cash benefits under a comprehensive social insurance system and a comprehensive public assistance system would be 8 per cent (including workmen's compensation). A universal, comprehensive health insurance system would require an additional 4 per cent.

These percentages of our gross national product do not represent an added expense to the nation. The loss of family income—resulting from unemployment, sickness, permanent disability, old age, and death—is a fact, whether or not protection is provided against it. The cost of medical care is a fact, whether or not protection is provided against it. Moreover, to the extent that this protection reduces dependency and stabilizes purchasing power, it actually increases our gross national product.

Thus, I believe that it is possible to abolish destitution in this country almost overnight through the establishment of a comprehensive contributory social insurance system, supplemented by a comprehensive public assistance system. We have not only the resources but the experience to do so. I have no doubt that eventually we will achieve the national consensus to act on the basis of that experience.

I have not attempted to submit a complete blueprint for the future, but merely to indicate some specific changes that I think should be made in the present system. Whether or not these particular changes are accepted, I should like to suggest some general considerations that I think ought to be kept in mind in making any changes. First of all, I think we should concentrate our attention on developing a system whose primary purpose is limited to protecting individuals from becoming destitute. We should undertake to realize this specific purpose in such a way as to promote general goals that are desirable from a social, political, and economic standpoint, such as better distribution of income, stabilization of purchasing power, control of the business cycle, and strengthening of our federal-state form of government.

I think it is essential that the federal government take the initiative and have continuing responsibility for the development of an effective nationwide social security system. However, I believe that we should explore fully the advantages of federal-state cooperation in the administration of various features of the system. The mistakes and failures of the past should be used as a guide, not a bar, to future cooperation. We should not blame the states for failure to act because of fear of unfair interstate competition when the federal law failed to protect them from that competition, nor for failure to provide sufficient funds because of lack of fiscal capacity. Insofar as the state legislatures may have been to blame for not having met their full responsibility under the present provisions of the Social Security Act, we should recognize that basic changes are now going on in voter registration and legislative reapportionment which are bound to affect future state legislatures.

I believe we should place maximum reliance on contributory social insurance. It seems to me that it fits in best with our economic and social institutions, because of the close relationship among benefits, contributions, and wages. Thus we can maintain individual equity by paying differential benefits to take account of variations in wage loss, at the same time that we make certain social adequacy is achieved by paying higher proportionate benefits to low wage earners.

In order to achieve these twin objectives, I believe it is desirable that a portion of the cost of social insurance benefits should be financed out of general revenues. I think paying a portion of the cost out of general revenues is desirable also because it introduces greater flexibility into the financing. Thus, the portion financed out of general revenues can be financed out of progressive taxes or borrowing, whichever seems warranted by prevailing economic conditions.

Of course, the goal of social security should be to provide the maximum amount of necessary protection against economic insecurity at a minimum cost. Therefore, a social security system should aim at providing a basic floor of protection upon which an individual can build more effectively a higher standard of living through home ownership, savings, and private insurance, and upon which employers and labor organizations can build health and welfare plans to provide additional protection.

It goes without saying that, in order to provide maximum protection at a minimum cost, it is necessary that we undertake to coordinate all governmental systems which provide economic security, so as to eliminate all gaps, overlaps, and anomalies. At the present time, duplicate benefits are being paid under the old age, survivors', and disability insurance and other government systems, such as federal and state workmen's compensation laws, the United States civil service retirement system, or the railroad retirement system, as well as through veterans' benefits and military personnel pensions.

Needless to say, I also think that the federal agency which would be charged with the administration of such an important program should not only be adequate in its organization and its staffing but also have a clear congressional mandate regarding its basic purpose. The heterogeneous character of the present Department of Health, Education, and Welfare has created needless administrative obstacles as well as confusion regarding our concept of social security.

It seems inevitable to me that the growing expansion of federal health, education, and welfare activities will require the establishment of a cabinet department for each of these three fields. This probable development will afford the opportunity to rectify the mistakes of the past which have led to downgrading and destroying the originally integrated character of social security administration. It will make it possible to group together social insurance, public assistance, and other related activities, without loss of identity or status of any of these activities.

Whether the new department is called "Department of Social Security" or "Department of Social Welfare" or some other name is less important than that it be a name that indicates its homogeneity and great purpose. Naturally, I would favor calling it the "Department of Social Security." This would serve to revive the original comprehensive concept of social security, which, in the course of the years, has been narrowed to refer only to the federal old age, survivors', and disability insurance system.

As I have said, I believe that it is possible to abolish destitution in this country almost overnight through the establishment of a comprehensive contributory social insurance system, supplemented by a comprehensive public assistance system. I do not mean to suggest that we would then have abolished the root causes of poverty arising out of the inability of individuals to find jobs which pay them enough to maintain themselves and their families in decency and health. The causes of this inability are both impersonal and personal. Neither contributory social insurance nor public assistance is a substitute for gainful employment at adequate wages. Furthermore, its receipt cannot abolish discrimination or automatically endow workers with the training, education, and other personal qualities necessary to take advantage of available employment opportunities.

But contributory social insurance can spread the wage-income of normally self-supporting workers over periods of non-earning, as well as over periods of earning. Both contributory social insurance and public assistance can furnish the income necessary for decency and health while these root causes of poverty are being eradicated. This income can be provided in a manner that maintains self-respect and promotes the desire to be self-sufficient. It can be accompanied by constructive social services, which make certain that all of a community's resources, both governmental and nongovernmental, including health and educational facilities, low-cost housing, and day-care centers, are actually used to enable recipients to be self-supporting.

The responsibility for marshaling a community's resources to enable recipients of public assistance to enjoy a satisfying and useful life rests, of course, upon the public welfare agency administering public assistance. But that same agency can and should be used to marshal these resources for all citizens of the community who need them. Thus, a public welfare agency can be a powerful factor in the "war on poverty."

It has come as a shock to the people of America that there should be so much poverty during this unprecedented period of prosperity. While much poverty has been prevented or mitigated because of the programs included in the Social Security Act, too much remains. Moreover, the same factors that have created our affluent society, such as increasing mechanization, industrialization, and urbanization, are responsible for most of this poverty.

The great changes that have occurred and will occur arise out of the very nature of a highly dynamic society based upon a system of free enterprise. Our problem is to retain all the advantages of a dynamic free enterprise system while we seek to eliminate its disadvantages.

I am sure that this great nation will succeed in solving this problem and that an improved social security system will be a main factor in the solution. We are indeed fortunate, in this land of ours, that we have the economic resources to achieve the good life for all our citizens. What we need to do is perfect our social organization to take full advantage of these resources.

In seeking to perfect our social organization, I am sure we shall keep in mind that our goal is simply a redistribution of welfare, whereby every citizen is assured genuine freedom of opportunity —which is both the promise and the challenge of our democratic way of life.

APPENDICES AND INDEX

Appendix I

Significant Events of Social Security, 1935–65

1935

January 17.—Report of Committee on Economic Security transmitted to Congress with recommendations for federal old age insurance, federal-state public assistance and unemployment compensation programs, and extension of public health services, maternal and child health services, services for crippled children, child welfare services, and vocational rehabilitation services. Economic security bill introduced.

August 14.—Social Security Act became law.

August 23.—Members of Social Security Board named by President: John G. Winant (Chairman), Arthur J. Altmeyer, and Vincent M. Miles.

August 29.—Railroad Retirement Act of 1935 and Carriers Taxing Act of 1935 signed by President (to replace Railroad Retirement Act of 1934).

1936

January 1.—Federal unemployment tax of 1 per cent of payrolls first applicable to employers of 8 or more, with credit offset for contributions paid to state unemployment funds.

February.—Public assistance payments to recipients first made with federal participation under Social Security Act in old age assistance (17 states), aid to dependent children (10 states), and aid to the blind (9 states).

March 5.—First federal grant for administration of state unemployment insurance law (New Hampshire) certified.

August 17.—First state unemployment benefit paid in Wisconsin.

November.—All states, the District of Columbia, Alaska, and Hawaii actively participating in program of maternal and child health services under Social Security Act.

1937

January 1.—Workers began to acquire credits toward old age insurance benefits. Employers and employees each subject to tax of 1 per cent of wages, up to $3,000 a year. Lump sum payments first payable to eligible workers, their survivors, or their estates.

Federal unemployment tax payable by employers of 8 or more increased to 2 per cent of payrolls.

May 24.—Constitutionality of old age and unemployment insurance provisions of Social Security Act upheld by United States Supreme Court (301 U.S. 495, 548, 619).

June 24.—Railroad Retirement Act of 1937 became law, amending portions of Railroad Retirement Act of 1935.

June 30.—Unemployment insurance legislation became nationwide with approved laws in all states.

1938

January 1.—Federal unemployment tax, payable by employers of 8 or more, increased to 3 per cent of payrolls.

June 25.—Railroad Unemployment Insurance Act became law.

September.—All 51 jurisdictions making old age assistance payments under Social Security Act.

1939

March 24.—All states, the District of Columbia, Alaska, and Hawaii actively participating in program of crippled children's services under Social Security Act.

July 1.—Federal Security Agency, set up by President's Reorganization Plan No. 1 of 1939, integrated into one unit the Social Security Board (to which was transferred the United States Employment Service), U.S. Public Health Service, Civilian Conservation Corps, National Youth Administration, and U.S. Office of Education.

August 10.—Social Security Act amended to provide, under old age and survivors' insurance, benefits for dependents and survivors, to advance payment of monthly benefits to 1940, to revise the benefit formula, to modify certain coverage provisions, and to hold contribution rates for employers and employees at 1 per cent each through 1942; under unemployment insurance, to modify definition of covered employment and make tax applicable only to first $3,000 in wages; to increase federal share of public assistance payments; to raise annual authorization for grants for maternal and child health, crippled children's, and child welfare services and to extend these programs to Puerto Rico. For unemployment insurance and public assistance, state personnel merit system made requisite for Social Security Board approval of state plan; also made a condition for federal grants for maternal and child health and crippled children's services.

1940

January.—Monthly benefits first payable under old age and survivors' insurance.

June.—All states, the District of Columbia, Alaska, Hawaii, and Puerto Rico actively participating in program of child welfare services under Social Security Act.

1942

February 9.—Social Security Board given certain responsibilities in program for aid to enemy aliens.

February 26.—Social Security Board authorized to administer monthly benefits, assistance, and services to civilians affected by enemy action.

April 29.—Rhode Island enacted first cash sickness insurance law, providing temporary-disability benefits to those covered by state unemployment insurance law.

August 28.—Emergency grants to states authorized for programs for day care for children of working mothers under plans approved by Children's Bureau and Office of Education, administered by Work Projects Adminstration.

October 21.—Old age and survivors' insurance contribution rates frozen at 1 per cent through 1943. (Increase again postponed in 1943, 1944, 1945, 1946, and 1947, through 1949.)

1943

March 18.—Medical and hospital care for wives and infants of enlisted men in the four lowest grades of armed forces authorized to be administered by Children's Bureau, through grants to state health departments.

March 24.—Wartime coverage under old age and survivors' insurance provided for seamen employed by or through War Shipping Administation.

1944

February 25.—Social Security Act amended to authorize appropriation, to old age and survivors' insurance trust fund, of any additional amounts required to finance benefits.

June 22.—Servicemen's Readjustment Act of 1944 (G.I. Bill of Rights) approved. Provided for special placement services through United States Employment Service and readjustment allowances for unemployed and self-employed veterans.

October 3.—Federal unemployment account authorized in the unemployment trust fund from which, up to July 1947, states might borrow when their own unemployment funds dropped to a certain level.

1946

July 16.—Under the President's Reorganization Plan No. 2 of 1946, Social Security Board abolished and its functions transferred to the Federal Security Administrator, who established the Social Security Administration to carry on programs of Social Security Board and those of the Children's Bureau. The Children's Bureau (except for its child labor functions) transferred to Federal Security Agency by same plan.

August 10.—Social Security Act amended to provide monthly benefits under old age and survivors' insurance for survivors of certain World War II veterans, coverage of private maritime employment under state unemployment insurance, temporary unemployment benefits to seamen with wartime federal employment, permission for states with employee contributions under their unemployment insurance laws to use such funds for temporary-disability insurance benefits, greater federal sharing in public assistance payments for a specified period, and larger grants for maternal and child health and child welfare, as well as extension of these programs to the Virgin Islands.

1947

August 6.—Social Security Act amended to hold old age and survivors' insurance contribution rate for employers and employees at 1 per cent for 1948 and 1949 and to schedule increases to 1½ per cent each for 1950 and 1951 and to 2 per cent each in 1952 and thereafter. Increased federal share in public assistance programs extended through June 1950. Authorization for appropriations to special federal unemployment account, from which states may borrow when their funds are low, extended through 1949.

1948

April 20.—Social Security Act amended to exclude certain newspaper and magazine vendors from coverage under old age and survivors' insurance and under the Federal Unemployment Tax Act.

June 14.—Definition of "employee" as used in the Social Security

Act limited and federal participation in public assistance payments increased.

July 29.—Administration of Federal Credit Union Act transferred to Federal Security Agency, and Bureau of Federal Credit Unions established in Social Security Administration.

1949

June 30.—Termination of emergency maternity and infant care program administered by Children's Bureau in cooperation with state health departments.

August 20.—Bureau of Employment Security transferred from Social Security Administration to Labor Department.

1950

January 1.—Old age and survivors' insurance contribution rates permitted to increase to 1½ per cent each for employers and employees.

August 28.—Social Security Act amended to extend coverage under old age and survivors' insurance to about ten million more persons (including most non-farm self-employed persons), to liberalize the eligibility conditions, to improve the retirement test, to provide wage credits of $160 a month for military service from September 1940 to July 1947, to increase benefits substantially, to raise the wage base for tax and benefit computation purposes, to provide a new contribution schedule, and to eliminate 1944 provision authorizing appropriations to trust fund from general Treasury; in public assistance, to establish program of aid to the permanently and totally disabled, to broaden for federal matching purposes aid to dependent children to include relative with whom child is living, and to extend federal matching provisions to aged and blind persons in certain public medical institutions and to payments made directly to doctors, hospitals, and others supplying medical care to recipients; and, in states making assistance payments to persons in institutions, to require standards for such institutions; in the programs for maternal and child health, crippled children's, and child welfare services, to raise maximum authorization for grants. Old age and survivors' insurance and public assistance programs extended to Puerto Rico and the Virgin Islands.

October.—First payments made under the federal-state program of aid to the permanently and totally disabled.

1951

January 1.—Old age and survivors' insurance contribution rate of 2¼ per cent of earnings effective for self-employed.

October 20.—Revenue Act of 1951 authorized certification of grants for public assistance to states with laws specifying conditions for public access to assistance records if such legislation bars the use of information thus obtained for commercial or political purposes.

October 30.—Railroad Retirement Act amended to coordinate railroad retirement and old age and survivors' insurance programs further by transferring to old age and survivors' insurance the wage records of workers who die or retire with less than 10 years' railroad employment; to provide for financial interchanges between systems so that old age and survivors' insurance trust fund will be placed in the same position it would have been if railroad and employment had always been covered under old age and survivors' insurance.

1952

July 16.—Veterans' Readjustment Assistance Act, which included unemployment compensation for veterans amounting to $26 a week minus any weekly unemployment insurance benefit payable under any other law, subject to a maximum total of $676.

July 18.—Social Security Act amended to increase benefits under old age and survivors' insurance, to extend the period of wage credits for military service through December 31, 1953, to liberalize the retirement test, and to liberalize the grant formula for public assistance payments to make additional funds available to the states.

1953

April 11.—Reorganization Plan No. 1 abolished Federal Security Agency and transferred all its powers and functions to Department of Health, Education, and Welfare.

May.—With approval of Nevada's plan for aid to the blind, all 53 jurisdictions administering such programs.

August 5.—Federal Unemployment Tax Act amended to cover federal seamen under unemployment insurance.

August 14.—Old age and survivors' insurance wage credits of $160 a month provided for active military service performed after 1953 and before July 1, 1955.

1954

January 1.—Rise in old age and survivors' insurance contribution rates effective, increasing to 2 per cent each for employers and employees and to 3 per cent for self-employed.

August 3.—Vocational Rehabilitation Act amended to call for cooperation of vocational rehabilitation agencies with state public assistance agencies, the Bureau of Old Age and Survivors Insurance, and other public agencies providing services related to vocational rehabilitation.

August 5.—Employment Security Administrative Financing Act provided that excess of collections of federal unemployment tax over employment security administrative expenditures be used to maintain permanent reserve of $200 million in federal unemployment account, which will lend funds to states with depleted reserves and divide the excess over $200 million among the states for benefit payments or administrative costs.

September 1.—Social Security Act amended to extend old age and survivors' insurance to farmers, self-employed members of specified professions, and additional farm and domestic employees; on a voluntary group basis, to members of state and local government retirement systems; and, at the election of the individual, to ministers and members of religious orders; to raise to $4,200 the earnings base for tax and benefit computation purposes; to raise ultimate contribution rates; to increase benefits; to liberalize the retirement test; to permit a dropout of 4 or 5 years of lowest earnings in computing benefits; and to protect benefit rights of disabled persons through a disability freeze provision.

Social Security Act amended by addition of new title XV to provide unemployment insurance benefits for federal civilian employees, financed by federal funds and paid by state agencies under their own benefit formulas.

Federal Unemployment Tax Act amended to include firms employing 4 or more in 20 weeks, after January 1, 1956, and to permit experience rating tax reduction to new or newly covered employers after one year's experience (instead of three).

1955

August 9.—Social Security Act amended to extend to April 1, 1956, the period during which wage credits of $160 a month could be provided for military service and extend the time for filing claims for lump sum death payments with respect to servicemen dying overseas and reburied in this country.

1956

June 7.—Dependents' Medical Care Act provided for medical and hospital care, on a uniform basis, for the dependents of the uniformed services in service facilities and, for certain dependents of those on active duty, set up the program of "Medicare," authorizing the use of civilian hospitals and physicians.

August 1.—Social Security Act amended to provide monthly benefits to permanently and totally disabled workers aged 50–64 under old age and survivors' insurance program; to pay child's benefits to disabled children (aged 18 or over) of retired or deceased workers, if their disability began before age 18; to lower to age 62 the retirement age for widows and female parents, and, on election of a reduced benefit, for wives and women workers; to extend coverage to self-employed professional persons (other than doctors of medicine), additional farm owners and operators, and certain state and local government employees; to set up a disability insurance trust fund to which ¼ per cent of contributions from employers and employees and ⅜ per cent from the self-employed are allocated and from which disability benefits are paid; to reimburse the trust fund for the costs of the gratuitous military wage credits granted veterans. Public assistance amendments revised the federal matching formula to increase the federal share in assistance payments; to establish a new basis for federal sharing in medical care for recipients, separately from money payments to them; and to authorize grants for the training of public welfare personnel. For child welfare services, the authorization for appropriations was increased. Grants were authorized for cooperative research or demonstration projects relating to the prevention and reduction of dependency.

Servicemen's and Veterans' Survivor Benefits Act amended the Social Security Act by extending regular contributory coverage under old age and survivors' insurance to members of the uniformed services on active duty.

1957

January.—First payments with respect to disability paid under old age, survivors', and disability insurance when benefits for this month went to retired or deceased workers' dependent children aged 18 or over with a permanent and total disability that began before age 18. Rise in old age, survivors', and disability insurance contribution rates effective, increasing to 2¼ per cent each for employers and employees and to 3⅜ per cent for self-employed.

July.—Monthly disability benefits first payable under old age, survivors', and disability insurance to insured workers aged 50–64.

July 17.—Social Security Act amended to modify the offset provision so that receipt of Veterans Administration disability compensation does not mean a reduction of the disability benefit under the Social Security Act.

1958

June 4.—Temporary Unemployment Compensation Act provided for paying, from July 1957 through March 1959, additional unemployment benefits to workers exhausting their benefit rights under the regular state program, with the federal government advancing the funds.

August 28.—Social Security Act amended to increase benefits under old age, survivors', and disability insurance, provide benefits for dependents of disabled worker beneficiaries, raise to $4,800 the amount of earnings taxable and creditable for benefit purposes, set new schedule for contribution rates, raise to $100 the amount of monthly wages a beneficiary with earnings higher than $1,200 a year may have without losing benefits, and repeal the provision that reduced disabled worker and disabled child's benefits by the amount of certain other disability payments received.

Public assistance amendments revised the formula for federal sharing in state assistance expenditures by shifting to an average single monthly limitation on the amount to which the federal government will contribute for money and medical care payments combined and by relating federal participation in part to the fiscal capacity of each state.

Child health and welfare programs amended to raise maximum authorizations for federal appropriations for all three programs, make grants available to Guam, remove the provisions relating to the use of federal child welfare funds in predominantly rural areas, revise the allotment formula for child welfare funds, provide for variable matching of child welfare funds (based on state per capita income), broaden provisions on use of federal child welfare funds for return of runaway children, and permit reallotment of federal child welfare funds.

August 28.—Title XV of the Social Security Act amended by Ex-Servicemen's Unemployment Compensation Act, which set up a permanent unemployment insurance program for ex-servicemen like that for federal employees.

1959

January 1.—Rise in old age, survivors', and disability insurance contribution rates effective, increasing to 2½ per cent each for employers and employees and to 3¾ per cent for self-employed.

March 31.—Program for additional unemployment benefits for workers exhausting benefits under regular state programs extended for three months.

1960

January 1.—Rise in old age, survivors', and disability insurance contribution rates effective, increasing to 3 per cent each for employers and employees and to 4½ per cent for self-employed.

September 13.—Title I of old age assistance amended to provide medical benefits for aged persons who are not old age assistance recipients but whose income and resources are insufficient to meet the costs of medical services. Old age and survivors' insurance amended to provide disability insurance benefits to disabled workers of all ages and to their dependents; to liberalize the retirement test; to liberalize the elegibility requirements; to liberalize the calculation of average wage on which benefits are based; and to liberalize orphans' benefits.

1961

March 24.—Temporary extended unemployment compensation provided for paying, until March 31, 1962, additional benefits to workers exhausting their benefit rights under the regular state program, with the federal government reimbursing the state.

June 30.—Old age, survivors', and disability insurance amended to permit male workers to elect a reduced retirement benefit at age 62; to increase minimum benefit payable; to liberalize the benefit payable to aged widow, widower, or surviving dependent parent; and to liberalize the retirement test and eligibility requirements. Public assistance titles temporarily amended to increase the federal share of cost and to make eligible for aid to dependent children the children of unemployed parents and children removed from unsuitable homes.

1962

July 25.—Public assistance titles amended to provide a greater federal sharing in the cost of rehabilitative services to recipients, applicants, and persons likely to become applicants for public assistance; to increase further the federal share in the cost of public assistance payments; to permit the states to combine the various categories into one category; and to make permanent the 1961 amendment extending aid to dependent children to cover children removed from an unsuitable home.

1963

January 28.—Reorganization order of the Secretary of Health, Education, and Welfare removed from the Social Security Administration and placed in a newly created Welfare Administration the Bureau of Family Services (formerly Bureau of Public Assistance), the Children's Bureau, and the Cuban Refugee Program; the order also placed in the Welfare Administration the Office of Aging and the Office of Juvenile Delinquency and Youth Improvement which formerly reported directly to the Secretary.

1964

October 13.—Eligibility for disability benefits of persons meeting eligibility requirements at time they became disabled was made fully retroactive by permanent legislation.

1965

July 30.—Social Security Act and Railroad Retirement Act were amended to provide protection against the cost of hospital and related care to persons aged 65 and over entitled to monthly retirement benefits under these acts (and to persons not so entitled who reach 65 before 1968); to permit all persons aged 65 and over to purchase protection against the cost of physicians' services, one half of such cost to be paid by the federal government out of general revenues; to liberalize the cash benefits, the retirement test, and the definition of disability under old age, survivors', and disability insurance; to liberalize the federal matching ratio for public assistance; to require a state which desires federal matching of the cost of medical care for medically indigent aged persons to provide similar protection to all needy persons for whom the state is receiving federal grants; and to increase the federal grants to the states for maternal and child health and welfare services.

Appendix II

Official Documents of Social Security, 1935–65

Basic Documents

U.S. COMMITTEE ON ECONOMIC SECURITY. *Report to the President.* Washington, D.C.: U.S. Govt. Printing Office, 1935. 74 pp.

————. *Social Security in America: The Factual Background of the Social Security Act as Summarized from Staff Reports to the Committee on Economic Security.* (Publ. by Social Security Board.) Washington, D.C.: U.S. Govt. Printing Office, 1937. 592 pp.

U.S. CONGRESS. HOUSE, COMMITTEE ON LABOR. *Unemployment, Old Age, and Social Insurance. Hearings, 74th Congress, 1st Session, on H.R. 2827, 2829, 185, and 10.* Washington, D.C.: U.S. Govt. Printing Office, 1935. 726 pp.

————. HOUSE, COMMITTEE ON WAYS AND MEANS. *Economic Security Act. Hearings on H.R. 4120, 74th Congress, 1st Session.* Washington, D.C.: U.S. Govt. Printing Office, 1935. 1,141 pp.

————. HOUSE, COMMITTEE ON WAYS AND MEANS. *The Social Security Bill.* (House Rept. 615 on H.R. 7260, 74th Cong., 1st session.) Washington, D.C.: U.S. Govt. Printing Office, 1935. 45 pp.

————. SENATE, COMMITTEE ON FINANCE. *Economic Security Act. Hearings on S. 1130, 74th Congress, 1st Session.* Washington, D.C.: U.S. Govt. Printing Office, 1935. 1,354 pp.

————. SENATE, COMMITTEE ON FINANCE. *The Social Security Bill.* (Senate Rept. 628 on H.R. 7260, 74th Cong., 1st session.) Washington, D.C.: U.S. Govt. Printing Office, 1935. 55 pp.

U.S. DEPARTMENT OF HEALTH, EDUCATION, AND WELFARE. SOCIAL SECURITY ADMINISTRATION. *Annual Report of the Social Security Administration.* Washington, D.C.: U.S. Govt. Printing Office, 1937————. (Reports for fiscal years 1936–46 were issued as *Annual Report of the Social Security Board.* Since 1953 the reports constitute a section of the *Annual Report of the Department of Health, Education, and Welfare.*)

288

Amendments of 1939

U.S. ADVISORY COUNCIL ON SOCIAL SECURITY. *Final Report . . . December 10, 1938.* (Senate Doc. 4, 76th Cong., 1st session.) Washington, D.C.: U.S. Govt. Printing Office, 1939. 29 pp.

U.S. CONGRESS. HOUSE, COMMITTEE ON WAYS AND MEANS. *Social Security. Hearings Relative to the Social Security Act Amendments of 1939, 76th Congress, 1st Session.* Washington, D.C.: U.S. Govt. Printing Office, 1939. 3 vols.

———. HOUSE, COMMITTEE ON WAYS AND MEANS. *Social Security Act Amendments of 1939.* (House Rept. 728 on H.R. 6635, 76th Cong., 1st session.) Washington, D.C.: U.S. Govt. Printing Office, 1939. 121 pp.

———. SENATE, COMMITTEE ON FINANCE. *Social Security Act Amendments. Hearings on H.R. 6635, 76th Congress, 1st Session.* Washington, D.C.: U.S. Govt. Printing Office, 1939. 554 pp.

———. SENATE, COMMITTEE ON FINANCE. *Social Security Act Amendments of 1939.* (Senate Rept. 734 on H.R. 6635, 76th Cong., 1st session.) Washington, D.C.: U.S Govt. Printing Office, 1939. 39 pp.

U.S. SOCIAL SECURITY BOARD. *Proposed Changes in the Social Security Act.: A Report of the Social Security Board to the President and Congress of the United States.* Washington, D.C.: U.S. Govt. Printing Office, 1939. 29 pp.

Amendments of 1946

U.S. CONGRESS. HOUSE, COMMITTEE ON WAYS AND MEANS. *Amendments to Social Security Act. Hearings . . . 79th Congress, 2nd Session, on Social Security Legislation.* Washington, D.C.: U.S. Govt. Printing Office, 1946. 3 vols.

———. HOUSE, COMMITTEE ON WAYS AND MEANS. *Social Security Act Amendments of 1946.* (House Rept. 2526 on H.R. 7037, 79th Cong., 2nd session.) Washington, D.C.: U.S. Govt. Printing Office, 1946. 42 pp.

———. HOUSE, COMMITTEE ON WAYS AND MEANS. SOCIAL SECURITY TECHNICAL STAFF. *Issues in Social Security. . . .*Washington, D.C.: U.S. Govt. Printing Office, 1946. 742 pp.

———. SENATE, COMMITTEE ON FINANCE. *Social Security Act Amendments of 1946.* (Senate Rept. 1862 on H.R. 7037, 79th Cong., 2nd session.) Washington, D.C.: U.S. Govt. Printing Office, 1946. 41 pp.

Amendments of 1950

U.S. ADVISORY COUNCIL ON SOCIAL SECURITY. *Recommendations for Social Security Legislation. A Report to the Senate Committee on Finance from the Advisory Council on Social Security.* (Senate Doc.

208, 80th Cong., 2nd session.) Washington, D.C.: U.S. Govt. Printing Office, 1949. 236 pp.

U.S. Congress. House, Committee on Ways and Means. *Social Security Act Amendments of 1949. Hearings on H.R. 2892 and H.R. 2893, 81st Congress, 1st Session.* Washington, D.C.: U.S. Govt. Printing Office, 1949. 2 vols.

―――. House, Committee on Ways and Means. *Social Security Act Amendments of 1949.* (House Rept. 1300 on H.R. 6000, 81st Cong., 1st session.) Washington, D.C.: U.S. Govt. Printing Office, 1949. 207 pp.

―――. Senate, Committee on Finance. *Social Security Revision. Hearings, 81st Congress, 2nd Session, on H.R. 6000, An Act To Extend and Improve the Federal Old-Age and Survivors Insurance System, To Amend the Public Assistance and Child Welfare Provisions of the Social Security Act, and for Other Purposes.* Washington, D.C.: U.S. Govt. Printing Office, 1950. 3 vols.

―――. Senate, Committee on Finance. *Social Security Act Amendments of 1950.* (Senate Rept. 1669 on H.R. 6000, 81st Cong., 2nd session.) Washington, D.C.: U.S. Govt. Printing Office, 1950. 319 pp.

Amendments of 1952

U.S. Congress. House, Committee on Ways and Means. *Social Security Act Amendments of 1952.* (House Rept. 1944 on H.R. 7800, 82nd Cong., 2nd session.) Washington, D.C.: U.S. Govt. Printing Office, 1952. 51 pp.

―――. Senate, Committee on Finance. *Social Security Act Amendments of 1952.* (Senate Rept. 1806 on H.R. 7800, 82nd Cong., 2nd session.) Washington, D.C.: U.S. Govt. Printing Office, 1952. 36 pp.

Amendments of 1954

Consultants on Social Security. *A Report to the Secretary of Health, Education, and Welfare on Extension of Old-Age and Survivors Insurance to Additional Groups of Current Workers.* Washington, D.C.: U.S. Govt. Printing Office, 1953. 32 pp.

U.S. Congress. House, Committee on Ways and Means. *Social Security Act Amendments of 1954. Hearings, 83rd Congress, 2nd Session, on H.R. 7199.* Washington, D.C.: U.S. Govt. Printing Office, 1954. 883 pp.

―――. House, Committee on Ways and Means. *Social Security Amendments of 1954.* (House Rept. 1698 on H.R. 9366, 83rd Cong., 2nd session.) Washington, D.C.: U.S. Govt. Printing Office, 1954. 98 pp.

―――. House, Committee on Ways and Means. Subcommittee

ON SOCIAL SECURITY. *Analysis of the Social Security System. Hearings, 83rd Congress, 1st Session.* Washington, D.C.: U.S. Govt. Printing Office, 1953 and 1954. 6 parts and appendices I and II.

————. SENATE, COMMITTEE ON FINANCE. *Social Security Amendments of 1954. Hearings, 83rd Congress, 2nd Session, on H.R. 9366.* Washington, D.C.: U.S. Govt. Printing Office, 1954. 746 pp.

————. SENATE, COMMITTEE ON FINANCE. *Social Security Amendments of 1954.* (Senate Rept. 1987 on H.R. 9366, 83rd Cong., 2nd session.) Washington, D.C.: U.S. Govt. Printing Office, 1954. 183 pp.

Amendments of 1956

U.S. CONGRESS. HOUSE, COMMITTEE ON WAYS AND MEANS. *Public Assistance Titles of the Social Security Act. Hearings, 84th Congress, 2nd Session, on H.R. 9120, 9091, 10283, and 10284.* Washington, D.C.: U.S. Govt. Printing Office, 1956. 358 pp.

————. HOUSE, COMMITTEE ON WAYS AND MEANS. *Social Security Act Amendments of 1955.* (House Rept. 1189 on H.R. 7225, 84th Cong., 1st session.) Washington, D.C.: U.S. Govt. Printing Office, 1955. 72 pp.

————. SENATE, COMMITTEE ON FINANCE. *Social Security Act Amendments of 1955. Hearings, 84th Congress, 2nd Session, on H.R. 7225.* Washington, D.C.: U.S. Govt. Printing Office, 1956. 3 vols.

Amendments of 1957

U.S. CONGRESS. HOUSE, COMMITTEE ON WAYS AND MEANS. *Public Assistance Medical Care Provisions of Social Security Act.* (House Rept. 496 on H.R. 7238, 85th Cong., 1st session.) Washington, D.C.: U.S. Govt. Printing Office, 1957. 9 pp.

————. SENATE, COMMITTEE ON FINANCE. *Medical Care Vendor Payments.* (Senate Rept. 473 on H.R. 7238, 85th Cong., 1st session.) Washington, D.C.: U.S. Govt. Printing Office, 1957. 13 pp.

Amendments of 1958

U.S. CONGRESS. HOUSE, COMMITTEE ON WAYS AND MEANS. *Social Security Legislation. Hearings, 85th Congress, 2nd Session, on All Titles of the Social Security Act.* Washington, D.C.: U.S. Govt. Printing Office, 1958. 1,205 pp.

————. HOUSE, COMMITTEE ON WAYS AND MEANS. *Social Security Amendments of 1958.* (House Rept. 2288 on H.R. 13549, 85th

Cong., 2nd session.) Washington, D.C.: U.S. Govt. Printing Office, 1958. 79 pp.

———. SENATE, COMMITTEE ON FINANCE. *Social Security. Hearings, 85th Congress, 2nd Session, on H.R. 13549.* Washington, D.C.: U.S. Govt. Printing Office, 1958. 448 pp.

——— SENATE, COMMITTEE ON FINANCE. *Social Security Act Amendments of 1958.* (Senate Rept. 2388 on H.R. 13549, 85th Cong., 2nd session.) Washington, D.C.: U.S. Govt. Printing Office, 1958. 78 pp.

Amendments of 1960

U.S. CONGRESS. HOUSE, COMMITTEE ON WAYS AND MEANS. *Hospital, Nursing Home, and Surgical Benefits for OASI Beneficiaries. Hearings, 86th Congress, 1st Session.* Washington, D.C.: U.S. Govt. Printing Office, 1959. 720 pp.

———. HOUSE, COMMITTEE ON WAYS AND MEANS. *Social Security Amendments of 1960.* (House Rept. 1799 on H.R. 12580, 86th Cong., 2nd session.) Washington, D.C.: U.S. Govt. Printing Office, 1960. 336 pp.

———. SENATE, COMMITTEE ON FINANCE. *Social Security Amendments of 1960. Hearings, 86th Congress, 2nd Session, on H.R. 12580.* Washington, D.C.: U.S. Govt. Printing Office, 1960. 531 pp.

———. SENATE, COMMITTEE ON FINANCE. *Social Security Amendments of 1960.* (Senate Rept. 1856 on H.R. 12580, 86th Cong., 2nd session.) Washington, D.C.: U.S. Govt. Printing Office, 1960. 301 pp.

———. HOUSE. *Social Security Amendments of 1960.* (House Rept. 2165, Conference Rept. on H.R. 12580, 86th Cong., 2nd session.) Washington, D.C.: U.S. Govt. Printing Office, 1960. 29 pp.

Amendments of 1961

U.S. CONGRESS. HOUSE, COMMITTEE ON WAYS AND MEANS. *Social Security Amendments of 1961. Hearings, 87th Congress, 1st Session, on H.R. 4571.* Washington, D.C.: U.S. Govt. Printing Office, 1961. 161 pp.

———. HOUSE, COMMITTEE ON WAYS AND MEANS. *Social Security Amendments of 1961.* (House Rept. 216 on H.R. 6027, 87th Cong., 1st session.) Washington, D.C.: U.S. Govt. Printing Office, 1961. 103 pp.

———. SENATE, COMMITTEE ON FINANCE. *Social Security Benefits and Eligibility. Hearings, 87th Congress, 1st Session, on H.R. 6027.* Washington, D.C.: U.S. Govt. Printing Office, 1961. 127 pp.

———. SENATE, COMMITTEE ON FINANCE. *Social Security Amendments of 1961.* (Senate Rept. 425 on H.R. 6027, 87th Cong., 1st

session.) Washington, D.C.: U.S. Govt. Printing Office, 1961. 105 pp.
———. HOUSE. *Social Security Amendments of 1961.* (House Rept. 611, Conference Rept. on H.R. 6027, 87th Cong., 1st session.) Washington, D.C.: U.S. Govt. Printing Office, 1961. 8 pp.

Amendments of 1962

U.S. CONGRESS. HOUSE, COMMITTEE ON WAYS AND MEANS. *Public Welfare Amendments of 1962. Hearings on H.R. 10032, 87th Congress, 2nd Session.* Washington, D.C.: U.S. Govt. Printing Office, 1962. 697 pp.
———. HOUSE, COMMITTEE ON WAYS AND MEANS. *Public Welfare Amendments of 1962.* (House Rept. 1414 on H.R. 10606, 87th Cong., 2nd session.) Washington, D.C.: U.S. Govt. Printing Office. 1962. 86 pp.
———. SENATE, COMMITTEE ON FINANCE. *Public Assistance Act of 1962. Hearings on H.R. 10606, 87th Congress, 2nd Session.* Washington, D.C.: U.S. Govt. Printing Office, 1962. 603 pp.
———. SENATE, COMMITTEE ON FINANCE. *Public Welfare Amendments of 1962.* (Senate Rept. 1589 on H.R. 10606, 87th Cong., 2nd session.) Washington, D.C.: U.S. Govt. Printing Office, 1962. 82 pp.
———. HOUSE. *Public Welfare Amendments of 1962.* (House Rept. 2006, Conference Rept. on H.R. 10606, 87th Cong., 2nd session.) Washington, D.C.: U.S. Govt. Printing Office, 1962. 11 pp.

Amendments of 1964

U.S. CONGRESS. HOUSE, COMMITTEE ON WAYS AND MEANS. *Medical Care for the Aged. Hearings, 88th Congress, 1st and 2nd Sessions, on H.R. 3920.* Washington, D.C.: U.S. Govt. Printing Office, 1964. 2103 pp.
———. HOUSE, COMMITTEE ON WAYS AND MEANS. *Social Security Amendments of 1964.* (House Rept. 1548 on H.R. 11865, 88th Cong., 2nd session.) Washington, D.C.: U.S. Govt. Printing Office, 1964. 58 pp.
———. SENATE, COMMITTEE ON FINANCE. *Social Security; Medical Care for the Aged Amendments. Hearings, 88th Congress, 2nd Session, on H.R. 11865.* Washington, D.C.: U.S. Govt. Printing Office, 1964. 728 pp.
———. SENATE, COMMITTEE ON FINANCE. *Report to Accompany H.R. 11865.* (Senate Rept. 1513 on H.R. 11875, 88th Cong., 2nd session.) Washington, D.C.: U.S. Govt. Printing Office, 1964. 137 pp.
———. HOUSE, COMMITTEE ON WAYS AND MEANS. *Report to Accompany H.R. 9393, A Bill to Provide Full Retroactivity for Disability*

Determinations, etc. (House Rept. 1279 on H.R. 9393, 88th Cong., 2nd session.) Washington, D.C.: U.S. Govt. Printing Office, 1964. 11 pp.

————. SENATE, COMMITTEE ON FINANCE. *Report to Accompany H.R. 9393, A Bill to Provide Full Retroactivity for Disability Determinations, etc.* (Senate Rept. 1516 on H.R. 9393, 88th Cong., 2nd session.) Washington, D.C.: U.S. Govt. Printing Office, 1964. 23 pp.

Amendments of 1965

U.S. CONGRESS. HOUSE, COMMITTEE ON WAYS AND MEANS. *Medical Care for the Aged. Hearings, 89th Congress, 1st Session, on H.R. 1 and other Bills Relating to Social Security.* Washington, D.C.: U.S. Govt. Printing Office, 1965. 898 pp.

————. HOUSE, COMMITTEE ON WAYS AND MEANS. *Report to Accompany H.R. 6675.* (House Rept. 213 on H.R. 6675, 89th Cong., 1st session.) Washington, D.C.: U.S. Govt. Printing Office, 1965. 264 pp.

————. SENATE, COMMITTEE ON FINANCE. *Social Security. Hearings, 89th Congress, 1st session, on H.R. 6675.* Washington, D.C.: U.S. Govt. Printing Office, 1965. 1255 pp.

————. SENATE, COMMITTEE ON FINANCE. *Report to Accompany H.R. 6675.* (Senate Rept. 404 on H.R. 6675, 89th Cong., 1st session.) Washington, D.C.: U.S. Govt. Printing Office, 1965. 563 pp.

————. HOUSE. *Conference Report on H.R. 6675.* (House Conference Rept. 682, 89th Cong., 1st session.) Washington, D.C.: U.S. Govt. Printing Office, 1965. 70 pp.

Appendix III

Memorandum for the President, 1937:
Amendments to the Social Security Act

September 11, 1937

Memorandum for the President
From Mr. Altmeyei
Subject: Amendments to the Social Security Act.

I should greatly appreciate an opportunity to confer with you relative to the above subject as soon as possible. The immediate reason is that, as you know, last February Senator Harrison as chairman of the Senate Committee on Finance acting at the request of Senator Vandenberg agreed to the creation of an advisory council on social security. The matter came up during the course of a hearing before the Senate Committee on Finance and it appeared at that time that there was no alternative but for the Social Security Board to agree, although reluctantly, to the creation of this advisory group. Some time thereafter an advisory group was appointed jointly by a subcommittee of the Senate Committee on Finance and the Social Security Board. Aside from the wisdom of the appointment of such a group, the mistake was made of not consulting the House Committee on Ways and Means. Nothing has been done to utilize the services of this advisory group although Senator Vandenberg has become more and more insistent that a meeting be called. I have talked with Senator Harrison several times about the matter. He still feels that it was wise to consent to the creation of this advisory group and that we ought to call a meeting. However, he suggested that before doing so I discuss the matter with you.

The problem of what to do with the advisory group is a part of the much larger problem of what we should look forward to by way of future amendments to the Social Security Act. This is likely to become a very hot partisan issue.

Some time ago we were warned that the Republican National Committee was already supplying material to various nationally known columnists relative to the Social Security Act the substance of

295

which, in a little more refined version, was that the payroll taxes constituted a method whereby the government was collecting pennies from the poor to finance a wasteful government. Recently, John Hamilton in his speeches has claimed as an accomplishment of the Republican members of Congress that they "forced the Democratic Social Security Board to start action to adopt the Republican proposal to increase and hasten old age benefits and to keep at a low level payroll taxes on employers and employees by doing away with a needless 47 billion dollar reserve." While these attacks are to be expected, nevertheless they need to be reckoned with because both the A.F. of L. and the C.I.O. labor leaders and unions have publicly indicated dissatisfaction with the present provisions of the Social Security Act and particularly the payroll tax provisions. While, of course, we should not be stampeded into taking unwise action, I think that it is most necessary to consider at this time the general character of the Administration's policy regarding amendment of the Social Security Act.

As a matter of fact, I think it is possible not only to offset these attacks on the Social Security Act, but really to utilize them to advance a socially desirable program, fully in accord with present fundamental principles underlying the Social Security Act and within our financial capacity. You will recall that some time ago at a conference in your office Harry Hopkins outlined a long term program dealing with unemployment and relief. I have indicated to Mr. Hopkins and the Secretary of Labor how the insurance approach in the Social Security Act should fit into this long term program and they have reacted favorably to the general idea. The discussions I have had with them may be summarized as follows:

1. The full reserve feature of the old age insurance system may be essentially sound, but is under considerable attack by both conservatives and liberals. The position of the liberals is more consistent than the position of the conservatives since they recognize more clearly that if we go off the reserve plan it is most important not only to bring the budget into balance, but provide for rapid retirement of the government debt through the imposition of higher progressive taxes. This necessity arises out of the fact that unless we do so we will reach a period in the future when we must either raise payroll taxes to almost twice the present contemplated maximum, or provide a large government subsidy which together with the service charges on the government debt may prove unbearable.

2. If we go off the reserve plan with our eyes open it is more desirable to do so by increasing and extending both the size and character of the benefits provided instead of reducing the present tax rates which are relatively low.

3. Specifically, we should convert our old age insurance system into an old age, *permanent* invalidity and survivors' insurance system, as follows:

(a) Start monthly benefit payments not later than January 1,

1939, instead of January 1, 1942, and liberalize the monthly benefits payable during the early years.

(b) Provide an extra allowance for wife of old age benefit recipient.

(c) Provide benefits for surviving widows and orphans, regardless of age of deceased.

(d) Provide benefits for permanent total disability.

4. As regards unemployment compensation it is feasible and desirable to extend the system so as to include unemployment due to *temporary* disability not arising out of the employment. This proposal would not meet with objection from the medical profession; in fact, it stands a good chance of eliciting active support from the medical profession. The increased cost would be less than 1% of the payroll.

5. The extension of a considerable part of this program to a greater proportion of the population, particularly agricultural workers, domestic employees and the self-employed can probably be accomplished through changing to a combined payroll and *earned income* basis for computing taxes and benefits. Such extension should be dependent upon solving the administrative problems involved and upon popular demand. Even now, important excluded groups, such as banks, seamen, and religious and charitable organizations are urging extension of coverage to them.

6. The foregoing program would supplement the program of unemployment and relief outlined by Mr. Hopkins and as time went on take care of a larger and larger segment of the problem, *without affecting the Federal budget during the next fifteen years and without the necessity of increasing the present total payroll taxes more than 1% (figured on the payroll) during that period of time.* Eventually it would be necessary to provide another step-up in payroll tax rates under the proposed old age permanent invalidity and survivors' insurance system so that instead of a maximum of 3% from the employer and employee, the maximum might be 4% from each. However, this step-up need not occur until 1952. Beginning some time after 1952, a government subsidy would be necessary which would increase each year, due chiefly to the fact that the system would not reach its maturity for about 40 years.

Because of the magnitude of the problems involved, I should like to suggest that you appoint a very small unofficial, unpublicized group, including Miss Perkins, Harry Hopkins, Henry Morgenthau, Henry Wallace, and myself to explore these problems and to report to you from time to time the course of their thinking.

I should also like to have your suggestion as to what to do about the advisory group described in the attached newspaper release of May 10, 1937.

Appendix IV

Correspondence with Congressman Curtis of Nebraska, Chairman of Subcommittee on Social Security of the Committee on Ways and Means, U.S. House of Representatives, 1953: Investigation of Social Security

WASHINGTON, D.C., June 9, 1953

Mr. Arthur J. Altmeyer
Fairfax Hotel
2100 Massachusetts Avenue, N.W.
Washington, D.C.

DEAR MR. ALTMEYER:

As you know, I have been appointed chairman of a Ways and Means Subcommittee to conduct a study of social security, with particular reference to the Federal programs dealing with income for the aged. I am determined that this shall be a thorough, objective, fact-finding investigation, which will enable the Ways and Means Committee to write legislation early in the next session.

In order to inform the members of the committee fully and accurately, I consider it indispensable to have presented a fair and complete statement of the principles underlying the present programs of Old Age and Survivors Insurance and Old Age Assistance. For such a statement, I know of no one better qualified than you, who have been associated with the Social Security Administration since its inception. Therefore, I should greatly appreciate it if you would prepare such a statement of principles for the subcommittee.

Responding to this request might, of course, be regarded by some as merely rendering a public service. However, since I regard you as the outstanding authority on the present system, I would expect to arrange for remuneration in a manner comparable with what we pay expert consultants.

I trust that I will hear from you at your earliest convenience. I am sure that we will have no difficulty in mutually agreeing on the scope and subject matter of this statement.

Sincerely yours,
CARL T. CURTIS
Chairman, Subcommittee on Social Security

MADISON, WISCONSIN, June 23, 1953

Honorable Carl T. Curtis
Chairman, Subcommittee on Social Security
Committee on Ways and Means
Washington, D.C.

DEAR SIR:

I have your letter of June 9, requesting me to prepare for you a "statement of the principles underlying the present programs of Old Age and Survivors Insurance and Old Age Assistance." You state that you would expect to arrange for remuneration for this service.

I am sorry to say that not only do I believe that the preparation of such a statement is unnecessary but that I believe compliance with your request would greatly harm rather than help the cause of social security.

You will find a complete discussion of the principles underlying our social security system, a description of the way the Social Security Act is functioning, and specific recommendations for improving it in the reports I have submitted annually to the Congress and in the testimony I have given before the Committee on Ways and Means on many occasions.

I very much regret being obliged to say to you further that I do not believe that any restatement I might prepare at this time would be likely to change your personal opposition to social insurance which you expressed when the Committee on Ways and Means considered the 1950 and 1952 amendments to the Social Security Act. You not only opposed these amendments which greatly improved the Act but you voted for the Gearhart Amendment in 1948 which took away the protection of the Old Age and Survivors Insurance System from a half-million workers.

Even after you became Chairman of this subcommittee you have continued to express your personal opposition to social insurance. Moreover, you have appointed as staff director a person who also is on record as opposed to social insurance.

Under these circumstances I must say that I do not see how it is possible for you to carry out your avowed determination that "this shall be a thorough, objective, fact-finding investigation." Therefore, I am of the opinion that my participation in the manner you propose would only serve to confuse and mislead the friends of social security as regards what I am constrained to believe is bound to be a biased investigation by you and your staff director.

I know that you say that you are for social security and are only opposed to what you allege are inequitable and unsound provisions in the present system. However, you have consistently attacked the basic principles underlying contributory social insurance and have advocated the abandonment of these principles. Specifically, you have opposed the payment of benefits as a matter of right; you have opposed the payment of benefits related to wage loss; you have opposed any long-range financing plan to provide assurance that future benefits will be paid. By criticizing the fact that insured persons who are well-to-do as well as persons without resources receive the benefits provided by law, you seem to be in favor of some sort of means test, and, of course, you have always contended that the Old Age and Survivors Insurance System is not insurance, although it is so designated in the law itself.

I trust you will believe me when I say that I find it painful to use such blunt language and that I am impelled to do so only because of the grave danger to social security which I believe your present views represent.

I should like to make it clear that I am not charging that the subcommittee as a whole is opposed to social security. I am not familiar with the views of the other majority members but I do know that the minority members have always been staunch advocates of social security and have played a leading part in the development of the present social security system. I would also hope that you yourself will modify your views as the committee proceeds with its deliberations.

I should also like to make it clear that I shall be glad to present my views to the committee when it undertakes the consideration of specific proposals and the report and recommendations of your staff.

Sincerely,
ARTHUR J. ALTMEYER

MADISON, WISCONSIN, September 25, 1953

Honorable Carl T. Curtis
Chairman, Subcommittee on Social Security
Committee on Ways and Means
Washington, D.C.

DEAR SIR:

I have just been served with a subpoena signed by you, directing me to appear before your subcommittee on social security on November 6. I have already made engagements which will take me away from Madison most of the month of October and the first week in November. Therefore, I would appreciate your permitting me to appear at least a week later. I would also appreciate your furnishing me with a list of the questions you wish to ask or at least the specific items you wish me to discuss. This will make it possible for me to assemble the necessary material so that my testimony may be helpful to the subcommittee.

As I indicated in my letter to you, dated June 23, you will find a complete discussion of what I consider to be the principles underlying our social security system, a description of the way the Social Security Act is functioning, and specific recommendations for improving it in the reports I have submitted annually to the Congress and in the testimony I have given before the Ways and Means Committee on many occasions. If you have not had the time to examine this material, I would suggest that you have your staff do so on your behalf.

As I also indicated in my previous letter, because all of the foregoing material is readily available, I felt that I could be most helpful if I presented my views to the subcommittee when it undertakes the consideration of specific proposals and the report and recommendations of its staff. Since your committee has been at work for some time it may be that you now have before you specific proposals and a preliminary report from your staff. If so, I would appreciate receiving a copy to study prior to appearing before your subcommittee.

Very truly yours,
A. J. ALTMEYER

Index

Addressograph Corp., "dog-tag" proposal of, 69

Administration: importance of, *vi;* need for focused and integrated character of, 166–68; involves interpretations and policy decisions, 262–65; and heterogeneous character of Department of Health, Education, and Welfare, 272–73. *See also* Merit systems for personnel; Patronage; Research, importance of; Social Security Administration; Social Security Board

Advisory Council on Social Security: 1937, 89–90, 91–92, 230, 295; 1947, 161, 163, 169

Agricultural Adjustment Act, 20, 56

Agricultural workers, 92, 97, 103, 181, 182, 184, 185, 217, 241, 244, 245–46, 247–48, 297

Agricultural Workers Union, 213

Agriculture, Secretary of. *See* Wallace, Henry

Aid to dependent children. *See* Dependent children, aid to

Allen, Robert S., 124

Amendments to Social Security Act: Clark, 32, 40–42; 1939, 99–114, 125, 138; McCormack, 104, 110–11, 113, 258; Connally, 111–12, 113; Johnson, 111, 113; Danaher, 131; 1944, 147–48; 1946, 154–57; 1947, 160; 1948, 163; 1950, 184, 185, 187, 204, 217, 233, 259–60, 299; Jenner, 190–91; 1952, 193–

99; McFarland, 198; 1953, 219; 1954, 240–48; 1965, 267, 268–69; Gearhart, 299

American Association for Old Age Security (American Association for Social Security), 4

American Association of Social Workers, 33

American Dental Association, 242

American Farm Bureau, 241, 248

American Federation of Labor, 32–33, 213, 214, 243, 254, 296

American Hospital Association, 253

American Life Convention, 253

American Medical Association: and Medical Advisory Committee, 27; opposition to health programs, 33, 57, 116, 146, 171, 254; meetings of House of Delegates, 33, 96, 116, 186; objections to Social Security Act, 55; and National Health Conference, 96; attacks Ewing, 176; opposition to disability benefits, 185–86, 196, 197, 242, 243; mentioned, 248–49n

American Public Welfare Association, 114

Appropriation Act of 1947, 159

Appropriations, administration of social security, 43–44, 49, 136–37, 147, 156, 164–65, 201n

Appropriations committees: House, 43, 164–65; Senate, 49, 50, 131

Atlantic Charter, 5, 129, 145

Attorney General, 7, 70, 228

Ball, Senator Joseph H., 158. *See also* Taft-Smith-Ball bill

Bane, Frank, 114

Berry, Senator George, 50

Beveridge, Sir William: report of, 5, 141, 142, 143; visits U.S., 144–45

Black, Senator Hugo, 39

"Blanketing-in" proposals. *See* Old age, survivors', and disability insurance

Blind assistance, 40–41, 42, 98, 104, 105, 156, 180

Blue Cross Association, 253, 262

Bolivar, Simon, 3n

Brandeis, Justice Louis D., 21

Brown, Dean J. Douglas, 143

Bryce, Lord James, 11

Buchanan, Congressman James P., 43

Bureau of Accounts and Audits (Social Security Board), 53

Bureau of Budget, 137, 217, 220

Bureau of Business Management (Social Security Board), 53, 117

Bureau of Employment Security: created, 117; and federal-state relations, 120; administers U.S. Employment Service, 176; transferred to Dept. of Labor, 178, 189; and California unemployment compensation agency, 183–84; mentioned, 141, 164, 219

Bureau of Federal Credit Unions, 164

Bureau of Federal Old-Age Benefits (Social Security Board), 53, 67–68

Bureau of Internal Revenue, and employer reporting, 66–67, 86–88

Bureau of Old Age and Survivors' Insurance (formerly Bureau of Old Age Insurance): increases staff, 119; administers Civilian War Benefits, 140; and 1950 amendments, 188; and 1952 amendments, 201–2

Bureau of Old Age Insurance (formerly Bureau of Old-Age Benefits), 68, 86–87, 119

Bureau of Public Assistance (Social Security Board): and state administration, 58, 59, 60–61, 65, 119–20; administers Civilian War Assistance, 140, 141; and 1950 amendments, 188; eligibility and amount of assistance, 191–93; mentioned, 53, 62

Bureau of Research and Statistics (Social Security Board), 56–57, 148

Bureau of Unemployment Compensation (Social Security Board): and state administration, 58; administrative problems of, 62–65; and U.S. Employment Service, 64, 117; mentioned, 53, 120

Burns, Dr. Eveline, 214

Business Advisory Council (Dept. of Commerce): on unemployment insurance, 23, 24, 258; mentioned, 33

Butler, Senator Hugh, 182, 183, 204

Byrd, Senator Harry F., 39, 59–60, 61, 216, 248n

Byrnes, Senator James F., 93, 106, 131

Cain, Senator Harry P., 183

Calhoun, Leonard, 155

California, unemployment compensation agency in, 183–84

Cardozo, Justice Benjamin, 56

Chamber of Commerce. *See* U.S. Chamber of Commerce

Chapman, Oscar (Assistant Secretary of the Interior), 94

Child labor laws, 15

Children's Bureau: established, v; administers infant and maternity benefits, vi, 36, 146; and aid to dependent children, 41; placed within Social Security Administration, 159; mentioned, 33, 52

Child welfare, 170. *See also* Dependent children, aid to

Churchill, Prime Minister Winston: on compulsory insurance, 142; addresses Congress, 144–45; mentioned, 5, 129

Civilian Conservation Corps, 117

Civilian War Assistance, 140

Civilian War Benefits, 140

Civil Service Assembly, 65

Civil Service Commission: selection of Board personnel, 47, 49; mentioned, 272. *See also* Merit systems for personnel

Clark amendment, 32, 40–42

Commerce, Secretary of, 7, 219

Commissioner for Social Security, 159, 169, 209, 220, 225–35. *See also* Social Security Administration

Commissioner of Social Security, 220

Commission on the Health Needs of the Nation, 194, 210, 212n

Committee on Economic Security: created, 3, 7; policy decisions of, 4, 14, 15, 16; Executive Director of, 7, 8–9; technical board of, 7, 8, 17, 18, 26; relations with Roosevelt, 8, 16–17; advisory council of, 8, 19, 24, 258; on old age insurance, 13, 24, 25, 26; unemployment insurance plans of, 17, 18, 19, 20–21, 86; and health insurance, 33, 55, 57–58n; continued, 114–15; and National Research Planning Board, 114–15; mentioned, 47, 67, 142, 214, 229

Committee on Education and Labor, 116–17, 158–59

Committee on Finance. *See* Finance, Senate Committee on

Committee on Retirement Policy for Federal Personnel, 217

Committee on Ways and Means. *See* Ways and Means, House Committee on

Connally amendment, 111–12, 113

Conference of State Governors (1931), 4

Congress of Industrial Organizations, 213, 243, 254, 296

Connecticut Manufacturers Association, 33

Connery, Congressman William P., 30–31

Constitutionality of social legislation: in policy considerations, 14–15; of unemployment insurance plans, 19–21, 32, 35, 61–62; of old age insurance programs, 25–26, 37, 40, 56, 69, 86; of Railroad Retirement Act, 39; of National Recovery Act, 44; mentioned, 51, 97, 232

Consultants on Social Security, 216, 240

Cooper, Congressman Jere, 30

Council of State Chambers of Commerce, 224, 242

Council of State Governments, 54, 114

Cummings, Homer (Attorney General), 7

Curtis, Congressman Carl T.: on contributory social insurance, 214, 221–23; comments on Department of Health, Education, and Welfare, 224; Chairman, Subcommittee on Social Security, 224–34, 235–36, 298; bill of, 236, 238, 240, 260; on "blanketing-in," 243–44; correspondence with Altmeyer, 298–301

Cushing, Dr. Harvey, 27, 94

Danaher amendment, 131

Davey, Governor Martin L., 75–77

Democratic National Committee, 52

Dependent children, aid to: grants to states for, 28, 33, 104, 174, 175, 180, 185; administration of, 36, 41, 42; and 1950 amendments, 183, 187–88; mentioned, 4, 16, 35, 82, 93, 98, 156, 225, 269. *See also* Public assistance

Dependents' benefits. *See* Old age, survivors', and disability insurance

Depression: cause of welfare proposals, 6–7, 9–11; and Federal Emergency Relief Administration, 44; mentioned, 47, 93, 258

Dewey, Governor Thomas E., 193n

Dictionary of Occupational Titles, 120–21

Dill, Senator Clarence C., 30

Dingell, Congressman John: bills of, 146, 158, 160; and national health program, 154; member, Subcommittee on Social Security, 228. *See also* Wagner-Murray-Dingell bill

Disability assistance, 174, 175, 182–83, 184, 188

Disability insurance benefits: in Wagner bill, 116; under Civilian War Benefits program, 140; amendment to Federal Unemployment Tax Act for, 157; postwar recommendations for, 159, 162, 189, 194; bill for, 170; and George amendment, 248–49n; mentioned, 91, 95, 134, 135, 143, 154, 239

——, for permanent total disability: recommended, 92, 162, 170, 193, 296–97; American Medical Association opposition to, 185–86; and preservation of other social insurance rights, 195–202, 212, 213, 240, 242, 243, 248–49n, 267, 283–84; mentioned, 97, 103, 173, 260

——, for temporary disability: recommended, 91, 98, 162, 170, 193, 267, 297; failure to provide, 103, 266; in Rhode Island, 147

Displacement benefits, 136

Division of Aid for the Aged (Ohio), 76

Dolliver, Congressman James I., 253

Domestic employees, 92, 97, 173, 181, 297

Donnell, Senator Forrest C. *See* Taft-Donnell-Smith bill

"Double-decker" plans. *See* Old age, survivors', and disability insurance

Doughton, Congressman Robert L., 29, 100, 107, 197

Douglas, Senator Paul, 31–32

Downey, Senator Sheridan, 124, 129

Early, Stephen, 122–23

Eaton, Congressman Charles A., 142

Eberharter, Congressman Herman P., 156

"Economic Insecurity in Old Age," 56

"Economic Security Act," 3

Education, Office of, 117, 139

Education and Labor, Senate Committee on, 116–17, 158

Eisenhower, President Dwight D.: and old age insurance coverage, 211, 217, 237–38; recommendations on unemployment insurance, 237, 250, 251–52; health program of, 237–38, 252

"Employee" in Social Security Act, definition of, 163, 173, 175, 182, 184, 263

Employees, federal, 97, 150, 200, 216–17, 241

Employees, state and local, 97, 173, 195, 198, 201, 217, 241

Employers' groups, 23, 33, 34, 178, 185, 242

Employment security administrative financing bill, 219–20, 249

EPIC (End Poverty in California), 12

Epstein, Abraham, 4, 32

Evening Star (Washington, D.C.), 107

Ewing, Oscar R. (Federal Security Administrator), 162–63, 176, 193n, 196–97

Fair Deal, 153, 212

Farley, James (Postmaster General), 50, 52

Farm operators, 174, 185, 205, 217, 241, 245, 246, 247

Federal Bureau of Investigation, 70

Federal Deposit Insurance Corporation, 164

Federal Emergency Relief Administration, 16, 36, 44

Federal Estate Tax Act, 21

Federal Security Administrator: and War Manpower Commission, 139; appointed Director of Office of Defense, Health, and Welfare, 140; and Commissioner for Social Security, 159, 165; mentioned, 134, 137, 164, 178, 190, 217. *See also* Ewing, Oscar R.; Hobby, Mrs. Oveta Culp; McNutt, Paul V.

Federal Security Agency: created, 117; Children's Bureau under, 159; Bureau of Federal Credit Unions under, 164; heterogeneous character of, 166–68; and 1949 reorganization plans, 176

Federal Security Agency Appropriation Act, 164

Federal-state relations: Roosevelt's insistence upon, 11, 17, 115, 257; and unemployment insurance program, 18–19, 62–63, 134–35, 161–62, 178, 220, 251–52; and old age insurance, 25; Social Security

Board and state administration, 46–47, 53–54, 58–59, 65, 74–78, 79–80, 138, 147–48, 264–65; and health programs, 115, 210, 261–62; and defense labor needs, 131–33, 147; and "disability freeze," 202; future for, 271

Federal Unemployment Tax Act, 156, 157, 163, 181, 183, 219, 220, 249, 250, 266. *See also* McCormack, Congressman John

Finance, Senate Committee on: and social security bill, 30, 31, 38–39, 40–41; and Vandenberg resolution, 88–89; advisory councils on social security of, 89–90, 91–92, 161, 163, 169, 230, 295; and 1939 amendments, 106–7, 110–11, 112; appoints Special Subcommittee to Investigate the Old Age Pension System, 124; and Revenue Act of 1942, 137; and 1946 amendments, 156–57; and 1950 amendments, 180, 181–83, 184; and "disability freeze" provision (1952), 197–99, 201; and 1954 amendments, 245–47; and employment security administrative financing bill, 249–50

Flanders-Ives-Nixon bill, 171–72, 262

Folsom, Marion (Undersecretary of the Treasury), 214, 215

Fortune Magazine, 146

Gallup poll, 146

Gearhart amendment, 299

General Accounting Office (Social Security Board), 55

General Counsel (Social Security Board), 53, 59, 61, 79, 117, 147

General Welfare Federation of America, 105–6

George, Senator Walter F.: introduces hospital construction bill, 128; on disability provisions, 201, 248–49n; and coverage of self-employed, 245–47

G.I. Bill of Rights, 149–50, 200

G.I. Bill of Rights for Korean Veterans, 199–200

Glass, Senator Carter, 49

Gore, Senator Thomas P., 38

Governors' Conference (1951), 193n

Great Britain, 66, 140n, 143, 178

Green, Senator Theodore, 130

Green, William (President, American Federation of Labor), 4, 32–33, 146n

Hamilton, John, 296

Harrison, Senator Pat, 30, 295

Hastings, Senator Daniel O., 41

Health, Education, and Welfare, Department of (formerly Federal Security Agency), 117, 166, 168, 224, 237, 246, 272–73

Health, Education, and Welfare, Secretary of. *See* Federal Security Administrator; Hobby, Mrs. Oveta Culp

Health programs: Roosevelt on need for, 14, 115, 126, 129; Medical Advisory Committee for, 27–28; reaction of American Medical Association to, 33, 57, 116, 146, 171, 185–86, 254; authorization for research on, 55, 56–57; report of Technical Committee on Medical Care, 94–95; National Health Conference on (1938), 95–96, 261–62; Social Security Board recommendations on, 98, 148, 154, 193–94; Senator Wagner on, 115–16; hospital benefits, 143, 193–94; for enlisted men, 146–47; Truman's national health program, 153–54, 159–60, 169–70, 171, 179, 189; Republican vs. Truman Administration proposals for, 160; action of Federal Security Administrator on, 162–63, 176; and National Health Assembly (1948), 163; public assistance grants for, 174, 185, 187, 188, 268; and 1952 presidential election, 202; Eisenhower position on, 237–38, 252–55; Taft bill for, 261; controversial nature of, 267–68; legislation of, for the aged, 268–69; mentioned, 117, 149, 157, 195, 209, 239. *See also* Flanders-Ives-Nixon bill; Interdepartmental Committee to Coordinate Health and Welfare Activities; President's Commission on the Health Needs of the Nation; Public health programs; Taft-Donnell-Smith bill; Taft-Smith-Ball bill; Wagner-Murray bill; Wagner-Murray-Dingell bill

Hearst press, 69

Helvering v. *Davis*, 56

Hill-Burton Act. *See* Hospital Survey and Construction Act

Hillman, Sidney (Office of Production Management), 132, 136*n*

Hobby, Mrs. Oveta Culp: appointed Federal Security Administrator, 211; personal characteristics of, 212*n;* appoints advisory group, 213–14, 215, 216, 240; and Commissioner's retirement, 220–21; Curtis comments upon, 224; and 1954 amendments, 241–42, 245; and health reinsurance bill, 252–53, 254–55

"Hobby Lobby," 214

Hoehler, Fred, 114

Holmes, Justice Oliver W., 6

Hopkins, Harry L. (Federal Emergency Relief Administrator): and unemployment insurance, 23, 297; and old age insurance, 28–29, 296; and aid to dependent children, 93; hospital construction program of, 95; health plan of, 126; mentioned, 7, 18

Hospital construction programs, 95, 126–28, 153, 157, 171, 252

Hospital Survey and Construction Act (Hill-Burton Act), 157, 252

Illinois Manufacturers Association, 33

Indiana, and Jenner amendment, 190

Insurance companies (private), 34, 70, 242–43, 248–49*n*

Interdepartmental Committee to Coordinate Health and Welfare Activities, 56–57, 93–96, 115–17, 126, 128, 261

Internal Revenue Service (formerly Bureau of Internal Revenue), 67*n*

International Labour Office, 72

International Monetary Fund, 108

Inter-Professional Association for Social Insurance, 31

Interstate and Foreign Commerce, House Committee on, 171, 253

Interstate Conference of Employment Security Agencies, 132–33, 178, 179*n*

"Issues in Social Security," 155

Ives, Senator Irving M. *See* Flanders-Ives-Nixon bill

Javits, Senator Jacob K., 262

Jenkins, Congressman Thomas, 78, 121

Jenner amendment, 190–91

Johnson, Senator Edwin C., 111, 113

Joint Congressional Committee on Railroad Retirement, 216–17

Journal of the American Medical Association, 27

Judiciary, House Committee on the, 121

Justice, Department of, 56, 141

Kaiser, Henry J., 212*n*

Kean, Congressman Robert W., 214, 217

Keefe, Congressman Frank, 165

Kennedy, Senator John F., 249–50

Knudsen, William S., 132

Labor, Department of: and administration of Social Security Act, 36, 41; administers U.S. Employment Service, 63–64, 154, 159, 161, 163, 176, 177, 178; mentioned, 93, 139, 179*n*, 183, 189, 194, 219, 251–52

Labor, House Committee on, 31

Labor, Secretary of, 64, 251. *See also* Perkins, Frances

Labor and Public Welfare, Senate Committee on, 160, 171

Labor organizations: regarding social security bill, 32; support Wagner-Murray-Dingell bill, 146; and Advisory Council on Social Security, 161; and Bureau of Employment Security, 178; oppose Chamber of Commerce plan, 215; criticize Subcommittee on Social Security and Curtis, 224, 234,

244–45; mentioned, 69, 214, 219, 248–49, 250–51

LaFollette, Senator Robert M.: and old age and survivors' insurance, 107–8, 110–11, 113, 115; mentioned, 40, 52, 124

Landon, Alfred M., 68–69

Latimer, Murray, 67, 108

Lenroot, Katharine (Chief, Children's Bureau), 52

Lewis, Congressman David J., 29

Life Insurance Association of America, 253

Long, Senator Huey: "share the wealth" movement of, 10, 257; filibusters by, 41, 44

Lundeen, Congressman Ernest, 30–31, 37

McCarl, John R. (Comptroller General), 44

McCormack, Congressman John, 104, 110–11, 113, 258

McFarland amendment, 198

McIntyre, Dr. Ross, 27

McKellar, Senator Kenneth, 50

McNutt, Paul V. (Federal Security Administrator): and Social Security Board, 116, 121–22; supports uniform pension plan, 122–23; mentioned, 117, 124

Maritime Commission, 156

Maritime employment, 156

Maternity and child health programs: Maternity and Infancy Act, vi; under Children's Bureau, vi, 36, 146; and Sheppard-Towner Act, 15; constitutionality of, 15, 20; opposed by American Medical Association, 33; and Wagner bill, 116; and national health program, 153; mentioned, 4, 5, 35, 171

Medical Advisory Committee (Committee on Economic Security), 27, 28, 94

Medical care. See Health programs

Medical education and research, 153, 171

Merit systems for personnel, 35–36, 65, 74–75, 79, 84, 93, 98, 105, 111, 138, 147–48, 177, 178, 264–65. See also Civil Service Commission

Merriam, Charles E., 114

Migratory workers, 18, 128

Miles, Vincent M. (Social Security Board), 45

Military personnel, benefits for, 145, 146–47, 149–50, 155–56, 195, 219, 241. See also Servicemen's Readjustment Act of 1944; Veterans' Readjustment Assistance Act of 1952

Millikin, Senator Eugene D., 181, 183, 247

Morgenthau, Henry, Jr. (Secretary of the Treasury), 7, 23, 28–29, 33–34, 103, 137, 297

Murray, Senator James, 116, 137, 154, 160. See also Wagner-Murray bill; Wagner-Murray-Dingell bill

Nation, The, 142

National Association of Commerce, 219

National Association of Manufacturers, 33, 242, 250

National Conference of Mayors (1934), 13

National Conference of Social Work (1953), 221–23

National Conference on Economic Security (1934), 13, 19, 25

National Employee Index, 87

National Health Agency, 158

National Health Assembly (1948), 163

National Health Conference (1938), 95–96, 115, 261

National Industrial Conference Board, 122–23

National Industrial Recovery Act, 44, 56

National Industrial Recovery Administration, 44–45, 47

National Management-Labor Policy Committee, 139n

National Manpower Program, 118

National Metal Trades Association, 33

National Physicians Committee for the Extension of Medical Service, 146

National Publishers Association, 33

National Reemployment Service, 83

National Resources Planning Board, 114, 143, 144
National Retail Dry Goods Association, 33
National Youth Administration, 117, 139
Navy, Department of, 139
Nebraska Association of County Officials, 234–35
New Deal, 12, 20, 56, 211, 212
Newspaper and magazine vendors, 163
Newspapers: and Ohio episode, 77, 78; attacks on old age insurance, 123–24, 297; on "Hobby Lobby," 214–15; mentioned, 4, 13, 31–32, 69, 107, 138, 220–21, 234, 246
New York, public assistance standards of, 191–93
Nixon, Congressman Richard, 171–72, 262. *See also* Flanders-Ives-Nixon bill

Ohio, maladministration of old age assistance in, 74–78, 121–22
Ohio Chamber of Commerce, 33
Old age assistance: need for, 25–26; federal grants for, 35, 157, 183, 236, 237, 245; administered by Social Security Board, 36; standards for, 39; confidential records of, 58–59, 190–91; and Ohio maladministration, 76–79, 121–22; and Roosevelt's Teamsters Union message, 126; and pension plans, 129; growth of, 169–70; and 1950 amendments, 180, 181; and U.S. Chamber of Commerce proposals, 207–8; policy decisions on, 263–64; mentioned, 75, 81, 98, 104, 105, 187, 298, 299. *See also* Public assistance
Old age, survivors', and disability insurance: and Committee on Economic Security, 4, 16; Roosevelt's plans for, 13, 91, 126, 128–29, 148–49, 257; initial policy decisions on, 25–26, 263; constitutionality considerations, 25, 40, 56; financing of, 28–29, 33–34, 66–67, 86–90, 92, 96–97, 100–101, 108–10, 156, 169–70, 179, 259–60,

296; eligibility conditions for, 34, 42, 107, 113, 203–4; administration of, 36, 65–68, 70–71, 72, 168, 177; Republican opposition to, 37–38, 47, 68–69, 295–96; local office personnel for, 50, 55; confidential records of, 58, 70; assignment of account numbers, 69–70; dependents' and survivors' benefits included, 90–92, 100–2, 296–97; coverage of, 91–92, 97, 128–29, 134, 135, 143, 163, 172, 182, 184, 213, 216–17, 296–97; postponements of increase in contribution rate, 103, 106, 137–38, 147, 149, 150, 154, 155, 160, 184, 218; "double decker" plans for, 124–26, 128–30, 181–82, 204–6, 207–8, 259–60; military service benefits of, 145, 147, 155–56, 218–19; and amendments to Railroad Retirement Act, 158, 189–90, 217; Truman recommendations on, 161, 162, 170, 179, 193; and 1950 amendments, 170–75, 179–88; and hospitalization benefits, 193–94, 269; and 1952 amendments, 194–99, 200–1; and 1952 presidential campaign, 202–3, 206–8; work clause and flexible retirement under, 203–4, 242; "blanketing-in" proposals for, 205–6, 215, 216, 238, 240, 243–44; Eisenhower's recommendations on, 211, 237–38; and Curtis, 221–23, 235, 243–44, 298–300; and Subcommittee on Social Security, 225–27, 231–35; and 1954 amendments, 240, 241–42, 245–48; mentioned, 39, 41, 74, 93, 130, 191, 210, 265, 267, 272, 273. *See also* Bureau of Federal Old-Age Benefits; Clark amendment; Disability insurance benefits; Health programs; Pension plans; Townsend plan

Patronage, 37, 41, 47–52, 138
Pearl Harbor, 130, 136, 138
Pearson, Drew, 124
Pennsylvania, patronage issue in, 138

Pension plans: and 1939 amendments, 105, 108–9; of Federal Security Administrator, 122–23; Senate subcommittee on, 124; and 1952 Republican platform, 203, 204–5, 238; and U.S. Chamber of Commerce, 206–8; and Curtis, 222, 225, 236; and Roosevelt's policies, 257; mentioned, 4, 55, 114, 125, 175, 183, 206–7, 224, 259–60. *See also* Old age, survivors', and disability insurance; Townsend plan

Perkins, Frances (Secretary of Labor): and Committee on Economic Security, 7, 31; and old age insurance, 13, 28–29; and Justice Stone, 15; attitude of Congress toward, 36–37; testifies before Finance Committee, 39; on health insurance, 57n; on unemployment insurance, 83; *The Roosevelt I Knew*, 142; mentioned, *ix*, 11–12, 23, 25, 137, 296, 297

Personnel. *See* Merit systems for personnel; Social Security Administration; Social Security Board

"Political Repercussions of Pending Social Security Act Amendments," 110

Postmaster General. *See* Farley, James

Post Office Department, 66, 68, 86

Presidential campaigns: 1936, 68–69, 88; 1940, 96, 117; 1948, 163, 169, 263; 1952, 202

President's Commission on the Health Needs of the Nation, 194, 210, 212n

Press, the. *See* Newspapers

Production Management, Office of, 136n

Public Administrative Clearing House, 114

Public assistance: and Committee on Economic Security, 4, 16–17; necessity for, 5, 269–70, 273–74; federal grants to states for, 16, 109, 110, 128, 143, 156, 157, 160, 163, 198, 242, 244, 245, 247; administration of, 36–37, 59–61, 74–78, 80–82, 168; confidentiality of records of, 58–59, 190–91; sanctions for maladministration of, 77, 138, 190–91, 192; inadequate state appropriations for, 82; personnel merit systems for, 84, 93; and 1939 amendments, 97–98, 104–5; variable grant proposal for, 111–13; wartime provisions of, 140–41; postwar recommendations on, 162, 170, 189, 193, 194–95; and 1950 amendments, 173–75, 180, 182–85, 187–89; statewide standards for, in New York, 191–93; and Subcommittee on Social Security, 232; Eisenhower recommendations on, 238–39; and 1954 amendments, 240, 241–42, 244, 245; retrospect on recommendations for, 260–61; and federal-state relations, 269–70. *See also* Bureau of Public Assistance; Connally amendment; Jenner amendment; McFarland amendment; Old age assistance

Public health programs, 4, 5, 16–17, 36, 171. *See also* Health programs

Public Health Service, 165–66

Public Law, 379

Puerto Rico, 173, 174

Railroad Retirement Act: and constitutionality considerations, 39, 40, 56; amendment to, 157–58, 189–90

Railroad Retirement Board, 67

Railroad Retirement Fund, 108

Railroad retirement system, 272

Railroad Unemployment Insurance Act, 82, 267

Railroad workers, 82, 216–17, 241

Rayburn, Congressman Sam, 43, 136, 145

Reed, Congressman Daniel, 38, 196–97, 217

Rehabilitation agencies, 188

Religious groups, 217, 241, 297

Reorganization Act of 1949, 175–76

Reorganization plans: 1939, No. 1, 117; 1947, No. 2, 161; 1949, No. 1, 176; 1949, No. 2, 176; 1953, No. 1, 220

Republican criticism: in 1935, 37–38, 47; in 1936 presidential campaign, 68–69; in 1937, 295–96

Research, importance of, 55–56

Revenue Act: of 1942, 137; of 1943, 149; of 1945, 154; of 1951, 190

Rhode Island, temporary disability insurance law of, 147

Roche, Josephine (Assistant Secretary of the Treasury): and health programs, 94, 95–96, 115, 117; mentioned, 23, 28

Rockefeller, Nelson (Undersecretary of Health, Education, and Welfare), 243–44

Roosevelt, President Franklin D.: conception of social security, 3, 4–5, 12–13, 142, 257–58, 261–62, 265; creates Committee on Economic Security, 3, 7; reaction of, to Beveridge report, 5, 141; and social reform, 6, 9, 10, 16–17, 24–25; and social security financing, 11, 29, 34, 112–13, 135–38, 142; insistence upon federal-state cooperation, 11–12, 17, 19, 115, 257; addresses National Conference on Economic Security (1934), 13; proposes increase in Supreme Court justices, 20, 56; and health insurance programs, 27, 57–58n, 94, 96, 117, 129, 151; signs Social Security Act, 42, 56; nominates Social Security Board, 43; on personnel difficulties, 49, 50, 84, 138–39; and amending Social Security Act, 90–91, 295–97; on old age insurance eligibility, 110; signs 1939 amendments, 113–14; and hospital construction bill, 117; vetoes Jenkins bill, 122; opposes uniform pension plans, 122–23; speech to Teamsters Union, 126; signs Atlantic Charter, 129; and national defense manpower needs, 130, 131; and report of National Resources Planning Board, 143, 144; on veterans' legislation, 145, 148–49

————, messages to Congress: 1934, 3, 9–10, 11, 13, 17, 24–25; 1935, 29, 43; 1937, 49; 1939, 99, 112–13, 115; 1940, 122, 126; 1941, 128, 129; 1942, 135–38, 141; 1944, 148–49; 1945, 150–51

Roosevelt, James, 27

Rosenman, Judge Samuel, 153–54

Russell Sage Foundation, 31

Selective Service Administration, 139

Self-employed persons, 92, 134, 143, 145, 181, 185, 217, 241, 244, 245–46, 247, 297

Senate Committee to Investigate the Old Age Pension System, 129

Senate Resolution 300, 184

Senate Special Committee on Social Security, 214

Servicemen's Readjustment Act of 1944, 149–50, 200

Servicemen's readjustment allowances, 118

Sheppard-Towner Act, 15

Simpson, Congressman Richard M., 218

Sinclair, Upton, 12

Smart, Joseph, 102

Smith, Senator H. Alexander. See Taft-Smith-Ball bill

Smith, Harold, 153n

Social Security Administration: appropriation for, 164–65, 166–67; 1949–50 annual report of, 189; and statewide standards, 190–91, 192; 1950–51 annual report of, 193–94; "double-decker" study by, 204, 206; on "blanketing-in," 205–6; 1953 annual report of, 209–10; and Republican administration, 238–39

Social Security Board: creation of, 36; administration of, 36–37, 41–53, 58–59, 117; and personnel, 46–52, 65, 67–68, 72, 75–78, 147; training program of, 53–54, 55; and state administration, 54, 75–82, 147, 191; research program of, 55, 56–57; and U.S. Employment Service, 63–64, 83–84, 132–34, 136n; and employer reporting systems, 66–67; headquarters for, 71–72; sanctions of, 75–78, 138; and Ohio maladministration, 76, 121–22; and Bureau of Internal Reve-

nue, 87–88; and old age insurance
reserves, 88–89; and 1939 amendments, 96–98, 118–19; placed
within Federal Security Agency,
117, 121–22, 165, 167–68; and
national defense manpower needs,
120; appropriation for, 120, 130–
31; newspaper editorial on, 123–
24; and "double-decker" system,
124–26; on federal-state unemployment insurance system, 134–
35, 162; and War Manpower
Commission, 139, 139–40n; and
wartime assistance programs, 140;
abolished, 159; and McCormack
amendment, 258–59; retrospect
on policies of, 258–61, 263–64
——, annual reports of: 1940–41,
134–35; 1941–42, 142–43; 1942–
43, 148; 1944–45, 154, 162
Social security concept: definition
of, 3–6; role of social insurance in,
4, 11, 16; and abolition of destitution, 271–72; and war on poverty,
273
Social workers, 33
Southern Labor Conference, 31
Special Committee to Investigate
Unemployment and Relief (1937),
92–93
Special Subcommittee to Investigate
the Old Age Pension System, 124
State Technical Advisory Service,
51, 65
Stevenson, Adlai, 204
Stone, Justice Harlan F., 15
Subcommittee on Social Security of
the Ways and Means Committee:
appointed, 218; and Curtis'
speech, 221–23; Altmeyer's appearance before, 223, 225–34,
298–301; membership of, 224; report of, 240–41
Supreme Court: attitude toward social legislation, 14–15; and constitutionality questions, 20–21, 25,
56, 61–62, 86, 225–26, 232–33;
and Railroad Retirement Act, 39–
40; mentioned, 30, 49, 74, 163,
263
Survivors' benefits. See Old age, survivors', and disability insurance

Taber, Congressman John, 37–38
Taft, Senator Robert A., 116, 121,
128, 157, 158, 181, 183, 259, 261.
See also Taft-Donnell-Smith bill;
Taft-Smith-Ball bill
Taft-Donnell-Smith bill, 171–72, 173
Taft-Smith-Ball bill, 160
Tawney, Richard, 144
Technical Committee on Medical
Care, 94–95
Temporary Extended Unemploy-
ment Compensation Act of 1961,
266
Time Magazine, 142
Townsend, Dr. F. E., 32. See also
Townsend plan
Townsend plan: described, 9–10;
Roosevelt's opposition to, 11, 257;
pressure for, 13, 32, 37, 61, 75, 99,
108, 123, 124, 129; considered by
House, 105–6; petition for (1954),
242–43
Treadway, Congressman Allen T.,
38
Treasury Department, 108, 119, 161,
219
Truman, President Harry S.: on unemployment insurance system,
152; administrative channels of,
152–53n; reconversion program
of, 154; abolishes Social Security
Board, 159; 1948 campaign of,
169; and reorganization plans,
175–76, 178; and 1950 amendments, 185; appoints President's
Commission on the Health Needs
of the Nation, 193; and "disability
freeze," 199
——, messages to Congress: 1945,
153, 158; 1946, 155; 1947, 159–
60; 1948, 161–63; 1949, 170–71;
1950, 179; 1951, 189; 1952, 193;
1953, 210–11

Unemployment Benefit Advisors,
Inc., 219
Unemployment insurance: Committee on Economic Security recommendations on, 4, 16–17; Roosevelt's recommendations on, 12, 13,
14, 16, 128–29, 148–49; development of state administration of,

17, 40, 42, 61–62, 82, 83, 84, 138; federal vs. cooperative federal-state system for, 17–18, 21–25, 40, 134, 135–36, 143, 161–62, 257–58; tax-offset vs. subsidy plan for, 17–21, 24, 31–32, 35, 40; constitutionality of, 20–21, 61–62; and employer experience rating, 22, 23–24, 35, 40, 85, 134–35, 179n, 250, 258; and federal administrative relations, 36, 62–65, 97, 103–4, 189; and public employment offices of U.S. Employment Service, 41–42, 62–64, 82–84, 176–77, 263; lack of minimum benefit standards in, 85–86, 258–59, 266; coverage of, 97, 103–4, 163, 219, 251, 266, 297; contributions for, 104, 108, 258–59; and benefits for servicemen, 118, 145, 149–50, 199–200; "federalizing" of, 132–36; and war displacement benefits, 136; federal supplementation of, 136, 154–55, 160, 219, 266; Truman recommendations on, 152, 161, 179, 193; transferred to Labor Department, 176; and 1950 amendments, 180–81, 187; use of excess tax receipts for, 219–20, 249–50; and Subcommittee on Social Security, 227–35 *passim;* Eisenhower rcommendations on, 237; and "employment security administrative financing bill," 249–52; mentioned, 28, 39, 55, 74, 157, 170, 171, 173, 194, 267. *See also* Bureau of Unemployment Compensation; Federal Unemployment Tax Act; Lundeen, Congressman Ernest; McCormack, Congressman John; Special Committee to Investigate Unemployment and Relief; U.S. Employment Service; Wagner-Lewis bill
United Nations, Declaration of the, 5
U.S. Chamber of Commerce: and disability benefits, 186; "double-decker" proposal of, 206–8, 215, 236–37, 240, 260; Committee on Social Legislation of, 213; and Hobby advisory group, 214–15; and unemployment insurance, 219,

250; and reinsurance health bill, 253–54; mentioned, 33, 211, 212, 234, 238, 242
U.S. Employment Service: financing of, 18; unemployment compensation payments through, 42, 62–63; related to unemployment insurance, 62–65, 176–78; created, 63; state offices of, 82–83, 130–33, 159; transferred to Social Security Board, 84, 93, 104, 117; and national defense manpower, 118, 120; federalizing of, 132–33, 159; transferred to War Manpower Commission, 139–40; administered by Labor Department, 154, 161, 163, 176–78; transferred to Social Security Administration, 164; mentioned, 41, 97, 108, 263. *See also* Bureau of Employment Security; Bureau of Unemployment Compensation; Danaher amendment; Unemployment insurance
U.S. Government bonds, 135
U.S. Public Health Service, 36, 94, 117, 153

Vandenberg, Senator Arthur H., 88–89, 124, 137, 295
Van Kleeck, Mary, 31
Veterans. *See* Military personnel
Veterans' Readjustment Assistance Act of 1952, 199–200
Vinson, Congressman Fred M., 30, 36, 48–49, 90, 100
Virgin Islands, 173, 174
Vocational rehabilitation, 5, 41, 42

Wadsworth, Congressman James W., 38
Wagner, Senator Robert F., 29, 39, 115–16, 128, 154, 160, 261. *See also* Wagner-Lewis bill; Wagner-Murray bill; Wagner-Murray-Dingell bill; Wagner-Peyser Act
Wagner-Lewis bill, 13–14, 17, 18, 19, 21, 30, 32
Wagner-Murray bill, 158
Wagner-Murray-Dingell bill, 146, 154, 160
Wagner-Peyser Act, 63

Wallace, Henry (Secretary of Agriculture), 7, 23, 297
War Department, 132, 139
War Manpower Commission, 139–40, 154
War Mobilization and Reconversion Act, 150
War Powers Act, 161
War Relocation Authority, 141
Warren, Governor Earl, 171
War Shipping Administration, 147
Washington *Post*, 4
Watson, General Edwin M., 125
Ways and Means, House Committee on: and social security bill, 29–30, 31, 34–36, 38; and selection of Board personnel, 47–51; and 1939 amendments, 99–106; and variable grants, 112; and Revenue Act of 1942, 137; and 1946 amendments, 152, 155–56; and reconversion unemployment legislation, 154–55; and 1950 amendments, 173–75; and 1952 amendments, 195–97; and Subcommittee on Social Security, 218, 221–23, 225–34, 298–301; hearings on extensions of Federal Unemployment Tax Act, 219; and "employment security administrative financing bill," 220; and 1954 amendments, 240–44; mentioned, 90, 107, 153, 157, 181, 192, 217, 245
Wilson, M. L. (Assistant Secretary of Agriculture), 94
Winant, John G. (Chairman, Social Security Board), 5, 45, 68, 72, 129, 144
Wisconsin: unemployment compensation in, *vii, viii*, 24, 82, 85; coverage of public employees, 219
Wisconsin Unemployment Compensation Act, 24
Witte, Dr. Edwin E. (Executive Director, Committee on Economic Security), 7–8, 11, 13, 14, 24, 25, 28–29, 31, 39, 227–28
Women's Army Auxiliary Corps, 212*n*
Woodrow Wilson's New Freedom, 211
"Workers' unemployment and social insurance bill," 30–31, 37
Work relief, 12, 13, 16
Works Progress Administration, 16, 44, 93, 126
World War I, 211
World War II, 5, 120, 204, 263

Date Due

DEMCO NO 295

			/	